T0305162

Minsky's Moment

NEW DIRECTIONS IN MODERN ECONOMICS

Series Editor: Malcolm C. Sawyer, *Professor of Economics, University of Leeds, UK*

New Directions in Modern Economics presents a challenge to orthodox economic thinking. It focuses on new ideas emanating from radical traditions including post-Keynesian, Kaleckian, neo-Ricardian and Marxian. The books in the series do not adhere rigidly to any single school of thought but attempt to present a positive alternative to the conventional wisdom.

For a full list of Edward Elgar published titles, including the titles in this series, visit our website at www.e-elgar.com.

Minsky's Moment

An Insider's View on the Economics of
Hyman Minsky

Piero Ferri

Professor Emeritus of Economics, University of Bergamo, Italy

NEW DIRECTIONS IN MODERN ECONOMICS

Cheltenham, UK • Northampton, MA, USA

Published by
Edward Elgar Publishing Limited
The Lypiatts
15 Lansdown Road
Cheltenham
Glos GL50 2JA
UK

Edward Elgar Publishing, Inc.
William Pratt House
9 Dewey Court
Northampton
Massachusetts 01060
USA

A catalogue record for this book
is available from the British Library

Library of Congress Control Number: 2018960801

This book is available electronically in the **Elgar**online
Economics subject collection
DOI 10.4337/9781788973731

ISBN 978 1 78897 372 4 (cased)
ISBN 978 1 78897 373 1 (eBook)

Typeset by Servis Filmsetting Ltd, Stockport, Cheshire

Printed and bound in Great Britain by TJ International Ltd, Padstow, Cornwall

To Camilla and Esther

Contents

PART V   THE ECONOMICS OF MINSKY IN A DYNAMIC
         SETTING

Preface

This book was written to celebrate the centenary of Hyman Minsky's birth in Chicago on September 23, 1919. His life covered most of what Hobsbawm (1994) called "The Short Twentieth Century", having died in 1996.

The relevance of this author in the age of the "Great Recession", sometimes also called the "Great Financial Crisis", and in its aftermath suggests that there is value in deepening his analysis and expanding his analytical apparatus that explains turbulences within a wider intellectual domain, ranging from the institutional school of Chicago to Schumpeter's and Keynes's analyses.

My approach to achieving this goal is based upon a precise strategy which starts with the three journal articles that we wrote together, one on methodology, one a critique of the neoclassical synthesis and one on our vision of the economy and a possible research agenda. These articles are then updated and the methodology deepened and expanded in order to enter Minsky's "black box". My attempt is to place his financial instability hypothesis within a dynamic perspective.

The result is neither a research on the history of economic thought nor a diary of our collaboration. The book's ambition is to extend Minsky's contribution.

Our collaboration started in 1978 at the University of Bergamo in Italy. Hyman attended an international conference on finance, where the main exponents of the new finance school were present. Minsky, as usual, represented a minority point of view. I liked that point of view and showed him a paper I was writing on the labor market and income distribution, trying to follow the suggestions put forward by Hicks (1974) in his *The Crisis in Keynesian Economics*. In fact, I got a DPhil in Oxford in 1971 and Hicks was my supervisor.

When Hyman invited me to Rome, where he was serving at Confindustria, having been invited for a sabbatical by his friend Jan Kregel, I discovered that my paper had been heavily corrected. He proposed to write a joint paper, which was published six years later.

In the meantime, many things had happened. In 1979 he started visiting Bergamo for vacations with his family, Esther and their two children Diana and Alan, and attended the university quite regularly. Eventually they bought a flat in the city. Subsequently, each summer we had long sessions of co-working. And if the summer was insufficient, I visited Washington University in St. Louis, a habit that I maintained even when Hyman retired to the Levy Economics Institute in 1990, in order to work with Ed Greenberg and Steve Fazzari.

While he was in Italy, Minsky visited most of the universities – Bergamo, Cattolica of Milan, Siena, Pavia, Cagliari, Rome, Perugia, Venice and Turin – where he gave talks and participated in conferences. Furthermore, he regularly attended the post-Keynesian summer seminars held in Trieste, in which scholars across the globe participated. Eventually, Bergamo became his hub from which to travel throughout the world.

During the gestation period of the first paper, two things happened. The first thing was that he published two books, *Can "It" Happen Again?* in 1982 and *Stabilizing an Unstable Economy* in 1986, both books being collections of papers. The second was that we started a diary of our meetings, because new projects were being planned.

At the beginning, we struggled to comprehend what each was saying, his Midwest accent not fitting well with my Oxonian English. So we decided to work in a Socratic way: I raised questions and he supplied answers. The dialogue was written on computers, which were relatively primitive at that time. To give a flavor of these colloquiums, some excerpts from them are included in the text. They are at the root of the other two articles that we published, one in 1989 and the other in 1992. Furthermore, a project for a joint book was laid down. However, we never succeeded in finishing it. In the meantime, I had become rector of my university, while Hyman had retired to the Levy Economics Institute. The personal and the family links remained, and still remain close, but the scientific collaboration was passed to younger generations.

In the front of his 1975 book, Minsky wrote: "To Piero Ferri, A collaborator, a colleague and a friend." In his Festschrift, published in 1992, he concluded: "Our collaboration has been rewarding. Many thanks." Many thanks to you, Hyman, for having enlarged my vision of economics and made more robust the Kantian approach to economics that I learned from Hicks.

I wish to thank the publishers of the *Journal of Post Keynesian Economics*, the *Review of Political Economy* and *Structural Change and Economic Dynamics* for having allowed me to reproduce the respective articles. I also thank Steve Fazzari, Anna Maria Variato, Annalisa Cristini, Riccardo Leoni and Fabio Tramontana for various forms of collaboration. Corrado Di Guilmi kindly reviewed Chapter 8. Finally, Stefania Varinelli, at the University of Bergamo, provided great bibliographical assistance.

Last but not least, I wish to thank Matthew Pitman of Edward Elgar Publishing and Malcom Sawyer for having favored the publication of the book, while Elizabeth Clack and David Adams provided valuable editorial support.

1.   Introduction

1.   THE FINANCIAL INSTABILITY HYPOTHESIS, A SEMINAL IDEA

According to *The Economist* (July 23, 2016a), six seminal economic ideas dominate modern economic theory. They are:

1.   Akerlof's market for lemons;
2.   Minsky's financial cycle;
3.   the Stolper–Samuelson theorem;
4.   the Keynesian multiplier;
5.   the Nash equilibrium;
6.   the Mundell–Fleming trilemma.

As with all hit parades, this list is neither perennial nor fully accepted by the economic community. However, it is important to stress that Minsky's contribution, above all in the aftermath of the Great Recession, would hardly be contested.

These seminal ideas represent analytical insights. They are often counterintuitive, sometimes irreverent, but surely interesting. Most of their originators have been rewarded with a Nobel Prize – all except Minsky and Keynes. Yet, many of them had difficulty getting their ideas published in mainstream journals (i.e. 1, 2 and 3). The insights refer both to micro, 1 and 5, and macro aspects and touch upon different subjects. Akerlof's main contribution is the foundation stone of information economics, where the agents are not supposed to share the same set of information. This principle has had an important impact on the theory of the labor market, the credit market, the firm and the insurance market. The Stolper–Samuelson theorem tried to challenge Ricardo on international trade and shed new light on the relationship between tariffs and wages. The Keynesian multiplier dealt with the paradox of saving and with the role of fiscal policy in the economy. The Nash equilibrium gave economics a way to make real-world predictions based on information about each person's incentives. Finally, Mundell–Fleming faced the trilemma represented by fixed exchange rate, monetary autonomy and free flow of capital and found their incompatibility.

Only 1,4 and 5 have a relationship with the Minskyan financial instability hypothesis, which is a cornerstone for the interpretation of the Great Recession.

2.   A POSTHUMOUS STAR

Economics, as happens in all other disciplines, makes progress under the combined pressure of internal analytical and methodological developments along with the emergence of new stylized facts in search for an interpretation. In the case of Minsky, it took the occurrence of the Great Recession to raise him to the upper echelons of the most important economists. Thirty years after his famous book *Can "It" Happen Again?* (1982), where "it" stands for the "Great Depression", it really happened again in the form of the "Great Recession", also named "The Global Financial Crisis" (see Wray, 2016).

As *The Economist* puts it:

> From the start of his academic career in 1950 until 1996, when he died, Hyman Minsky laboured in relative obscurity. His research about financial crises and their causes attracted a few devoted admirers but little mainstream attention . . . So it remained until 2007, when the subprime-mortgage crisis erupted in America. Suddenly, it seemed that everyone was turning to his writings as they tried to make sense of the mayhem. Brokers wrote notes to clients about the "Minsky moment" engulfing financial markets . . . And he became a posthumous star. (*The Economist*, July 30, 2016b)

In this sense the age of the Great Recession and its aftermath can be labeled as Minsky's moment, when his work eventually became well known to both academia and the business and financial milieu.

3.   MINSKY MOMENTS

"Minsky moment", however, also means something more pregnant than mere fame in the media. In fact, it is nowadays used as an indicator of financial crises. It was Paul McCulley of PIMCO, a fund management group, who coined the term "Minsky moment", using it to describe the Russian financial crisis of 1998, and so it existed long before the Great Recession. It signifies the capability of Minsky's financial instability hypothesis to interpret – and in a sense to anticipate the possibility of – "great turbulences", characterized by debt levels reaching breaking point and asset prices starting to plunge.

It might seem reductive to consider Minsky's contributions as if they were epitomized by the so-called Minsky moment, in either of the two meanings that this term has been assigned. In fact, his fame could risk mimicking that of the Great Recession: as soon as the economy recovers to its pre-crisis levels, Minsky moments will disappear and so will the author.

However, this forecast is too pessimistic because it does not consider the dominance of the financialization of the economy, run by the so-called money managers. It represents a new structural characteristic of the economy that is bound to last, and this circumstance increases the likelihood of new turbulences being generated and therefore new Minsky moments occurring. *The Economist* (May 2, 2018), for instance, writes: "The genesis of the next crisis is probably lurking in the corporate debt. Investors are getting less reward for the same amount of risk. Consider this with the declining liquidity . . . and you have a recipe for the next crisis."

As one can see, the fundamentals are represented by yields, risk and liquidity. Furthermore, *The Economist* makes it clear which ingredients must be present to generate a financial crisis:

1. excessive borrowing;
2. concentrated bet;
3. mismatch between assets and liabilities.

However, one precautionary adjective is lacking: potential. In fact, when all these factors are present, there is only the possibility of a crisis. A crisis actually takes place only if it succeeds in defeating the thwarting forces that try to counter it.

In this perspective, Minsky's contribution assumes a deeper relevance. It becomes urgent to better define the Minsky moments and to identify their relationships with Minsky's economics. This is the precise task of the present book.

4.   THE AIM OF THE BOOK

The aim of this book is different from that of Leijonhufvud (1968), who in writing about Keynes juxtaposed Keynesian economics to the economics of Keynes. The hiatus between what Keynes actually wrote and the successive interpretations had become so wide that a critical re-examination was needed. The integrity of the original message was in danger and had to be restored.

Instead, this book on Minsky does not imply that the vast literature existing on the so-called Minsky moment is necessarily a misrepresentation of his original thought; it only stresses the necessity of inserting what has been recently discovered about Minsky's analysis during the Great Recession into his lifelong research program in order to obtain a more complete picture of both his vision and his analytical apparatus.

In this perspective, the task is not simply to re-propose Minsky's original ideas but to verify how they are capable of meeting the challenges deriving from the evolution of both the economy and the discipline. It follows that the deep purpose of the book is more to broaden the perspective of the debate than to develop a "destruens" approach with respect to the current literature. In particular, it does not intend to participate in the debate as to whether Minsky would have been known much earlier had he not encapsulated his financial instability analysis within a heterodox framework.

These questions, although very important and fascinating, will not be directly tackled in this book. Rather, its ambition is to try to present the financial instability hypothesis as a particular case of his general vision about the evolution of complex dynamic systems. The thesis put forward is that the financial instability hypothesis can be better understood within a theoretical framework marked by three fundamental characteristics:

1. an interdependence between monetary and real aspects;
2. the presence of endogenous destabilizing market forces countered by thwarting devices;
3. the existence of complex dynamics where these opposite forces stimulate an evolution of the economic system that is far from being a mechanical process.

These characteristics must be jointly considered and analyzed through their evolution over time in order to obtain a satisfactory picture of the economics of Minsky. However, to meet the challenges deriving both from the presence of new stylized facts and from the developments of the discipline, one must enter Minsky's black box in order to deepen and broaden his analysis.

5.   BUILDING BLOCKS

To pursue these objectives, different strategic choices have been put forward. Even though some of them will be introduced later, it is important to underline now that Minsky's contribution will be analyzed by focusing almost exclusively on his books. Minsky wrote two groups of books that can be easily categorized.[1] While he was still alive, he published the following three books:

1. *John Maynard Keynes* (1975);
2. *Can "It" Happen Again?* (1982);
3. *Stabilizing an Unstable Economy* (1986a).

Post-mortem, the Levy Economics Institute supported the publication of two more:

4. *Induced Investment and Business Cycles* (2004) edited by D.B. Papadimitriou;
5. *Ending Poverty: Jobs, Not Welfare* (2013) edited by D.B. Papadimitriou, L. Randall Wray and J. Kregel.

Book 4 is simply Hyman's dissertation (1954), while book 5 is a collection of essays on the labor market written in the 1960s.

All the listed books will be considered in the following analysis, though with different degrees of attention. The main emphasis will be put on books 2 and 3. The reason is simple: the main attempt of this book is to try to reconcile these two books; or, to put it differently, to insert the financial instability hypothesis developed in book 3 within his dynamic apparatus put forward in book 2.

The reasons behind my strategic choice are at least twofold. On the one hand, some of these books are simply collections of papers, and this simplifies the analysis. On the other, they allow one to capture the evolution of his ideas in a compact way. Since the present analysis is not a research on the history of economic thought but, on the contrary, has the ambition to follow the methodological strategy suggested by Hicks in his *Capital and Growth* (1965), the decision to focus on the main books is particularly fruitful. In fact, Hicks (1965) suggested that in order to grasp the fundamental contributions of the most important authors it is necessary to study ideas vis-à-vis the technicalities with which they are expressed. Within his perspective, very close to a Kantian approach, it is legitimate to wonder whether there are discontinuities between the various contributions of Minsky or whether evolution is the more appropriate answer. I refrain from anticipating any detailed answer at this stage of the analysis. It is sufficient to state that there is a substantial continuity in the vision and differences in the analytical apparatus.

6.   AN INTERPRETATIVE GRID

One of the suggestions contained in Hicks's book (1965) is to refer to the following canonical triptych in order to reveal the backbone of the various contributions:

1. the temporal dimension;
2. the transaction structure;
3. the aggregation strategy.

These categories have been used amply, for instance by Leijonhufvud (1968), and they may also help to characterize Minsky's various contributions. Furthermore, they are also useful to understand the successive attempts at developing his analysis. In this perspective, while Minsky's (1982) *Can "It" Happen Again?* underlies point 1, his *Stabilizing an Unstable Economy* (1986a) refers mainly to the transaction structure of the economy. Finally, *John Maynard Keynes* (1975) has implications for the aggregation strategy, a subject also discussed in his dissertation (Minsky, 1954/2004).

The objective is to try to link the various contributions and therefore the various dimensions. In particular, as has been already mentioned, it is worth considering whether the financial instability hypothesis, which was mainly developed in *Stabilizing an Unstable Economy*, can be analyzed within the dynamic perspective suggested by *Can "It" Happen Again?*

The challenge is twofold. On the one hand, it is important to understand whether the financial instability hypothesis is already present "in nuce" in these early writings. On the other, one has to understand whether these early writings offer suggestions in order to develop it and cast it in dynamic terms, a priority for both modern macroeconomics and Minsky.

7.   THE TEMPORAL DIMENSION

There is no doubt that Minsky's vision (to use a familiar Schumpeterian term) was cast in dynamic terms, as is shown in *Can "It" Happen Again?* (1982). This is also evidenced by the following sentence that we co-authored:

> . . .we argue that the current state of economic theory as well as the perform- ance of capitalist recent years support the view that the path through time of a capitalist economy is best described as the result of the interaction between the system's endogenous dynamics, which if unconstrained would lead to complex paths that include periods of apparent growth, business cycles and economic instability, and the impact of institutions and interventions which, if apt, constrain the outcomes of capitalist market processes to viable or acceptable outcomes. We call these institutions and interventions thwarting systems. (Ferri and Minsky, 1992, p.79, reproduced in Chapter 7).

From the above quotation, it follows that Minsky was neither a doomster nor a Panglossian believing in the self-adjusting capability of the market process (see also Ferri and Minsky, 1989, reproduced in Chapter 6). He believed that policies and institutional changes could be of the utmost importance in checking the endogenous instability tendencies.

This complex vision is present "in nuce" in his initial papers collected in the volume *Can "It" Happen Again?* As stressed by Ferri (1992 and 2011), there are three analytical characteristics that are worth considering:

1. the model, based upon the interaction between the accelerator and the multiplier, tends to generate instability if unconstrained;
2. the presence of ceilings and floors can constrain the dynamics;
3. these constraints need not necessarily represent physical barriers but they may imply changes in policy and institutions triggering the presence of new initial conditions that allow the dynamic system to make a new start.

These characteristics are not confined to the initial accelerator–multiplier models considered by Minsky. They are robust to changes in the model and therefore can be utilized for more complex kinds of analysis that deserve to be considered.

8. THE TRANSACTIVE STRUCTURE

Even though there is no doubt that Minsky always had it in mind to operate within a monetary economy of production, it is not straightforward to find a point of contact between his early analysis and the so-called financial instability hypothesis. A possible and fruitful strategy is to understand where the financial aspects are hidden in his early approaches. The answer is to be found in his dissertation (Minsky, 1954/2004), which also offers some insights on his aggregation strategy.

According to Minsky, finance can have an important impact on the values of the parameters of the investment function that may reflect, *ceteris paribus*, different financial conditions. There are three main implications of this analysis. The first one is that real and financial aspects are always interconnected. In this perspective, neither the Modigliani–Miller (1958) approach nor purely monetary approaches seem to hold. The second implication is that the parameters of the (real) equations are subject to change when the financial conditions are different. It follows that, and this is the third implication, the working of the system is not necessarily a mechanical succession of numbers but the result of the interaction between complex forces.

According to Minsky: "Money matters most of the time, at some rare but important time it is all that matters, and sometimes money hardly matters at all" (1969, p. 228). The main methodological implication of this insight is that, within a monetary economy of production, money matters even though a financial sector is not specifically formalized. This does not imply that its presence is redundant. On the contrary, it allows the capturing of further processes of interdependence that cannot be generated in its absence. This is the value added of the financial instability hypothesis with respect to the early writings and to all those contributions that insist more on the financial nature of investment than on the presence of a fully specified financial system.

9.   MICRO–MACRO

There is a widespread view that Minsky did not trouble himself to explain methodology in detail in his publications, even though his writings have stimulated observations on his methodological choices. Ferri (1992), for instance, has insisted on detailing the methodological problems faced in his dynamic analysis, while Vercelli (2001) has stressed the difference between dynamic and structural instability, the latter characterizing Minsky's analysis but absent in Keynes's work.

The posthumous publication of Minsky's PhD dissertation (see Minsky, 1954/2004) has certainly contributed to challenging the view of a supposed neglect of methodological problems, and this has stirred further discussions (see Toporowski, 2008, p. 726).

Among the various topics considered in the dissertation, micro–macro relationships deserve special attention. As is well known, Minsky has been accused of being too macro oriented and, at the same time, laying himself open to fallacies of composition. In fact, according to some authors, he seemed to have relied mainly on national account identities. On the contrary, Lavoie and Seccareccia (2001) claim that his analysis is micro oriented so that fallacies of composition are inevitable when he tries to reach macro conclusions from micro analyses.

While the lack of microfoundations would assimilate Minsky to the neoclassical synthesis authors, the second kind of criticism includes Minsky among the supporters of the representative agent strategy. However, from a deeper analysis, Minsky is not reducible to either of these two alternatives. In fact, he offered many solutions to the micro–macro problems that will be considered in detail later on (see Chapter 8). At this stage of the analysis it is important to stress that they are suitable to be developed according to the new methodologies put forward in recent times.

10. SPECIAL LENSES

"The insider's view" qualifying the title of the book represents the second strategic choice followed in getting to the core of Minsky's economics, after the supremacy allowed to his books. The insider's view means that priority is given to the ideas that I learned directly from Minsky. These were developed through three different channels. The first one consists of the works that we co-authored during a two-decade period. The jointly published work is represented by three articles:

1. "Prices, employment, and profits" (1984);
2. "The breakdown of the IS–LM synthesis: implications for post-Keynesian economic theory" (1989);
3. "Market processes and thwarting systems" (1992).

These articles have a strong correspondence with the first three books quoted earlier, even though they do not respect their chronology and do not correspond one to one. The reasons behind the first peculiarity lie mainly in the idiosyncrasy that Hyman had not so much in writing papers as in publishing them, so that the official chronology does not fully reflect the dates of actual writing. The second peculiarity is a result of the fact that we tried to reach a unitary vision, so there was an overlap between the various contributions.

The three articles are reproduced in Part II of the book to provide a glimpse of our collaboration. They constitute the starting point of the book. Successively, they are updated and then, eventually, extended. The aim is to not so much to show the fruitfulness of that collaboration as to use them as a vehicle to get to the core of Minsky's contributions.

Along with the channel of published work, I have to mention a particular approach that I have called "Socratic colloquiums". These colloquiums consist in a series of questions raised by me and answered by Hyman. Both questions and answers were written on computers. A few of them have been published in the book just to provide a glimpse of our intense interactions. Someday they might be made available in full if the appropriate technology and the available human capital can be found.

The third channel is represented by book projects that were never finished. Whenever possible they will also be quoted, because they are important for understanding the background of the research agenda.

These three channels do not exhaust all the possibilities for grasping Minsky's ideas. A special mention must be reserved for conferences. Some of them were held while he was alive,[2] and a subset of them were published (see, for instance, the Festschrift edited by Fazzari and Papadimitriou,

1992). Others were organized post-mortem. In this case, I learned Minsky's ideas from the lessons of others (see Bellofiore and Ferri, 2001a, 2001b). The remaining were collected in books (Papadimitriou and Wray, 2010) or in journals (e.g. *International Journal of Political Economy*, vol. 39, 2010).

11.   THE VISION

The vision underlying Minsky's analysis is clearly stated in our joint work "Market processes and thwarting systems". This was the last paper that we wrote together, and it represents the pinnacle of our collaboration, at least from my point of view. Although dated 1992, it reads as though it was written after the Great Recession and not almost 20 years before.

It is worth reproducing it for at least three different reasons. First, it clearly states our common vision, even though we came from different intellectual backgrounds. Second, it indicates the main driving forces of a complex dynamic system. They are a mixture of endogenous tendencies countered by thwarting systems. And finally, it fixes a research agenda for future developments that I tried to follow as much as possible.

These elements are at the root of Minsky's interpretation suggested in this book as well as of the attempts at further developing his analysis – in particular, the efforts to insert his financial instability analysis into a broader complex dynamic framework. To achieve this insertion, I have to enter his black box of tools in a deeper way than he himself tried to do.

12.   INSTABILITY, INTEGRATION AND THE ROLE OF INSTITUTIONS

A complex dynamic system is not simply a mechanical sequence of events but represents a struggle between endogenous destabilizing forces thwarted by the adoption of suitable policies and the presence of adapting institutions. This vision creates a distance from those views that underline the exogenous nature of fluctuations. At the same time, it does necessarily lead to the conclusion that the system will inevitably experience runaway situations.

These endogenous destabilizing forces need not necessarily originate in the financial system, even though when this circumstance happens the turbulence tends to become particularly severe. This circumstance, however, does not dispense with considering what happens in the other markets, that is, the so-called real economy. In this perspective, the Minskyan financial instability hypothesis is deeply conceived within a monetary economy of production, where the role of the labor market and the nature of institutions are important. They must be integrated with the financial analysis, and this is why these aspects will be considered in this book.

The emphasis on the labor market represents my value added in the collaboration with Minsky. This does not imply that Hyman neglected this field, as his posthumous book *Ending Poverty: Jobs, Not Welfare* (2013) clearly shows. His expertise was really broad. In a sense, he was a classical economist.

13. THE STRUCTURE OF THE BOOK

Beyond the present introductory chapter, the structure of the book is characterized by five parts, each containing three chapters. In more detail, Part I, called "'It' happened again", describes the characteristics of the Minsky moment vis-à-vis Minsky's economics (Chapter 2), while Chapter 3 presents a synoptic view of the financial instability hypothesis. Chapter 4 illustrates the implications of an insider's view for both understanding Minsky's analysis and putting forward a research agenda.

Part II includes the three articles that Hyman and I co-authored. On the one hand, this inclusion serves the practical function of making them available in a unitary way since they are rather old articles. On the other, they represent the backbone of the book. They not only bear witness to the deepness of our collaboration, but are used to interpret and develop Minsky's analysis. Specifically, these articles are updated, deepened and broadened in order to meet the challenges that the new stylized facts of the economy and the developments of the discipline put forward.

Part III starts updating and deepening some methodological aspects present both in these three articles and in Minsky's works. Specifically, the triple classification suggested by Hicks will be followed. Chapter 8 deals with the micro–macro relationship in Minsky's analysis. Chapter 9 deals with the foundations of dynamics not only to compare Minsky with the so-called DSGE (discrete stochastic general equilibrium) literature (which was not yet put forward when the article reproduced in Chapter 6 was written) but also to fix the tenets of an endogenous dynamics. Chapter 10 updates the 1984 article on prices and profits. In so doing, it presents new tools for producing nonlinear dynamics.

Part IV enters the so-called black box of instruments used by Minsky. It is aimed at broadening Minsky's analysis in order to consider phenomena such as income distribution, inequality and productivity. In other words, it does not only consider the dynamic suggestions contained in his 1982 book, but tries to link growth and the labor market in a medium-run perspective. Chapter 11 develops a model where drivers, adapters and constraints coexist and where unemployment is generated by both aggregate demand and aggregate supply. Chapter 12 introduces the role of technical change and its implications for unemployment. Chapter 13 underlines the structural properties of the labor market. The results of the three chapters are compared with Minsky's ideas put forward in his 2013 posthumous book.

Part V utilizes this analytical apparatus in order to revisit the financial instability hypothesis in the dynamic setting put forward in Part IV. Chapter 14 stresses the novelty of the Great Recession and its analytical challenges. Chapter 15 develops a meta-model encapsulating the financial instability hypothesis in a broader context. Chapter 16 concludes by stressing the results achieved and the work that remains to be done.

NOTES

1. A full list of the publications of Minsky is to be found in Wray (2016).
2. For instance, we organized a conference on Keynes and Schumpeter at Washington University in 1983. On the contrary, with Riccardo Leoni we were preparing a conference on unemployment, but because of Hyman's sickness it never took place.

PART I

"It" happened again

2. The Minsky moment and the economics of Minsky

1. A TWO-FACED JANUS

Minsky has been a two-faced Janus. In fact, he played the role of the economist with the bankers, and taught banking to the economists. As an economist he was marked by the Great Depression and therefore he was minded to deal with turbulences. As a banker he gained hands-on experience, serving on the board of Mark Twain Bank of St. Louis, Missouri.

This double role explains his fate in the literature. It is not true that Minsky remained far from the limelight throughout his life. Nor is it correct to claim that the blame lay on his approach, which shunned academic convention by not exploiting his mathematics degree and instead using a narrative convention.

During the 1950s Minsky published in the major mainstream journals, offering important contributions on the theory of endogenous business cycles. He competed with the most important authors on the subject (such as Hicks, Kaldor, Goodwin and Kalecki). Most of these analyses lost their centrality when the quantitative methods based upon a stochastic interpretation of the business cycle became prominent, while the so-called neoclassical synthesis eliminated any reference to the Great Depression. In this perspective, occasional stock market busts (such as the 1987 Wall Street episode) or currency crashes are allowed, but modern economies had, it was claimed, defeated their worst demons (see Lucas, 1987).

Those (old) themes did not disappear but simply lost center stage, being kept alive only in the post-Keynesian tradition. However, Minsky, with his second face, the financial one, survived these changes that culminated with the so-called dynamic stochastic general equilibrium (DSGE) models. His Schumpeterian background led him to pay attention to innovations, not so much those in the real market as those in the financial sector. This was a decisive strategic factor in the era of financialization and securitization that accompanied the process of globalization.

For these reasons, being at the same time an insider and a scholar having long-run and broad views, he remained well known in the financial milieu and in Wall Street. The Great Recession ignited the process of contagion

14

of his popularity, which spread among a wider community of people. At the same time, it cannibalized most of the post-Keynesian writings. However, he had only a marginal impact on mainstream journals, which remained resilient to his analysis. This does not imply that new innovative approaches capable of contemplating Minsky's vision are not developing, as will be shown later.

2. THE BACKGROUND

Minsky moments are grounded upon the so-called financial instability hypothesis. Essentially, this hypothesis is an endogenous explanation of both business cycles and episodes of instability. It simply asserts that long stretches of prosperity sow the seeds of the next crisis. In this perspective, the 1920s were the incubator of the Great Depression, while in order to understand what happened in the "Great Recession", one has to search in the previous period of buoyancy.

The financial instability hypothesis did not appear out of the blue in Minsky's analysis. It had a long gestation in both the freshwater and saltwater schools. This dichotomy has been introduced only recently in the literature to distinguish between the new neoclassicists and the new Keynesians, the former concentrated in Chicago and the latter at Harvard. During Minsky's time, however, these places were different from what they are now. Chicago was the place where Minsky met Simon and Lange and learned the necessity of grounding any theory within a precise institutional context. Money and finance were precisely two of the most important examples of these institutions. At Harvard, where Hyman wrote a dissertation under the supervision of Schumpeter and then Leontief, he got acquainted with Keynesian thought enriched by possible innovations in the financial markets.

As stressed by Papadimitriou (2004): "It should be understood that Harvard, where Minsky undertook graduate studies, had not been as much of an influence on him as his undergraduate years at the University of Chicago. His recollections were of disappointment as topics discussed were treated in rather a mechanic manner and also in a most unstructured way" (p.x). And as the same author underlined some years earlier (1992): "[Alvin] Hansen, the leading disciple of Keynes in America, interpreted Keynes . . . [by] virtually ignoring the significance of money and finance. Furthermore, uncertainty, which was fundamental in Keynes' understanding of the capitalist economy, was left out" (p.18).

Even if it is true that these authors have always remained present in Minsky intellectual production, it is also true that his theory has been strongly shaped by some decisive facts, the most important being the Great Depression. As he wrote in his *Can "It" Happen Again?* (1982):

> Fifty years ago, in the winter of 1932–33, the American financial and economic system came to a halt: the collapse was well nigh complete. Two generations of the public (and the politicians they elect) have been haunted by the spectre of "It" (such a great collapse) happening again. We cannot understand the institutional structure of our economy, which was largely put into place during the first years of the Roosevelt era, without recognizing that a major aim of the reformers was to organize the financial and economic institutions so that "It" could not happen again. (p. vii)

Although formulated in the mid-1950s, the financial instability hypothesis received a definite form in the mid-1960s at Washington University in St. Louis (Missouri), where he taught until his retirement (1990).

3. A SYNOPTIC VIEW

Minsky's financial instability hypothesis had the Great Depression as a source of inspiration. This turbulent period has been studied not only by contemporaneous authors, such as Fisher (1933), who coined the term "debt deflation",[1] but also by successive scholars who have reflected on this experience (see Galbraith, 1961 and Kindleberger, 1978). However, it is important to stress that Minsky's contribution is fundamentally original, largely because he tried to apply the financial instability hypothesis to a context that was changing due to the occurrence of the Great Depression. In particular, the world of deflation was being replaced by a different set of policy options and institutions.

The financial instability hypothesis has been formalized in different ways (see Taylor and O'Connell, 1985, being one of the first examples. See also Fazzari et al., 2008), with contributions increasing enormously during the Great Recession and its aftermath. To give a glimpse of these various contributions, it is useful to refer to Table 2.1, which is based upon the same methodological grid used in Chapter 1.

The financial instability hypothesis implies different characteristics that are not always considered to their full extent. It follows that, even within the same paradigm, there can be different positions. However, the financial instability hypothesis has been studied within different paradigms, as will be shown in Chapter 3. The bulk of the contributions comes from the post-Keynesian world, which is a variegated one. One can find Kaldorian (Ryoo, 2016) and Kaleckian approaches (Lavoie, 2014), along with studies based upon Goodwin (Passarella, 2010), where income distribution matters.

Table 2.1   Classifying the contributions to the financial instability hypothesis

Temporal	Short-run	Business cycles	Medium-run
Transaction	Real	Monetary	
Aggregation	Capital goods	Financial sector	

These contributions present differences in at least one of the elements illustrated in the grid. Some are statics, while others are dynamics. Some include the banking sector, while others ignore it (see Nikolaidi, 2017 and Andreassen, 2017 for surveys).

Still others analyze the financial instability hypothesis within an agent-based approach (see Di Guilmi and Carvalho, 2015 and Delli Gatti et al., 2011), as will be considered later.

4.   THE CORE OF THE FINANCIAL INSTABILITY ANALYSIS

The variety of contributions that have been mentioned capture many of the analytic and methodological aspects of the financial instability hypothesis. Furthermore, some of them contribute to developing the idea in a substantial way. However, before proceeding, it is important to try to understand which are the aspects that can be considered the core of the Minskyan theory. Four of them are fundamental.

The first is that the financial instability hypothesis rests on endogenous forces. This is the main dividing line with those approaches that refer to exogenous financial shocks. The dichotomy endogenous–exogenous is a classical distinction in the theory of business cycles. It can also be used for financial turbulence situations.

The second core aspect is that although the seeds are cast in the financial market, they produce important effects because they interplay with real markets, in general, and investment, in particular. According to Minsky, investment is a dynamic activity bridging past and future. This implies the existence of an exchange of money today for money tomorrow. While money tomorrow comes from the operation of the activity in the form of cash flow, money today can come from either the firm's own cash or that of others. This latter way can take the form of either equities or debt.

According to the Modigliani–Miller theorem (1958), this different mixture should not affect the evaluation of the firm. This depends on the fundamentals, that is, how productive is capital, and not on finance mixture, which depends on the relative prices in the financial markets. For Minsky, on the contrary, the functioning of the economy depends also on the balances between the various financial channels. This is a fundamental divide separating Minsky's economics from the various versions of mainstream economics that have prevailed on the international stage. This is the Keynesian legacy of the monetary economy of production.

The third aspect is that the banking sector plays an important role in aggravating the quantity amplifying mechanisms that are operating in the system. Banks provide flexibility, but at the same time can be a source of instability. This dual nature is not typical of banks, but of the economic variables in general.

The fourth aspect is that the struggle between these forces can generate runaway situations. However, these do not necessarily take place, because there are thwarting forces operating in the system.

This is the reason why the dynamics of the system is so complex and cannot be examined by mechanical devices. And this is also the reason why nobody, not even Minsky, can foretell with precision the coming of a Minsky moment in the near future.

5.   DIFFERENT KINDS OF INSTABILITY

Minsky claimed that the financial instability hypothesis is a particular case of instability of complex systems such as capitalist economies. He was aware that these instabilities could assume different forms, as exemplified by Figure 2.1.

During his life, Minsky studied most of these kinds of instabilities, which had origins in different markets, and above all studied the conditions under which they might generate runaway situations. In this perspective, financial crises were particularly important. However, they remained a species within a well-studied genus.

6.   BUSINESS CYCLES AND FINANCIAL KEYNESIANISM

Minsky taught that endogenous fluctuations are a normal state for the economy, even though they may differ because of the intensity, the nature of the markets involved or the evolution into a runaway situation.

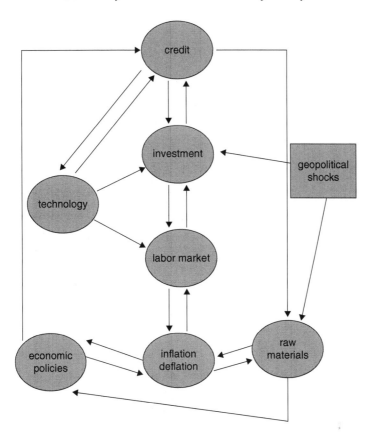

Figure 2.1   Different sources of instability

Among the various possibilities illustrated in Figure 2.1, Minsky[2] supposed that the canonical business cycle in the post-war period could be
characterized by the following seven stages:

1. Expansion accelerates and this brings about an increase in inflation.
2. Central Bank fights inflation by increasing the rate of interest.
3. This intervention might break the financial markets.
4. In this case, the Central Bank intervenes again.
5. Investment falls, income follows the same pattern as do inflation and
    the rate of interest. Unemployment rises.
6. Government expands the deficit.
7. The decline is halted while expansion has a new beginning.

As one can see, it is an endogenous explanation of the business cycle with the following two basic characteristics. On the one hand, real and monetary aspects are both present. On the other, policies and institutions play a fundamental role.

The possibility of checking these further feedbacks that are not present in the traditional business cycle depends on both the presence of the Central Bank as a lender of last resort and the role of fiscal policy in steering aggregate demand.

The goal is to understand how this canonical cycle, which characterized the post-war period until the Great Recession, can generate Minsky moments which fundamentally remain dynamic phenomena. To reach this goal, one has to consider how the financial instability hypothesis can be inserted into this canonical business cycle profile. To achieve this, one must introduce an investment function based upon both real and financial aspects. This endeavor has also been named "financial Keynesianism", a first step towards a full-blown financial instability hypothesis.

7. A FORMALIZATION

Consider the following investment equation specified in an intensive form, that is, deflated by (last period) income:

$$i_t = \frac{I_t}{Y_{t-1}} = \eta_0 + \eta_1 g_t^e + \eta_2(1-\omega)(1+g_t^e) - \eta_2 \frac{R_t d_t}{(1+\pi_t^e)} \qquad (2.1)$$

In this equation, g_t^e represents the expected rate of growth, while the remaining terms represent the expected cash flows in real terms, that is, the expected profit share (ω being the labor share) diminished by the debt service. R_t is the nominal rate of interest (it appears in this expression because interest payments are fixed in nominal terms in a monetary economy), while d_t represents the debt ratio, as will be shown below.[3]

This specification of the investment function stresses the interdependence between nominal and real aspects. Hicks (1989) named this approach the "balance sheet" perspective. This perspective becomes very important when the business cycle is not based mainly on the process of stock decumulation as happens in the very short run but is generated by the whole process of accumulation. This specification (see also Fazzari et al., 2008) is based upon a real and a financial kind of accelerator and assumes the existence of asymmetric information and uncertainty (see also Stiglitz and Greenwald, 2003 and Variato, 2001 and 2004).

Furthermore, one has to specify the pattern of debt, which is also defined in intensive form in the following way:

$$d_t = \frac{D_t}{P_{t-1} Y_{t-1}}$$

where P_{t-1} are (last year) prices. The dynamics are given by the following formula:

$$d_t = \frac{d_{t-1}(1 + R_{t-1})}{(1 + g_{t-1})(1 + \pi_{t-1})} + \frac{i_{t-1}}{(1 + g_{t-1})} - (1 - \omega) \tag{2.2}$$

where π_t is the inflation rate.

This formula will assume a different specification when, later on, consumer debt will be placed at the center of the analysis. Initially, the labor share will be considered exogenous.

In the present model, prices and wages are determined in non-competitive markets (see Hicks, 1989, Layard et al., 1991 and Asada et al., 2006), while productivity dynamics are considered exogenous. This hypothesis will be dropped later on. With a fixed markup, the inflation rate is given by:

$$\pi_t = \alpha \pi_t^e - \sigma_1 (u_{t-1} - u_0) + (1 - \alpha)\pi_{t-1} \tag{2.3}$$

where π_t^e is the expected rate of inflation and u_{t-1} one period lagged rate of unemployment.[4]

To close the model, the following equations must be appended.

$$u_t = 1 - e_t \tag{2.4}$$

$$e_t = e_{t-1} \frac{1 + g_t}{1 + \tau} \tag{2.5}$$

$$R_t = R^* + \psi_1 (\pi_t^e - \pi_0) + \psi_2 (g_t^e - g_0) \tag{2.6}$$

$$g_t = c_1(1 + g_t^e) + c_2 + c_3 \frac{R_t d_t}{(1 + \pi_t)} + i_t - 1 \tag{2.7}$$

Equation (2.4) defines unemployment, given labor supply (normalized to 1), where e_t is the employment ratio. Its dynamics are determined from (2.5). They depend on the ratio between the growth rate of the product (g_t) and the (given) productivity rate (t). Equation (2.5) determines the nominal rate of interest from a version of the Taylor rule, where the target values are set equal to the expected values. Finally, equation (2.7) represents aggregate demand, where consumption is made dependent on both past and expected rates of growth.

Given the expected values g^e and π^e and the dynamic of productivity (τ), it is possible to specify a temporary equilibrium for a system of seven equations in seven unknowns: π_t, u_t, e_t, i_t, d_t, R_t and g_t.

8.   SIMULATING THE DYNAMICS

To study the dynamics of the model, one has to formulate some hypotheses about expectations. Initially, we refer to a quasi perfect foresight hypothesis, where the qualifier is necessary because no assumption of market clearing has been put forward (see Turnovsky, 2000). Later on this assumption will be dropped (see Chapter 15), because a learning process will be considered. The reason behind this choice of a quasi perfect foresight hypothesis is twofold. On the one hand, it shows that the existence of an endogenous business cycle does not depend on the assumption of naïve hypotheses about expectations. On the other, this assumption reduces the dimension of the system and this may allow for a more analytical approach, as will be shown in the next chapter.

Therefore, the following equalities are put forward:

$$\pi^e_{et} = \pi_t$$
$$g_{et} = g_t$$

In this case, the system can be written in the following way, before being simulated. First, the inflation equation can be written as (see Ferri, 2011):

$$\pi_t = -\frac{\sigma_1}{1-\alpha}(u_{t-1} - u^*) + \pi_{t-1} \qquad (2.3)\ bis$$

Second, R_t, g_t and i_t are determined simultaneously:

$$\begin{bmatrix} 1 & -\psi_1 & 0 \\ \dfrac{c_3}{(1+\pi_t)(1-c_1)} & 1 & -\dfrac{1}{1-c_1} \\ \dfrac{\eta_3}{1+\pi_t} & (-\eta_2 + \eta_3\theta(1-\omega)) & 1 \end{bmatrix} \begin{bmatrix} R_t \\ g_t \\ i_t \end{bmatrix} =$$

$$\begin{bmatrix} R^* + \psi_1(\pi_t - \pi_0) - \psi_2 g_0 + \psi_3 \\ \dfrac{c_1 + c_2 + c_3 - 1}{1 - c_1} - \dfrac{c_3}{(1 - c_1)(1 + \pi_t)} \end{bmatrix}$$

Table 2.2 The parameters of the simulations

$\tau = 0.0075$	$\sigma_1 = 0.03$	$\sigma_2 = 0.04\sigma_1$	$r = 0.015$	$\eta_1 = 0.1344$ $\eta_2 = 0.150$
$\eta_3 = 0.345$	$c_1 = 0.40$	$c_2 = 0.4$	$c_3 = 0.025$	$\psi_1 = 1.1$
$\psi_2 = 0.65$		$R^* = 0.01$		

Finally, the remaining equations can be solved in a recursive way.

The parameters of the simulation are shown in Table 2.2. The parameters chosen are within the range established by econometric research. The dynamic pattern is shown in Figure 2.2. Persistent cycles are generated for the most important variables, like the growth rate, the rate of inflation and unemployment. This also holds true for the interest rate and the financial burden. Finally, loops in the Phillips curve are generated, after an initial period of transitory dynamics.

The purpose of the simulations is twofold. First, they set a benchmark for other simulations based upon different expectational hypotheses. Second, they show that persistent fluctuations can be obtained even in the presence of perfect foresight. It follows that the seven-stage cycle discussed at the beginning can be described by the above model, which represents a step towards a full-blown financial instability hypothesis.

The financial instability hypothesis, when it is taken into account, raises many questions. According to some, it would be a micro theory that does not hold in a macro environment. In a Kaleckian framework, to which Minsky referred, investment creates profits and if debt let investment take place there is not an increase in the debt ratio because profit also rises. This is the so-called paradox of debt that seems to prevent the financial instability hypothesis from becoming operative, since the increasing leverage ratio, one of the pillars of the theory, cannot materialize.

The results of our simulations are in contrast with these conclusions. This does not imply that the "paradox of debt" cannot be generated. It all depends on the complexity of the interaction between real and monetary factors that take place in a dynamic environment. If one assumes that the financial conditions change in an expansion phase, then the financial

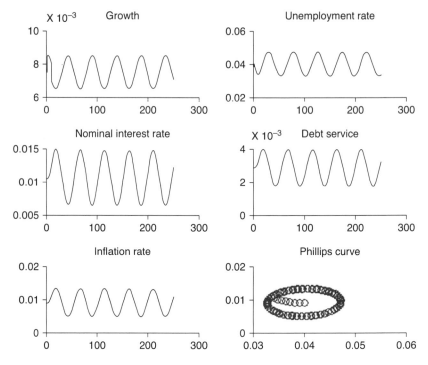

Figure 2.2   The dynamics with a financial accelerator

instability hypothesis becomes a macro possibility where the relative speed
of investment, cash flows and debt service are not necessarily the same.

   One final aspect is to be underlined. While in the pre-World War II
world deflation caused debt to peak after the crisis had taken place, in the
post-World War II world described by the model debt has a pro-cyclical
pattern, driven by cash flows and debt services.

9.   ADVANTAGES AND LIMITATIONS OF THE MODEL

The model discussed presents many analytical attributes. For instance,
one advantage of the model is that it shows how the financial instability
hypothesis can be inserted within the stylized fact of a seven-stage cycle
without creating any fallacy of composition. The financial instability
hypothesis is a dynamic hypothesis that cannot be tested within a static
environment. In a dynamic context, what matters is the relative speeds

of growth and debt accumulation, and these can generate different levels of leverage as shown in the above model. As already anticipated, another advantage is the capability of generating endogenous cycles without refer- ring to backward expectations, even though the assumption of perfect foresight in a world of uncertainty is particularly out of place.

This leads to the insufficiencies of the model. In fact, although it allows the possibility of runaway situations, which happens when the values of the parameters are changed, it does not analyze them in detail. It follows that it is not suited to considering extreme cases such as the Great Depression or the Great Recession. However, in order to proceed in this direction, the model need not be abandoned; rather, it must be simply refined. In fact, it contains most of the elements necessary to deal with such extreme situations.

NOTES

1. The importance of this author has been underlined by Eggertsson and Krugman (2013).
2. See our unpublished and unfinished book, P. Ferri and H.P. Minsky: "Business Cycles and Economic Instability" (1988).
3. In other words, investment is a function of expected cash flow, defined as:

$$CF_t^e = P_t(1 - \omega) Y_t^e - R_t D_t$$

Expressing in terms of ratios, defined below, one obtains the formula in the text that generates non-neutralities due to the presence of predetermined debt burden.
4. The presence of this lag implies that wages are set after the unemployment determination. In the perfect foresight model it is useful because it allows some recursivity in the model. However, later on, when the linearized version of the model is considered, it can be changed.

3. A synoptic view of the financial instability hypothesis

1. "IT" HAPPENED AGAIN

Can "It" Happen Again? was published in 1982. It contains many articles that were written much earlier. In those writings the Great Depression ("it") was a legacy of the past and only a possibility for the future. The fact that "it" did not happen until 2008, that is, almost 12 years after Minsky's death and 26 years after the publication of the book, raises two questions:

1. why did "it" not happen for such a long period of time?
2. why did "it" happen in 2008?

To answer these questions, one has to refer to Ferri and Minsky (1992), who have shown (see Chapter 7) that the actual outcome of an economy depends on the interaction between endogenous destabilizing market forces and thwarting processes. Given this premise, the first question may be answered in the following way: it did not happen for such a long time because the market destabilizing forces have been checked by particularly strong thwarting devices that were rooted in the aftermath of the Great Depression. In other words, while the policies put forward in the "New Deal" era have been effective in stopping debt deflation and stimulating the economy, the ensuing institutional reforms had a longer-run impact on the working of the economic system. In this perspective, the triad, big government, big firms and big unions, allowed a period of prosperity that lasted from the end of World War II until the late 1960s.

The second question cannot be answered by referring to our joint work, even though the answer can be extrapolated from it: these thwarting forces were not powerful enough to prevent the 2008 crisis from taking place. In turn, this answer suggests new questions because one has to understand what undermined the power of these forces vis-à-vis a stronger destabilizing impact deriving from the market processes.

The Great Recession calls for an explanation that is not necessarily the same as that put forward for the Great Depression. And it is exactly for this reason that it is also challenging for Minsky's theoretical apparatus, epitomized by his financial instability hypothesis. In other words, dropping the question mark in "Can 'It' Happen Again" has far-reaching analytical consequences that deserve to be brought to surface.

2.   THE PECULIARITIES OF EXTREME EVENTS

Extreme events, such as the Great Depression and the Great Recession, differ not only from the canonical business cycle that characterized the post-World War II period but also from so-called financial crises, which happen when the financial sector in general, and banks in particular, is involved. Usually, these crises last longer and have a more profound impact on the economy than the canonical business cycle (see Romer and Romer, 2017). The extreme events just mentioned are a subset of these crises and are characterized by:

1.   the speed of the events;
2.   the broadness of the sectors involved;
3.   the deepness of the impact on the financial institutions;
4.   the creation of massive unemployment;
5.   the long duration;
6.   the use of unorthodox measures of economic policy;
7.   the reshaping of institutions.

In what follows, the objective is not so much to produce a narrative describing these extreme events as to understand their structural differences. In this regard, two details are worth considering.

The first is that the process of debt creation has been different in the Great Recession compared to the Great Depression. In the latter, firms were the players, and debt deflation at that time hit firms and banks. In the Great Recession, on the contrary, the players have been households and, of course, the banking system as a whole. The banking system has always been on the stage, though in the last episode the so-called shadow banking must also be considered.

As will be considered in the following chapters, these differences in the debt process partly reflect differences in income distribution. In fact, in the Great Recession, a falling labor share has been accompanied by an increased debt ratio for households.

The second refers to policies, which explains why debt deflation was not so important in the Great Recession. Policies this time have been implemented more rapidly, and are different from those adopted in the 1930s.

There is no doubt that monetary policy has been used more intensively and effectively this time. The lender-of-last-resort power of the Federal Reserve has been used promptly and in an innovative way, by implementing so-called quantitative easing measures. These measures have prevented the banking system from going bankrupt. Differently from what happened in the 1930s, the contagion effect was halted at the first round, stopping further rounds from taking place.

On the contrary, fiscal policy has not been used as intensively as before. Apart from the beginning of the crisis, the philosophy of the Ricardian intertemporal constraint has dominated. This switch of policy has not only had a direct impact on the functioning of the economy, but also an indirect one through an increasing level of inequality. As shown in Ferri (2016), the capital gains that the quantitative easing has allowed, not only in the capital markets but also in the value of housing or in the value of land, have favored the richest section of the population. At the same time, the lack of fiscal policy has not helped the poorest section of the population, either in terms of income or in terms of employment.

3.   THE ANALYTICAL IMPACT

One would have expected that the first analytical consequence of the Great Recession would have been the abandoning of the predominant vision of business cycles, which assembles different positions, ranging from the more radical, such as the obsession for its obsolescence (see Bronfenbrenner, 1969) or its complete eradication by policy (see Lucas, 1987), to the more traditional view based upon an exogenous explanation.

Unfortunately, this methodological change did not occur – at least, it did not take place on a grand scale. Many researchers have tried to study the financial instability hypothesis as a particular case of a credit cycle model (see Liu and Wang, 2011 and Cerra and Saxena, 2017), even though van Eeghen (2014) has shown that DSGE (discrete stochastic general equilibrium) models cannot capture the complexity of this phenomenon. They are usually based upon a stochastic driver and ignore the interaction between the monetary and real sectors.

Others have deepened only the final part of the process, when sudden events can stop the dynamics of business cycles (see Mendoza, 2006). These approaches refer mainly to a short-run perspective and are based upon exogenous shocks. In this case, however, they are not of the i.i.d. (independent and identically identified) kind because the idea is to assimilate the turbulence to a rare event (Gabaix, 2008), also called a "Black Swan". In these episodes, there is a flight to quality and fire selling that destabilize the economy (see Caballero and Krishnamurthy, 2008 and Geneakoplos, 2003 and 2010, for a general equilibrium perspective).

The extreme events, however, are also challenging for the theories based upon the endogenous explanations of the business cycle. In this perspective, the model presented in Chapter 2 can also be challenged.

4. GENERATING RUNAWAY SITUATIONS

Let us reconsider the model of financial Keynesianism illustrated in the previous chapter (see also Ferri, 2010) and linearize it in order to obtain the following system:

$$d_t = D_1 d_{t-1} + D_2 i_{t-1} - D_3 g_{t-1} + D_4 R_{t-1} - D_5 \pi_t \qquad (3.1)$$

$$i_t = I_1 g_t - I_2 R_t - I_3 d_t + I_4 \pi_t \qquad (3.2)$$

$$g_t = G_1 i_t + G_2 R_t + G_3 d_t - G_4 \pi_t \qquad (3.3)$$

$$\pi_t = P_1 l_t + \pi_{t-1} \qquad (3.4)$$

$$l_t = l_{t-1} + L_1 g_t \qquad (3.5)$$

$$R_t = \psi_1 \pi_t + \psi_2 g_t + \psi_3 R_{t-1} \qquad (3.6)$$

All the variables are expressed as deviations from the steady state value, while the values of the multipliers are given in the Appendix to this chapter.

The system can be written in a compact way:

$$x_t = A^{-1} B x_{t-1}$$

In this case, the eigenvalues and the eigenvector of the system can be computed. Given the values of the parameters shown in Table 3A.1, one finds a couple of eigenvalues, which are complex and their modulus is equal to 1. This is a necessary condition in order to have a Neimark–Sacker kind of bifurcation. (For the other conditions, along with the dynamic property of the invariant curve, see Kuznetsov, 2004.) This is the situation underlying Figure 2.2 in Chapter 2 (the parameters of the linearized version are almost the same, as appears in the Appendix).

To obtain runaway situations, one must increase the values of the destabilizing parameters, such as coefficient η_1 and coefficient η_2 in the investment equation. These runaway situations, which are typical of the so-called extreme events, cannot only be simulated but can be proved analytically since the model is reducible to 3-D.

5. INSTABILITY IN A 3-D MODEL

The system can be written in the following way (see Appendix):

$$\begin{bmatrix} \pi_t \\ d_t \\ l_t \end{bmatrix} = \begin{bmatrix} 1 & 0 & P1 \\ DDD2 & DDD1 & 0 \\ L43 & L42 & L41 \end{bmatrix} \begin{bmatrix} \pi_{t-1} \\ d_{t-1} \\ l_{t-1} \end{bmatrix}$$

This 3-D system shows that the ultimate determinant of the dynamics are inflation, employment and debt. Employment reflects growth, inflation is related to the rate of interest and debt is linked to investment.

To study its stability, one has to refer to the polynomial underlying the matrix, which is represented by the following expression:

$$x^3 + d_2 x^2 + d_1 x = d_0$$

$$d_2 = -(DDD1 + L41 + 1);$$
$$d_1 = (DDD1 + L41 + DDD1*L41 - P1*L43);$$
$$d_0 = -(DDD1*L41 + P1*DDD''*L42 - P1*DDD1*L43).$$

According to Farebrother (1973) (see also Beavis and Dobbs, 1990 and Gandolfo, 1996), the stability requires the following inequality to hold:

$$1 + d_1 - |d_2 + d_0| > 0$$
$$1 - d_1 + d_2 d_0 + d_0^2 > 0$$
$$d_1 > 3$$

In this specific case, an increase in the values of the coefficient of the investment function can violate these conditions and therefore create runaway situations. It is important to stress that Minsky considered this procedure to be legitimate, as he made clear in his 1982 volume. For instance, when the monetary environment changes, it may impact on the existing investment equation by modifying its parameters. These changes can generate runaway situations.

However, in order to enter the core of his financial instability hypothesis, other elements of the economics of Minsky must be considered.

6. THE TWO-PRICE-LEVEL THEORY

The first element to be considered is the two-price-level theory of investment. This is a theory that distinguishes between the price of output and the price of investment and capital goods. This is a new analytical tool that enriches his financial theory of investment and that can eventually strengthen his financial instability theory. It was published in his *John Maynard Keynes* (1975), which was the result of his sabbatical year spent in Cambridge, UK, even though the foundations are to be found in his early work on financial instability, and his contacts with post-Keynesians on both sides of the Atlantic, such that Hyman recognizes: "Joan Robinson, G.L.S. Shackle, Nicholas Kaldor, Sidney Weintraub, Paul Davidson, Robert Clower, and Axel Leijonhufvud are prominent among the dissidents who affected my thinking"(p. vi).

The second legacy of that sabbatical is the Kaleckian theory of profits. In his view, cash flows, the buzzword in almost all his writings, had major functions:

1. to signal whether investments undertaken were based on sound decisions;
2. to provide funds needed by firms to fulfil payments;
3. to assist in the decision-making process for future investment financial conditions.

However, along with these functions, there was a feedback that can be considered the missing link between micro and macro: investment feeds profits. Following the sabbatical in Cambridge, this relationship was never forgotten. In a sense he closed a double gap: the one separating American Keynesianism from the European ones, and the one distinguishing his early works from the final ones.

These two legacies imply two analytical features that must be at the root of his financial instability analysis: the interdependence between real and monetary aspects and the role of income distribution in affecting both cash flows and the level of debts.

7. DEEPENING THE FINANCIAL ASPECTS

The financial instability analysis requires two further features: heterogeneity and complex expectations. These become essential in order to deal with a more sophisticated financial system. In this perspective, Minsky distinguishes between three kinds of financing (see also Ferri and Variato, 2010b):

1. Hedging;
2. Speculative;
3. Ponzi.

They differ according to the different relationships existing between cash flow, interest and debt. Hedge financing is the safest form because firms rely only on their future cash flow (*cf*) to repay all their borrowings (*D*):

$$\sum_1^t cf_i > D_t$$

Here, one has to make an important distinction between exante and expost. Firms that are hedgers exante do not necessarily remain the same expost; it all depends on expectations and realization, as will be discussed shortly.

Speculative finance is riskier because firms rely on cash flows to repay the interest on their debts. Therefore, they must roll over their debts to repay the principal:

$$\sum_1^t cf_i > \sum_1^t rD_i$$

The risk in this case is determined by the possibility of a downturn that would compromise the situation.

Finally, Ponzi financing is most dangerous because cash flows cover neither principal nor interest. Entrepreneurs are betting only that the underlying asset will appreciate by enough to cover their liabilities:

$$\sum_1^t cf_i < \sum_1^t rD_i$$

If this does not happen, they will be left exposed. Over-optimism by firms and by banks is at the root of this result. It is important to stress that these categories can be attributed to sectors and not only to agents. In this case, Table 3.1 can be helpful.

The Great Recession, also named the Great Financial Crisis by Wray (2016), belongs to the first row, while the Great Depression concerned mainly row 2. Finally, row 3 catches what happened in the southern countries of the European monetary system, the Economic and Monetary Union (EMU), which has a constitutional architecture that ignores the possibility of financial instability crises.

Table 3.1   The possibility of "Ponzi" finance in the various sectors

Agents	Sector
Households	Consumption
Firms	Investment
State	

In a world of perfect information and rational expectations, these phenomena are very unlikely to happen (even though the oxymoron "rational exuberance" has been coined), so there emerges a methodological contrast between those theories that assume these properties and those which deny them.

This is the reason why Minsky theory is accompanied not only by analytical conflicts but also by deeper divisions concerning the vision on the working of the economy.

8.   FROM MICRO TO MACRO

As interesting as this tripartition might be, it remains within the boundaries of microeconomics. Every banker could come across one or more of these situations. The challenge is to understand how they translate into macro phenomena.

It goes without saying that economies dominated by hedge financing are the most stable, while the prevalence of the other two forms creates fragility and instability.

If asset values start to fall, the most indebted firms will be forced to sell their positions. This further undermines asset values, causing troubles for even more firms. An amplifying feedback reaction is set in motion.

In this situation, four relevant analytical questions arise from a macro point of view, neglecting for the moment the more methodological ones:

1.   What triggers a Minsky moment?
2.   What is the role of uncertainty and asymmetric information?
3.   Why are financial crises so potentially devastating?
4.   What stops the process?

Each of these questions will be considered in the remaining part of the chapter.

9.   THE PARADOX OF TRANQUILLITY

One has to investigate what could turn a canonical business cycle into something more turbulent which "makes 'it' happen again", where "it" is notoriously the Great Depression or any other "extreme event". Minsky always thought that these events were within the set of probabilities, and this created a great distance with respect to the mainstream literature.

One of Minsky's (1975) main theses is that tranquillity is destabilizing.

Tranquillity favors the development of particularly risky investment that is the driver of business cycles. At the same time, as has already been mentioned, the proportion of speculative and Ponzi finance increases considerably, also helped by financial innovations.

The paradox of tranquillity has provoked much perplexity in the literature. However, it must be remembered that it is a general principle underlying any explanation of fluctuations based upon endogenous elements. For instance, it is at the root of the so-called accelerator–multiplier model so intensively studied by Minsky. In this case, the acceleration of investment creates its own seed of inversion. In a parallel way, the presence of a protracted buoyant period induces firms and bankers to ignore the increasing risk that they are collectively generating.

10. ASYMMETRIC INFORMATION AND UNCERTAINTY

The notions of asymmetric information and uncertainty are at the root of the previous analysis. Their possible coexistence explains the contrast between different theoretical paradigms. For instance, most so-called new-Keynesian authors tend to exclude the presence of uncertainty. In other words, according to the dichotomy put forward by Knight (1921) and based upon the distinction between risk and uncertainty, the new Keynesians and the so-called DSGE models choose to focus on risk, a measurable concept by some statistical methods.

Anna Variato (2004) has shown how the two forms can coexist. However, uncertainty, a non-measurable concept, must play an essential part in the story, as Keynes himself claimed and Minsky confirmed. This vision opens the way to two consequences. On the one hand, it creates a sharp contrast with modern macroeconomics, which is all based upon the hypothesis of rational expectations. This partly explains why Minsky's analysis has not been considered in the mainstream literature even after the Great Recession. On the other hand, the presence of uncertainty is a structural characteristic of a complex dynamic system that cannot be eliminated. It can only be tamed. This is the fundamental reason why destabilizing forces are present in the system.

11. THE ROLE OF THE BANKING SYSTEM

In stock–flow relationships (see Hicks, 1965 for a definition), where balance sheet phenomena impact on the economy, one might wonder why losses and gains do not cancel out in the aggregate so that they are neutral with respect to the real economy.

To understand this, once again heterogeneity must be introduced into the analysis. In this case, however, it must also be referred to sectors and not only to agents. In this way, one can understand why an increase in debt does not create the same and counterbalancing effect of an increased amount of credit. In this perspective, the advantages deriving to households for not honoring a debt are smaller than the disadvantages to the economy deriving from banking bankruptcies.

When the banking system is hit, the economy becomes more unstable while fluctuations differ from their canonical properties. As shown in the literature (see Reinhart and Rogoff, 2011), crises become both longer and deeper and impact on many more markets.

These results illustrate three fundamental points. The first is the pervasive role of banks in the system. Even though the development of capital markets has diminished the role of banks in financing investment by firms, it remains true that the role of banks in these capital markets has increased. The second is that the banks respond endogenously to the requirements of the markets and, by means of innovations, as Minsky stressed, can stimulate the financialization of the economy. Finally, this process can increase the presence of fundamental uncertainty that cannot be covered by any financial device. These are the reasons why the financial system creates flexibility and instability at the same time.

12. THWARTING DEVICES

Contrarians claim that Minsky guessed five out of the two actual crises that took place. To admit the possibility of a crisis does not imply the capability of forecasting it. This is beyond the possibility of any economist, Minsky included.

This is not the point at issue. The difference is that if one does not believe in the self-correcting capacities of the market one is keener to suggest policies and institutional devices capable of thwarting the instability forces.

In this perspective, both the destabilizing forces and the thwarting ones are not mechanical events but, on the contrary, history dependent, and there is feedback between them. In this sense, Lucas's critique struck a nerve when he underlined the impact of changing policies on expectations. Unfortunately, the suggested solution, to refer to fundamentals lying outside history, is not tenable.

One needs to consider a meta-model where endogenous forces and thwarting devices interact to create a complex dynamic system. In this system, financial instability is a possibility but not an inevitability if the right policies and institutions are set in place.

At this stage of the analysis the effort is directed in two directions. On the one hand, one has to study how this complex view evolved in Minsky's contributions. On the other, it is worth studying how it can be modified to meet the challenges deriving from both the evolution of the economy and the development of the discipline.

The safety net of welfare had been partly dismantled in the decades before the Great Recession, starting from Thatcher/Reagan era, and was not replaced by any great reform, as happened during the 1930s. Furthermore, the labor market this time was affected by the double impact of globalization and information technology that in the 1930s were absent. At that time, the world was dominated by beggar-my-neighbor policies, while technical change was not so pervasive.

Both globalization and technical change have contributed to weakening the market power of unions so that the wage share has kept falling. The productivity plus the inflation rate of wages growth that characterized the economy in the golden ages has been definitively broken down, and this has weakened consumption that relied on debt.

Although these long-run forces will remain backstage in the present analysis, they cannot be ignored along with the process of innovation in the financial sector.

The Great Recession, therefore, has been characterized by a prompt monetary policy but no reforms in the labor market, while those in the financial markets have been soft. It follows that the role of policies as thwarting forces has undergone profound change that must be considered for understanding what happened both during and after the crisis.

APPENDIX: A 3-D LINEARIZED SYSTEM

A.1 The Multipliers of the Extended Model

The extended model can be expressed in the following matrix form, where unemployment has been dropped and only the employment ratio has been considered:

$$
\begin{bmatrix}
1 & 0 & 0 & 0 & 0 & P_1 \\
0 & 1 & 0 & 0 & 0 & 0 \\
-\psi_1 & 0 & 1 & 0 & -\psi_2 & 0 \\
-I_4 & I_3 & I_2 & 1 & -I_1 & 0 \\
G_4 & -G_3 & -G_2 & -G_1 & 1 & 0 \\
0 & 0 & 0 & 0 & -L_1 & 1
\end{bmatrix}
\begin{bmatrix}
\pi_t \\ d_t \\ R_t \\ i_t \\ g_t \\ l_t
\end{bmatrix} =
$$

$$
\begin{bmatrix}
1 & 0 & 0 & 0 & 0 & 0 \\
-D_4 & D_1 & D_5 & D_2 & -D_3 & 0 \\
0 & 0 & \psi_3 & 0 & 0 & 0 \\
0 & 0 & 0 & 0 & 0 & 0 \\
0 & 0 & 0 & 0 & 0 & 0 \\
0 & 0 & 0 & 0 & 0 & 1
\end{bmatrix}
\begin{bmatrix}
\pi_{t-1} \\ d_{t-1} \\ R_{t-1} \\ i_{t-1} \\ g_{t-1} \\ l_{t-1}
\end{bmatrix}
$$

The following are the multipliers used in the matrices:

$$
\begin{aligned}
P_1 &= \frac{\partial \pi_t}{\partial l} = \frac{\sigma_1}{1 - \alpha} \\[2mm]
D_1 &= \frac{\partial d_t}{\partial d_{t-1}} = \frac{1 + R_0}{(1 + g_0)(1 + \pi_0)} \\[2mm]
D_2 &= \frac{\partial d_t}{\partial i_{t-1}} = \frac{1}{(1 + g_0)} \\[2mm]
D_3 &= \frac{\partial d_t}{\partial g_{t-1}} = \frac{i_0 + (1 + r_0) d_0}{(1 + g_0)^2} \\[2mm]
D_4 &= \frac{\partial d_t}{\partial \pi_{t-1}} = \frac{(1 + R_0) d_0}{[(1 + g_0)(1 + \pi_0)]^2} \\[2mm]
D_5 &= \frac{\partial d_t}{\partial R} = \frac{d_0}{(1 + g_0)(1 + \pi_0)}
\end{aligned}
$$

$$\left| \begin{array}{lll}
I_1 = \dfrac{\partial i_t}{\partial g_{t-1}} = & & \eta_2 + \eta_3 \theta (1-\omega) \\[3mm]
I_2 = \dfrac{\partial i_t}{\partial R_t} = & & \dfrac{\eta_3}{(1+\pi_0)} \\[3mm]
I_3 = \dfrac{\partial i_t}{\partial d_t} = & & \dfrac{\eta_3 R_0}{(1+\pi_0)} \\[3mm]
I_4 = \dfrac{\partial i_t}{\partial \pi_{t-1}} = & & \dfrac{\eta_3 R_0 d_0}{(1+\pi_0)^2} \\[3mm]
G_1 = \dfrac{\partial g_t}{\partial i_t} = & & \dfrac{1}{1-c_1} \\[3mm]
G_2 = \dfrac{\partial g_t}{\partial R_t} = & \dfrac{c_3}{1-c_1} \dfrac{1}{(1+\pi_0)} = G_3 = \dfrac{\partial g_t}{\partial d_t} \\[3mm]
G_4 = \dfrac{\partial g_t}{\partial \pi_t} = & & \dfrac{c_3}{(1-c_1)} \dfrac{R_0 d_0}{(1+\pi_0)^2}
\end{array} \right|$$

Table 3A.1   The values of the parameters

$\tau = 0.0075$	$\sigma_1 = 0.03$	$\eta_1 = 0.15$	$\eta_2 = 0.40$
$\eta_3 = 0.40$	$c_1 = 0.40 = c_2$	$c_3 = 0.05$	
$\psi_2 = 0.2$	$\alpha = 0.6$	$R^* = 0.0028$	$\psi_1 = 1.376$

The values of the parameters are slightly different from those of Table 2.2.

A.2   Reducing the System to 3-D

The system can be reduced to 3-D in the following variables: π_t, d_t and l_t.

To obtain this result, one has to proceed through two steps. The first consists in eliminating R_t and g_t. To proceed in this way, the following super-multipliers have been used.

The equations in R_t and g_t must be replaced in the remaining four equations in π_t, d_t, i_t and l_t, by using the above super-multiplier. In turn, this substitution creates these other super-multipliers.

Table 3A.2   The first group of super-multipliers

$RR1 = \dfrac{\Psi_1 - \psi_2 G_4}{1 - \Psi_2 G_2}$	$RR2 = \dfrac{\Psi_2 G_1}{1 - \Psi_2 G_2}$	$RR3 = \dfrac{\Psi_2 G_3}{1 - \Psi_2 G_2}$
$GG1 = G1 + G2*RR2$	$GG2 = G2*RR1 - G4$	$GG3 = G2*RR3 + G3$

Table 3A.3   The second group of super-multipliers

$DD1 = D1 + D5*RR3 - D3*GG3$	$DD2 = D2 - D3*GG1 + D5*RR2$	$DD3 = D5*RR1 - D3*GG2 - D4$
$II1 = (I1*GG2 - I2*RR1 + I4)/(1 - I1*GG1)$	$II2 = (I1*GG3 - I2*RR3 - I3)/(1 - I1*GG1)$	
$LL1 = L1*GG1$	$LL2 = L1*GG2$	$LL3 = L1*GG3$

Table 3A.4   The final group of super-multipliers

$DDD1 = DD1 + DD2*II2$	$DDD2 = DD2*II1 + DD3$	
$LLL1 = LL1*II1 + LL2$	$LLL2 = LL1*II2 + LL3$	
$L41 = 1 + LLL1*P1$	$L42 = LLL2*DDD1$	$L43 = LLL1 + LLL2*DDD2$

Finally, the system can be reduced to 3-D by eliminating i_t. Furthermore, we need to eliminate contemporaneous values in the l_t equation by referring to the following super-multipliers.

A.3   The Stability of a 3-D System

Eventually, the system can be written in the following way, which is discussed in the text:

$$\begin{bmatrix} \pi_t \\ d_t \\ l_t \end{bmatrix} = \begin{bmatrix} 1 & 0 & P1 \\ DDD2 & DDD1 & 0 \\ L43 & L42 & L41 \end{bmatrix} \begin{bmatrix} \pi_{t-1} \\ d_{t-1} \\ l_{t-1} \end{bmatrix}$$

In spite of the simplifications introduced, the interpretation of the "composite" parameters remains far from straightforward.

4. An insider's view

1. THE CHALLENGES

One of the characteristics of this book is that it offers an interpretation of Minsky starting from the work we carried out together. There is a dual risk in such an approach. On the one hand, there is what can be called the Chateaubriand risk: "Je parle éternellement de moi". In other words, there is the possibility that I might exploit Minsky in order to talk about myself. On the other hand, Minsky may have dropped topics that he considered to be outside my scientific agenda, which he knew was centered on macroeconomics and on the working of the labor market, but did not include finance.

The ensemble may appear biased, one-sided and perhaps obsolete. In fact, it might appear odd to refer to such old articles, mostly written during the 1980s. This pessimistic scenario, however, can be challenged. First, to follow this strategy does not necessarily imply putting forward an arbitrary subjective interpretation. On the contrary, it is simply based on the experience and the judgments accumulated in co-authoring with Minsky himself. It is worth stressing that the results of this cooperation not only include three published articles, which are reprinted in Part II of this book, but also refer to an unpublished book along with a series of colloquiums that were put on record and lasted for more than a decade.

Second, it is correct to claim that the one-sidedness is manifest in the first article, published in 1984, which ignores financial aspects. However, this is also true for many of the articles included in his 1982 volume. In spite of this absence, they are eligible to be enriched by financial considerations because they refer to a monetary economy of production, to use Keynes's terminology.

Finally, obsolescence is challenged through first making some revisions, followed by an attempt at generalization. The overall result may be the building of a prism reflecting Minsky's deepest ideas.

2. A FELIX ASTRAL CONJUNCTION

At this stage of the analysis, two kinds of preliminary investigation are necessary. The first delves into the genesis of these articles. The second tries to understand their relationships with Minsky's most important publications.

The story of the production of these articles starts in 1978, when Minsky attended an international seminar on finance at the University of Bergamo in Italy. What was special about that conference was the simultaneous presence of scholars belonging to three schools of thought:

1. supporters of the Modigliani–Miller theorem (1958);
2. founders of the new finance school based upon the efficiency theory of the markets (ETM);
3. theorists of financial instability.

Franco Modigliani discussed intensively with Eugene Fama (1970) and Robert C. Merton (1973) the relationships between the two main strands of theories, 1 and 2, and occupied center stage. The only representative of the third strand was Hyman P. Minsky, who seemed very determined, in spite of being practically isolated, in supporting the minority view that risks are not divisible *ad libitum* and that there are possibilities of financial turmoil. He was not disturbed by the mathematics but by the fallacy of composition that tried to extend to the system results that were hardly valid for singular cases.

As is well known, Nobel Prizes were assigned to the first two strands, even though history seems to have vindicated that tall professor who defended his position in total isolation.

On that occasion, I tried to socialize with Minsky and gave him a preliminary paper on the dynamics of wage share. He invited me to Rome, where he was visiting professor at Confindustria. He came back to Bergamo for the summer. From then, we spent every summer together until he died.

3. FROM HICKS TO MINSKY

My paper on the dynamics of wage share tried to exploit some ideas contained in Hicks's book titled *The Crisis of Keynesian Economics* (1974). I studied at Oxford with Hicks, who supervised my DPhil thesis on "Unemployment in Italy". I had the privilege of being received every Wednesday at 11 o'clock for three years at All Soul's. He was a fantastic supervisor, who never tried to impose anything but simply applied a maieutic method that I subsequently tried to maintain with Hyman.

My approach to the labor market has always been macro and inserted within a growth perspective.[1] It was therefore natural to extend the analysis to income distribution, a theme that I was developing when I first met Minsky. His stressing of the role of cash flows had points of contact with my interests in the theory of income distribution.

4.   SERENDIPITY

The first article that I co-authored with Minsky had a long gestation period. When I first visited him in Rome in May 1978, I found my paper had been totally ravaged. Corrections were everywhere, including on the backs of pages. In those times, computers were in their infancy, so corrections were made in pencil. Unfortunately, I found his handwriting even harder to understand than his accent.

What I did understand was that he liked the paper but that it needed some profound transformations. In fact, Hyman twisted the model. Mainly, he considered wage share to be one determinant of cash flow, a concept at the root of his financial instability hypothesis. This is one of the reasons why it took almost six years to complete the paper and get it published. Meanwhile, he suggested studying two papers, one by himself and one by Robert May, and gave me a programmatic agenda, as will be revealed shortly.

The paper eventually got published under the title "Prices, employment, and profits". It was totally different from my initial project, and I discovered afterwards that it tried to link the dynamic analysis contained in *Can "It" Happen Again?* (1982) with the Kaleckian theory of profits that was collected in his *Stabilizing an Unstable Economy* (1986a).

The paper was published in the *Journal of Post Keynesian Economics*. (It is reproduced in Part II as Chapter 5 and deepened in Part III in Chapter 10.) In the six-year interval from inception to publication, we started to plan further work together. His buying a house in Bergamo certainly made it easier to work together, the Internet still being a chimera.

5.   A DYNAMIC TENET

When we started working together, Hyman had just published *John Maynard Keynes* (1975) and was trying to go beyond the results obtained. His main worry, as will be shown shortly, was the static nature of the analysis along with an unsatisfactory theory of profit determination. In this regard, he published a series of papers on the Kaleckian theory of profits (1986b), to be possibly utilized for his financial instability hypothesis.

The dynamics aspects, however, continued to be absent, and this was the most important objective of the joint paper. In other words, to link the new research on profits and cash flows with his dynamic studies done in the 1950s and reproduced in the volume *Can "It" Happen Again?* seemed to be an enticing research agenda.

In order to achieve this result, he suggested (though it would be more accurate to add the adverb "strongly") utilizing two papers: his "A linear model of cyclical growth"(1959), which was not included in the 1982 volume, and an article by May (1976) that was setting the basis for a new nonlinear dynamic theory capable of generating chaotic movements.

The first article was useful for developing his piecewise technique based upon changes in the initial conditions and capable of generating interesting dynamics. In fact, in "Prices, employment, and profits", two results are obtained. The first is a dynamic reduced form reproducing the formula of the accelerator–multiplier model. In this case, however, it refers to prices, employment and profits, even though the dynamic considerations are similar. The second includes a way of reconciling micro behavior and macro results. Both of these will be developed in Part III.

The second article was the strategic one. May had just published "Simple mathematical models with very complicated dynamics". According to Hyman, my most important task was that of following these new mathematical developments, them being better capable of encapsulating his theory of economic functioning. It was a form of long-term human capital investment capable of analyzing the complex dynamics of an evolving economic system where monetary and financial aspects are interlinked and technical progress takes place along with the accumulation process. This strategy led me to meeting Ed Greenberg and Steve Fazzari at Washington University, with whom I started a lifelong collaboration. Furthermore, Richard Day, at the University of Southern California, and Laura Gardini and Fabio Tramontana, at the University of Urbino in Italy, supplemented their mathematical background at various stages.

6.   A GLIMPSE OF SOCRATIC COLLOQUIUMS

The long gestation period of the paper obliged me to take a stand on the respective positions. In order to maintain a record of my discussions with Minsky, a particular kind of Socratic method was adopted. I formulated my questions on my computer, while Hyman replied on his. Eventually, floppy disks were exchanged. In the present book, only a glimpse of them will be provided.

For instance, a preliminary question was how to set our 1984 paper in relation with Minsky's previous work. In particular, it was urgent to relate Minsky 1 ("Monetary systems and accelerator models", published in *American Economic Review* in 1957 and reproduced in *Can "It" Happen Again?*, 1982), Minsky 2 ("A linear model of cyclical growth", 1959) and Minsky 3, the financial instability hypothesis contained in *John Maynard Keynes* (1975). Minsky gave the following answer.

> The first answer is I don't know, but this is not true. Minsky 1 was a formal investigation of how money might interact with the process that determines aggregate demand. Minsky 2 was quite mechanical but made it clear that the initial conditions were important. Both Minsky 1 and Minsky 2 recognized that the accelerator coefficient in particular had to be treated as an endogenous variable, and the role of money could very well be in determining the size of the acceleration coefficient rather than just determining the ceiling or floors. Minsky 3 being rooted in interpreting Keynes was too damned static and unfortunately could be interpreted as another equilibrium model.
>
> The liquidity preference as determining the price level of capital assets conception has not caught on, but the PK function shifts when money market changes of significance occur. In terms of the models of Minsky 1 and 2, Minsky 3 would have PK considerations determine the beta coefficient even as the finance constraints in the M supply function determine new initial conditions as needed.

These observations are clear-cut, head straight to the main points and are very stimulating.[2]

7.   THE GRAND AGENDA

After many years of summer colloquiums, in the late 1980s (August 1988) we tried to work out a long-run project. At this time his third book *Stabilizing an Unstable Economy* (1986a) had been published, and so most of Minsky's contributions had been completed.

The idea was to write a book on "Business Cycles and Economic Instability" that would extend Minsky's research agenda and at the same time refer to new theoretical devices capable of producing complex dynamics.

It is important to consider the contents page because it helps in understanding not only the development of the research that took place afterwards but also in trying to grasp some of Hyman's deepest aspirations. In particular, it emerges that the claim that Minsky was indifferent to a formalization of his ideas is totally groundless. The question is what kind of formalization he had in mind.

The contents were as follows:

1.   The priors
2.   Historical paradigms
3.   A taxonomy
4.   The tools
5.   Real explanations
6.   The financial instability hypothesis
7.   An integrated approach
8.   Some formalizations
9.   The impact of innovations
10. Challenges

Though the book was started, it was never finished. Facts of life and competing projects were at the root of this unfinished task. Minsky's priority was more to work on the frontier of finance than to systematize his knowledge.

I published some of these chapters (3, 4 and 5) with Ed Greenberg in *The Labor Market and the Business Cycle Theories* (1989) and *Wages, Regime Switching and Cycles* (1992). Furthermore, they had been in the back of my mind when I wrote my 2011 and 2016 books and when I started to plan this volume.

It may be interesting to reproduce the comments made by Minsky (HPM) in relation to some of these chapters. They are presented because they can stimulate some reflections and give at the same time some guidelines for further research.

As far as the priors are concerned, Minsky claimed that the basic reference is Reder's (1982) anti-Chicago piece in the *Journal of Economic Literature (JEL)*.

> Reder's line was that the Chicago methodology started by knowing the empirical (econometrics) results they wanted to get and never rested until results compatible with the theoretical priors were achieved. A current book on war games indicates that the gamers rig the game to get results that they want to achieve. All gaming results are suspect and much of econometrics. Reder called the Chicago way of doing economics "tight priors".
>
> In contrast to the Chicago school which draws its priors from a simple minded equilibrium but taut model, our priors are loose in that we hold that abstract non-constrained models indicate that market mechanisms are likely to degenerate into incoherence and that institutions constrain either the values that variables can take on, this imposing new initial conditions from the dynamics, or the reaction parameters, thus changing regime.

In good part we are faking it, for though our references are to Day and other sophisticated types, our point of reference really is to the simple accelerator multiplier model with either floors and ceilings or changing alphas and betas.

In my book *Macroeconomics of Growth Cycles and Financial Instability* (2011), I actually went back to the more sophisticated approach. Some parts of these contributions are reflected in parts III, IV and V of the present book.

8.   A SECOND-BEST CHOICE

Instead of completing the book, the second-best strategy consisted in working on shorter efforts. To this end, two more papers were published. The first one, "The breakdown of the IS–LM synthesis: implications for post-Keynesian economic theory" (1989) was written as a result of the solicitation by a new post-Keynesian journal.

The paper has both a "destruens part" and a "construens part". The negative part is fundamentally a criticism of the mainstream of that time, that is, the so-called neoclassical synthesis. The lack of uncertainty, the misrepresentation of the accumulation process and the minor role attributed to financial factors are the main aspects underlined.

It might seem odd to refer to these old controversies. However, they are still relevant because most of these limitations also extend to modern versions of this synthesis, that is, the DSGE (discrete stochastic general equilibrium) models. These modern versions, however, have two further claims. They pretend to be microfounded. Furthermore, they claim that they can be emended in order to deal with new circumstances such as the Great Recession. These aspects will be expanded upon later (see Chapter 9).

The "construens part" of the paper shows our vision of the economy that is particularly developed in the last article, "Market processes and thwarting systems" (1992). Before dealing with this article, however, it is important to stress other concepts.

9.   THE ZENITH

"Market processes and thwarting systems" (1992) represents the pinnacle of our collaboration, at least from my point of view. The reason I want to reproduce it is that it seems fairly up to date to me. It reads as though it was written after the Great Recession and not almost 20 years before.

The paper was prepared while Minsky was about to retire from

Washington University. This happened in June 1990, when he moved to the Levy Economics Institute at the Bard College in Annandale-on-Hudson, New York. It was published in the same year as the Festschrift edited by Steven Fazzari and Dimitri Papadimitriou *Financial Conditions and Macroeconomic Performance* (1992).

At that time I did not imagine it would be our last work together. My responsibilities as rector of the University of Bergamo had in the meantime increased, while the grand project we were working on was too ambitious, as already mentioned.

I only visited the Levy Economics Institute three or four times, when international seminars were held. However, our summer meetings in Bergamo remained a splendid tradition. They were interrupted only by his attendance of the post-Keynesian meetings in Trieste, which sometimes I also did. Minsky had meanwhile strengthened his relationship with the so-called two cats, Delli Gatti and Gallegati, who represented the continuation of his Italian links. For my part, I strengthened my relationship with his former colleagues at Washington University, Ed Greenberg and Steve Fazzari in particular.

10. THE GUIDELINES OF THE PAPER

The paper "Market processes and thwarting systems" (1992), which culminated 15 years of collaboration, was at the same time a synthesis of our previous work, written or simply discussed, and an agenda for future projects.

The paper is characterized by four tenets that are worth considering. The first tenet is the *pars destruens*: it stresses the limitations of the mainstream economics, at that time represented by the so-called IS–LM synthesis model, even though attacks from the new classical school of Lucas were already spreading. In part, this criticism replicates that contained in the 1989 article.

The second tenet insists on the necessity of developing a Keynesian model cast in dynamic terms, where the interdependence of various markets is considered. The product market, the labor market and the financial markets are supposed to interact in dynamic and endogenous ways. In other words, the analysis must be integrated.

The third tenet refers to the methodological need of devising a dynamic system which is capable of producing a rich variety of dynamic patterns but that does not necessarily explode.

This double characteristic calls for the identification of thwarting forces, which is the last tenet. It contains an important message: the system is endogenously unstable but instability can be checked by appropriate policy measures and precise institutional settings.

These tenets represented the guidelines of our research agenda and provide a structure also for the present book.

11.   A DIFFERENT SYSTEM ANALYSIS

The paradox of the so-called DSGE models is that, while they claim to refer to the general equilibrium, in fact they refer to a representative agent, whose behavior is supposed to microfound macroeconomics.

One point that needs to be stressed is that complex interdependent systems are not restricted to the neoclassical general equilibrium framework. As now constituted, the general equilibrium framework means that the theory starts with:

1. "agents" (individualism bias) who are fully characterized by well-behaved utility functions that are invariant through time and are not subject to change from the use of resources (advertising must be information, not a way to control tastes and preferences).
2. "technology" characterized by well-behaved production functions, which in particular need to lead to well-measured marginal products so that the combination of utility and profit maximization distributes income. There is no need for a separate theory of income distribution, because income distribution is just a particular part of the pricing process.
3. profit and utility maximization, which are best approximated by the competitive markets.

According to Minsky's colloquiums,

> The General Equilibrium system of economics is a rather 'vulgar' copy of various modes of thinking in physics. Walras was quite clear that he was following the physicists' model, the biological analogy of Marshall fell by the way side. I am rather impressed by the Ingrao–Israel (1987) paper. Their contentions are:
>
> 1. The existence proof of Arrow–Debreu holds, but really only because they set the assumptions so that the economic model was in a 1–1 correspondence with the fixed point theorem; the proof of the existence of the competitive equilibrium is no more or less than a proof of the fixed point theorem.
> 2. The equilibrium is not unique.
> 3. A general proof of stability requires assumptions that are not readily rationalized economically.

Keynes's original model was an intermarket complex system that was not Walrasian general equilibrium. The Orwellian analogy was explicit, the parameters within which consumers behaved and workers lived were mainly set in the no government case by the willingness of businessmen and their bankers to finance spending on investment goods. In the post-Keynes world deficits were honorary investment in their impact on profits and aggregate demand determination details.

Furthermore Keynes's model and its modern applications are open to organizations and institutions such as trade unions to affect outcomes. Similarly industrial organizations and institutional arrangements by which technology is determined and innovations financed affect the outcome of the complexly interdependent system.

The lesson is that "Walrasian general equilibrium" is just a special case of a system approach to the economy. Other theories that try to understand the evolution of the whole system are badly needed.

Even though the accelerator–multiplier model has been used as a metaphor for representing the dynamics of economic systems, it has some limitations that are worth stressing:

1. It is very difficult to generate a cycle. To generate robust cycles you need to introduce either nonlinearities, as Goodwin did, or refer to ceilings and floors.
2. In this case, it has difficulty in explaining lower turning points. Rose (1967) suggested that an income distribution variable needs to be introduced.
3. It has no well-formulated expectation elements. In other words, it has to deal with Keynes after Lucas.
4. It ignored money.

Minsky tried to amend some of these problems by referring to the technique of changes in initial conditions that allowed explosive patterns to be checked by institutional and policy measures to thwart the market processes.

But what about the other aspects?

12. THE NEW RESEARCH AGENDA

At that time Minsky suggested an agenda for future research that nowadays is still valid. The fact that the Great Recession has taken place, that is, that "it" happened again, has reinforced the need for the new developments – analytical, methodological and empirical. However, they are more in the spirit of deepening the Minskyan vision than in revolutionizing it.

The main theme in the research agenda is an understanding of the complex dynamics generated by a system characterized by the existence of long-term assets and by the presence of a sophisticated financial system. The dynamic dimension is an essential part of the Minskyan analysis.

The second theme is the coexistence of endogenous destabilizing forces accompanied by thwarting forces. These assume the form of policies but also of suitable institutions. The triad "big firms, big unions and big government" that was prominent from the end of the World War II to the period of the oil shocks has vanished. One has to realize how the new institutions that replaced them had an impact on the working of the system. This is particularly true for the labor market, the power concentration of firms and the invasive importance of finance.

Finally, one has to consider that these changes are not once and for all, but rather there is a continuous process of innovation, not only technological but also institutional. The financialization process is a typical example. It produces new channels that must be challenged by a process of reforms.

Even though these themes are linked, the main focus of the book will be on the first one, although references to the workings of the labor market will be considered.

The aim is to define a meta-model that has a medium-run horizon, that integrates the various markets and that is general enough to cover both aggregate demand and aggregate supply aspects. It generates endogenous fluctuations while runaway situations cannot be excluded. It is a meta-model simply because it is not closed only by a possibility, but rather is open to various options. Within this framework, financial instabilities are possible, where Minsky moments can become a distinctive feature of the economy.

NOTES

1. A recent contribution with Fazzari and Variato (2018) reconsiders these themes.
2. Anna Variato, University of Bergamo, aims to make these records available, conditional on the overcoming of some technological constraints.

PART II

Co-authoring

5. Prices, employment, and profits

Hyman P. Minsky and Piero Ferri*

1. INTRODUCTION

Simultaneous inflation and unemployment, which has led to the coinage of terms like stagflation and slumpflation,[1] appears to be a non-transitory characteristic of advanced capitalist economies. This combination together with unimpressive growth in these economies since the mid-1960s is the result of both the behavior of labor and output markets and the system of government interventions that have aimed either to achieve a closer approximation to full employment or to prevent financial market incoherence. Thus stagflation has roots in both the structure and performance of markets and the behavior of macro-processes.

To understand the path of prices (P) and employment (N), we need to explain: (1) the dynamics of wage (W) and P behavior that reflect institutional characteristics; (2) how aggregate relations determine the set of possible P and N combinations; and (3) how these two determinants are reconciled to yield evolving reality.

2. THE INSTITUTIONAL ASSUMPTIONS

Today's institutional framework is characterized by: (a) firms and labor organizations which possess market power; (b) big government, whose monetary and fiscal measures constrain the "downward potential" of aggregate profits and influence the realized P-N outcomes; (c) a financial system which intermittently seems to verge on crisis; and (d) central bank interventions which prevent any system-wide financial disaster from fully developing.

Thus market power is exercised within aggregate conditions which set limits to possible realized conditions. Neither market power not aggregate explanations of the realized P-N combinations suffice. We need a framework that integrates the two.

Market power of firms leads to administered prices able to assure managers of an easy life and persuade financiers that profit margins will not collapse when excess capacity (unemployment) prevails. This assurance facilitates the financing of expensive capital assets. Thus a modern capitalist economy has a debt structure that requires continuous validation by profit flows and a banking/financial structure which must function smoothly if investment is to take place. We will forego technical analysis of the banking and financing system in this paper; we merely assume that the managers of administered prices and the negotiators of wages *know* that both the Treasury and the Central Bank will intervene to prevent a "free fall" of the financial system.

Negotiated wages ensue from trade union power, which we take to be an organizational imperative in a democratic society. Negotiated and contractual wages also tend to make costs comparable among the "independent" firms that share market power. Labor's market power may have its genesis in the political power of workers, rather than in the economic power of unions.[2]

Big government mainly operates by way of transfer payments, defense spending, and taxes. Big government ordinarily implies a need for high taxes. Both the spending and taxing schedules are related to GNP so that the government will be moving towards deficit or surplus depending on whether the economy is in an upswing or downswing.

As mentioned earlier we postulate that a Central Bank exists and that it will jump in to prevent full-fledged chaos from developing.[3] We assume that the W and P processes take place in an environment in which it is known that the Central Bank will accommodate the financial needs of governments and will assure that a deep debt-deflation will not occur.[4]

Big government, along with activist Central banks, has modified the nature of business cycles. A full-fledged debt-deflation and a deep and long depression are less likely, for when income drops a huge deficit well-nigh automatically occurs. The deficit sustains business profits which, in turn, enable business to fulfill its debt obligations. As a result, the value of business capital and the means to redeem debt commitments are maintained. Hence investment activity is at higher plateau during modern recessions than otherwise.

Because deficits sustain – and even increase – profits during recessions, the markup per unit of output does not fall in recession. The exercise – real or potential – of trade union strength and the constraint upon the fall in output that follows from the government deficit limit the money wage fall that takes place during recessions. The very relations which moderate the income decline tend to at least attenuate any tendency for P's to fall during periods of high unemployment. The N, P and Q characteristics of the business cycle have thus been transformed by post-World-War-II institutional adaptations.

3. THE ANALYTICAL FRAMEWORK

There are two aspects to the P and W formation in our economy: (1) a combination of bargaining that sets money wages and the exercise of market power which leads to the markup on unit labor costs; (2) the aggregate relations that yield the total obtainable markup on wage costs. The aggregate relations thus determine the P and Q combinations that can prevail. Both aspects yield markups, but each reflects different determinants of the flux of the economy.

4. BARGAINING AND MARKET POWER

The determination of prices and wages by bargaining and market power may be represented by two interacting equations over time:

$$P_c(t) = \gamma \frac{W_c(t)}{A_c(t)} + \alpha P_c^*(t) \qquad (5.1)$$

$$W(t) = g(X(t), P_c(t)) + \beta P_c^*(t) \qquad (5.2)$$

where $P_c(t)$ and $W(t)$ represent price and wage levels and $A(t)$ traces average productivity, while $P_c^*(t)$ reflects the price expectations and $X(t)$ stands for a vector of real variables (for instance, expected productivity gains, taxation . . .).[5]

The price equation reflects the market power of firms. The γ markup factor ($\gamma > 1$) reflects market power, history, and cash payment requirements imposed by the liability structure of firms.

As far as the wage equation is concerned, we live in a world in which trade unions exist and money wages are largely the result of bargaining and negotiations. Any explanation of wages must take this into account.[6] Unemployment (U) affects the wage boosts but, so long as catastrophic and prolonged unemployment has been averted, the effect of today's unemployment rate on wage bargains has been subdued. This implies that today's U rate can be omitted from equation (5.2) as an explicit variable,[7] although *chronic* high U's can erode the market power of unions and thus affect the W, P reaction. The price variable in the wage equation captures the explicit or implicit, full or partial, indexing of wages.

Substituting (5.2) into (5.1) we obtain (under particular specifications)[8] a second order equation:

$$P_c(t) - (E+F)P_c(t-1) + FP_c(t-2) = 0 \qquad (5.3)$$

which resembles the reduced form of the accelerator–multiplier trade cycle models.[9] The general solution to such an equation is given by:

$$P_c(t) = B_1\mu_1^t + B_2\mu_2^t \qquad (5.4)$$

where the roots μ_1 and μ_2 depend upon the parameters E and F, while B_1 and B_2 are determined by initial conditions. If the parameters are constant, the same holds for the roots μ_1 and μ_2. If the roots take on values greater than one, the model will tend to explode. The linear second order form to which we reduced the iterative wage-price determination process is a "gross simplification" of the interactions in the economy. It is unable to generate the complex paths that nonlinear systems do, but it can generate paths equally unacceptable as a stand-in for economic outcomes. The explosive result is as unacceptable as the incoherent or turbulent paths that nonlinear iterative processes generate.[10]

Acceptable, nonexplosive results can be obtained if meaningful constraints on the variables are introduced. For time series that tend to explode (or collapse), these constraints become ceilings and floors. If the ceilings and floors reflect economic processes, then the economic model can be characterized as "nonlinear." Analytically the positing of ceilings and floors is a technique for converting complex nonlinear processes into piecewise linear systems.[11]

5. MACROECONOMIC PRICE DETERMINANTS

The markup in equation (5.1) includes a factor allowing for price anticipations, for firms do not always succeed in attaining their price, quantity, and profit objectives. There are macro-constraints which limit firms' price power; these determine whether in the aggregate the profit objectives of firms can be validated.

Gross capital income, or profits (R), is the difference between total revenue and labor costs. For the consumption sector this is equal to:

$$R_c = P_c Q_c - W_c N_c \qquad (5.5)$$

From Kalecki[12] we have

$$R_c = W_1 N_1 + Df + C_R - S_W \qquad (5.6)$$

where N_I and W_I refer to investment goods, C_R equals consumption out of profits, and S_W equals saving out of wages, while Df equals government deficit.[13]

Combining (5.5) and (5.6), one obtains:

$$P_c Q_c = W_c N_c + W_I N_I + Df + C_R - S_W \tag{5.7}$$

Rearranging, we find that this becomes:

$$P_c = \frac{W_c}{A_c}\left(1 + \frac{W_I N_I + Df + C_R - S_W}{W_c N_c}\right) \tag{5.8}$$

For convenience, we can write (5.8) as:

$$P_c = \frac{W_c}{A_c}(1 + MK_c) \tag{5.9}$$

where MK_c = average markup in the C-goods. Equations (5.8) and (5.9) reveal that P_c can be viewed as a markup on unit labor costs.[14] This macroeconomic relation has to be integrated with the market processes that determine price and wages.

6. THE PATH OF PRICES AND EMPLOYMENT: THE ECONOMICS OF STAGNATION

We therefore have two sets of relations which are involved in determining the paths of P and N. These reflect different aspects of the mechanisms of a modern economy. One reflects the market power of firms and the bargaining that sets wages. The second reflects: (1) the course of I, (2) the fiscal posture of G; and (3) the distribution of income in concert with the consumption propensities of the "classes" of income recipients. Both sets of relations reinforce the proposition that P_c is a markup on unit labor costs, but in one case it reflects market power and in the second it is a by-product of the structure of aggregate demand.

The actual P_c-path depends upon the interaction of the relations. Thus we require a reconciliation process. From (5.7) we can write:

$$\left(P_c\frac{Q_c}{N_c} - W_c\right)N_c = W_I N_I + Df + C_R - S_W \tag{5.10}$$

Profit per unit of labor in C-production (the expression within the parentheses) times the number employed (this equals R_c) equals the sum of wages in investment production, the government deficit, and the saving and spending proclivities out of W and R incomes.

The course of aggregate R_c through time parallels the various

R-components.[15] For purposes of this argument, the right-hand terms are determined *outside* the system. The path of profits, as determined by aggregate relations, is thus amenable to influence by monetary policy, although the effects may be remote. Thus, in the following exercises the behavior of the aggregate R_c is taken as given and R_c becomes a rectangular hyperbola in profit per unit of labor and employment.

Given that:

$$P(t)_c \frac{Q_c(t)}{N_c(t)} \equiv P_c(t) A_c(t) \tag{5.11}$$

is the revenue per unit of employment and that $Q(t)/N(t) = A(t)$, then profit per unit of *C*-employment is equal to:

$$\frac{R_c(t)}{N_c(t)} = r_c(t) = A_c(t) P_c(t) - W_c(t) \tag{5.12}$$

By substituting (5.1) and (5.2) into (5.12), we obtain, for a given *A*, the solution equations:

$$r_c(t) = B_1' \mu_1'^t + B_2' \mu_2'^t \tag{5.13}$$

This portrays the *time profile* of profit in *C*-production *per employee* as determined by market processes. Inasmuch as profit per unit of employment is the price minus wages per unit of employment P_c will conform to equation (5.13).

Let us assume that the macroeconomic relations are set so that aggregate $R_c = \bar{R}_c = r_c N_c$ (see the solid curve in Figure 5.1). Let us also suppose that the profit rate per employee as shown in equation (5.13) increases ($\mu > 1$ and *t* increases).

Beginning at point N_f, where an approximation to full employment exists, if profit per employee surges, then P_c will increase relative to W_c – see equation (5.12) – and *N* will slump. Points ($N_1 P_1$ and $N_2 P_2$) in Figure 5.1 represent the *P* and *N* progression typical of stagflation: *P*'s can zoom even as *N* tumbles.

The drop in *N* may hit an "unemployment barrier" (N_m) at which either government fiscal intervention or a breakdown in the price–wage process takes place.

Here the realized money wage *W* and P_c reactions no longer conform to equation (5.2). At N_m, new initial conditions are imposed for the further evolution of *P* and *N*.

In Figure 5.2 the aggregate profit constraint of equation (5.10) is

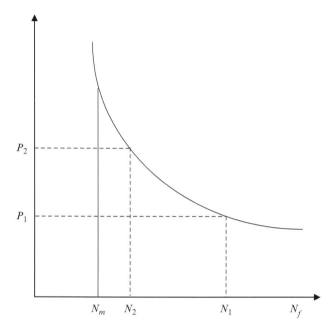

Figure 5.1   The stagflation profile, fixed total profits

increased (see lines I, II, III in the figure), even as unit R is guided by a
process summarized in (5.13).[16]
In the example, starting from N_f and r_0, the (R/N) outraces the constraint
shifts, so that r_1 (and hence P_1) is compatible with N_1, r_2 is associated with
N_2, and r_3 with N_3. On the path $N_f r_0$, $N_1 r_1$, $N_2 r_2$, and $N_3 r_3$ total profits and
profits per unit of employment increase even as employment decreases.

At r_3 an effective maximum inflation barrier is posited where the limitations of the financial system and conventional anti-inflationary monetary
and fiscal measures take hold. These drive private investment downward,
even as the government deficit escalates. A sharp rise in U and the new
aggregate constraint on the P-N combinations imply that new initial
conditions are imposed on the price equation (equation 5.13) so that, for a
time, ΔW and ΔP increases are moderated. At such time an expansion of
aggregate attainable profits will mainly lead to a rise in employment.

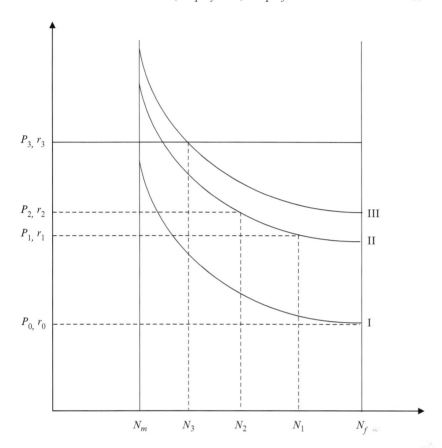

Figure 5.2   A changing total profit constraint

7.   CONCLUSIONS

This has been an exercise in integrating a market process explanation of the price movements, with the constraints upon prices and employment that reflect the aggregate characteristics of the economy.

In our model U does *not* check inflation, but is the *result* of inflation when the total profits constraint is specified. Policy to constrain aggregate profits will not usually decrease inflation. In our model monetary policies that might increase investment or fiscal policy, which would enlarge the deficit, would *not* increase the accelerating rise in P during a "free fall" period in which the rise in P conforms to the market process dynamics of equation

(5.13). Higher N's would be associated with unchanging rising P's if the aggregate profit constraint is sufficiently relaxed.

The "explosive accelerator-multiplier relation is a representation of the migration of the economy towards an incoherent state: "floors" and "ceilings" prevent the migration to "incoherence" from occurring. In general, any system as complex as an economy will of its internal functioning drive towards incoherent situations. Floors and ceilings, imposed by institutional structures, "automatic" stabilizers, customary usages, and policy maneuvers will override the endogenous thrust to "incoherence" by substituting the value of a constraint for the run-away "free market" values.

A major implication of this type of analysis is that appropriate institutional arrangements and policy interventions are necessary to prevent a market economy from periodically degenerating into incoherence.

NOTES

*   This is a reprint of the article: Hyman P. Minsky and Piero Ferri (1984), "Prices, employment, and profits", *Journal of Post Keynesian Economics*, VI(4), 489–99, 1984. The authors gratefully acknowledge the publisher Taylor & Francis for giving permission to reprint this article.
1. A detailed description and interpretation of the various situations are to be found in Weintraub (1978, p. 76).
2. The experience of 1982–83 shows that in the United States the market power of labor can be attenuated by unemployment, profit squeezes, and a hostile government. It is therefore an open question as to whether stagflation has been replaced by a "permanent" repression of employment in the United States. We believe that the success against inflation of 1982–83 is transitory unless the trade union fundamentals have been broken.
3. For a discussion of these aspects, see Minsky (1982).
4. Our argument does not lead to the monetarist conclusion that money income or prices are determined by the money supply and velocity, but that Central Bank interventions that prevent debt-deflations are part of the environment within which investment takes place. On the money, wages, and markup nexus, see Weintraub (1981b).
5. Because the wage level is affected by the price level, the "P's of this analysis are the prices of consumer goods. It will be evident in the argument about the aggregate determinants of prices and wages that the aggregate argument most immediately relates to the prices and wages of consumer goods. It is easy to assume that the wage level in consumer and investment goods is in a fixed relation one to the other and that prices of investment goods are markups on labor costs. Thus equations (5.1) and (5.2) might refer to both consumer and investment goods prices.
6. For discussion see Weintraub (1978), in particular, his Chapter 5: "Money Wages: Phenomena in Search of Theory."
7. This coincides with what the New Cambridge School, based on the target real wage hypothesis, has done. See Cripps and Godley (1976).
8. For instance, with extrapolative expectations:

$$P^*(t) = P(t-1) + \theta(P(t-1) - P(t-2))$$

and if wages vary according to the following formula, then:

$$W(t) = \lambda P(t-1)$$

and if output per man is given, then by substituting into equation (5.1), it follows that:

$$P(t) = \left(\frac{\gamma\lambda}{A} + \alpha + \alpha\theta\right) P(t-1) - \alpha\theta\, P(t-2)$$

It is worth stressing that this is just an example. The model can be specified in other forms.

9. For a discussion of these models see Samuelson (1939), Hicks (1950), and Minsky (1959).
10. For an analysis of nonlinear systems, see Day (1982).
11. Ceilings and floors break the iterative process by "not allowing" the results of the process in time t to occur and be fed into the determination of the variable in time $t+1$, etc. . . . The characteristics of the time path generated by a model with an explosive process that is constrained depend on how the rate of growth of the ceiling (constraint) compares to the minor root (μ_2). For a mathematical proof, see Minsky (1959).
12. See Kalecki (1971).
13. The definition of the deficit implied by this formula is (slightly) different from the one used by National accounts. On the spending side, acquisition of pre-existing assets and spending to refinance businesses need to be excluded. On the revenue side there is a need to exclude revenues that reflect "transfer of wealth" such as death duties, fines, and capital levies.
14. On Weintraub's assumption (1981a), according to which

$$P_c Q_c = \alpha WN$$

(5.8) becomes.:

$$P_c = \alpha\left(\frac{W}{A_c}\right) N/N_c$$

For a "generalization of the generalized" α concept, see Ferri (1983).

15. In a small government capitalism, the course of R_c depends upon N, W, and non-C production. Obviously, investment depends upon realized gross profits, but not in a simple way for the liability structure, financing conditions, and the market prices of existing capital assets are *determinants* of investment. See Minsky (1975).
16. As P_c and W_c increase, W_I also increases. Total investment equals $W_I N_I + R_I$ and $W_I N_I$ is a determinant of R_c. Therefore it is "logical" to assume that the total profits available for the producers of C-goods will increase as wages and prices increase; an outward moving R_C curve is entailed by rising W's.

6. The breakdown of the IS–LM synthesis: implications for post-Keynesian economic theory*

Piero Ferri and Hyman P. Minsky

1. INTRODUCTION

The inauguration of a new journal with a post-Keynesian perspective is a fit occasion for taking a longer view, for looking at how post-Keynesian economic theory and policy postures relate to developments in more orthodox and, to speak the truth, more accepted economic theory. The initial unifying element in the thinking of post-Keynesian economists was negative[1] (Chick, 1973; Davidson, 1972; Kregel, 1973; Minsky, 1975; Weintraub, 1966). Some 20 years ago post-Keynesians rejected the then dominant IS–LM formalization of The General Theory as:

1) a valid interpretation of Keynes, and
2) an appropriate theory for an understanding of capitalist economies.

Point 2) is more important than point 1). It followed from it that the IS–LM model was a poor analytical basis for formulating economic policy.

In particular, the post-Keynesians rejected the neoclassical synthesis, especially the version which added a labour market with a dominating equilibrium to the commodity and money markets of the simple IS–LM formulations (Modigliani, 1944; Patinkin, 1956). This version leads to propositions first, that unemployment results from rigidities and secondly, that the rigidities can be overcome by increasing the real value of money, either by increasing the money supply through monetary and fiscal policies or by having the price level and money wages fall. In this synthesis the flaws capitalist market economies exhibit are trivial, being due to the way labour or other markets are structured, and not fundamental, resulting from the need for the production and financial facets of capitalist economies to be coordinated by markets. In the labour market version of neoclassical

Keynesianism the message of Keynes was interpreted to be that all would be well if only labour behaved properly.

To post-Keynesian economists the flaws in financially sophisticated capitalist market economies are fundamental. In such economies the signals from markets can be such that the behaviour of rational agents, each acting in an attempt to maximize income, wealth, or utility, can lead to a disequilibrium (unemployment or an insufficiency of profits flows). Furthermore, the response of units to an initial disequilibrium may make the disequilibrium worse, not better. Modern mathematical analysis of the potential of complex dynamical systems to breed incoherence validates post-Keynesian insights that the results of the reactions of market participants to opportunity are not always benign (Ingrao and Israel, 1985; 1987; Day, 1982; 1983; Day and Shafer, 1986; Baumol and Benhabib, 1989).

Therefore post-Keynesians define the problems of Political Economy as:

1) to understand the dynamics of *an accumulating capitalist economy, with complex and evolving financial, product and labour markets*, where the dynamics may lead to explosive growth, implosive decline or complex business cycles rather than sustained exponential growth, and
2) to develop policies which thwart such disruptive dynamics and sustain employment, growth and price stability. As the underlined passage emphasizes, the subject of post-Keynesians is always a capitalist economy with complex financial structures, product markets and labour relations. In the post-Keynesian view institutional arrangements are not a veil: they affect the behaviour of the economy.[2]

Over the past 20 years the IS–LM model was displaced from the centre of macroeconomic analysis.[3] Unfortunately this was accomplished not by post-Keynesian thinking but by what started as a revival of pre-Keynesian monetary theory or monetarism (Friedman, 1956; 1959; 1968; Brunner, 1968; Brunner and Metzler, 1972). In the 1970s and the early 1980s the rout of IS–LM as the basis of macroeconomic thinking was completed by the development of the new classical economics (Lucas and Sargent, 1981).[4]

Over the past 20 years the economic environment, the problems economists attack and the way they are attacked have changed. The economic environment exhibited bouts of instability, a rapid evolution of financial institutions and usages, and profound changes in the power and acceptability of trade unions. Economists have been engaged in modelling expectation formation, market structures and information as determinants of market behaviour. High technology mathematics and econometrics have become the dominant tools of economic research. The importance in the economist's tool kit of knowledge of economic institutions and history has diminished.

With IS–LM routed and with no consensus view dominant, macroeconomics is searching for a new footing. It is now quite clear that the new classical economics was more successful as a critique of prior theory and policy analysis than as a rich basis for relevant research. The new classical economics led to the birth of a new Keynesian economics, which accepts the standards of economic argumentation of the new classical economists but derives what are taken to be Keynesian results. Much of the thrust and counter thrust among the new classicals and the new Keynesians shows how small differences in formal assumptions lead to large differences in propositions asserted.[5]

In the context of the breakdown of the IS–LM synthesis and the emergence of new Keynesianism, it is worth setting forth some basic post-Keynesian precepts which may act as a foundation for further work in macroeconomics. The perspective we advance stems from three post-Keynesian concerns: the role of money and finance in capitalist economies, the determinants of the movement of money wages in calendar time, and the impact of market power on prices, employment and investment. In this paper the main emphasis is upon the first two of the three, the role of money and finance and the movement of money wages. Somewhat lesser emphasis is placed upon market power although it seems clear that the cited emphasis by Keynes about the ". . .characteristics. . .of the actual economy in which we live. . ." encompasses the industrial structure.

Our argument is advanced in six sections:

1) the influence of events in the rout of IS–LM
2) a scorecard of the players
3) expectations, learning and information
4) the treatment of capital asset prices
5) the role of labour and product market institutions
6) the fundamentals of post-Keyensian economics.

This is followed by some concluding remarks.

2.   THE IMPACT OF EVENTS ON THE IS–LM SYNTHESIS

The IS–LM framework served as a partial basis for the big government interventionist capitalist regime that was put in place in the USA and the other advanced economies in the years following the second world war.

This regime reflected a combination of insights into the characteristics of a capitalist economy that were derived from the conventional interpretation of Keynes with specific market interventions that reflect largely pre-Keynesian views about the market failures that led to the great depression. An era of tranquil, successful capitalism followed the end of the second world war and lasted until the end of the 1960s. This successful perform-ance reinforced the dominance of Keynesian orthodoxy as both the way to do economics and as a guide to policy.

The 1970s were marked by stagflation, episodes of financial instability, and a breakdown in the postwar international monetary system. The turbulent performance of the capitalist economies in the 1970s (and the 1980s) fell short of the standard set in the first two decades after the second world war. Nevertheless, no serious, deep and long lasting recession or depression occurred. However the shortfalls in performance associated with inflation, problems arising from fighting inflation, and a deteriora-tion of the efficacy of various interventions in markets led to political changes which in turn led to the partial rejection of the policy synthesis that served the capitalist economies well throughout the 1950s and 1960s.[6] These economic and political developments also undermined the legiti-macy of the IS–LM approach to policy analysis and conferred legitimacy on the critics of Keynesian economics.

Although the IS–LM synthesis and the econometric forecasting models they spawned had logical holes, which monetarist and the new classi-cal critics made evident, their "fall", as a central concern of economic research, was due more to their inability to generate effective prescriptions for the failures of the economy than to the abstract analytical strength of the alternative analysis.

3. YOU CAN'T TELL THE PLAYERS WITHOUT A SCORECARD

In a *Night at the Opera* the great Groucho Marx disrupts the overture by selling programmes, calling out, as if he were in a baseball stadium, "You can't tell the players without a score card". In a similar vein a score card is needed to trace the thrusts and counterthrusts in the evolution of macroeconomic thinking over the past two decades. As we mentioned ear-lier such score cards have been provided in review articles by Leijonhufvud (1987) and Mankiw (1987). We will not replicate their detailed account, we have other axes to grind.

The initial position for developments in mainstream macroeconomics since the 1960s is the Phillips curve augmented IS–LM model that was and remains the analytical underpinning of the commercial econometric forecasting models.[7] These models had succeeded in reducing Keynes to banality, in particular they ignored Keynes's deep analysis of capital asset pricing, money and finance.

In developing the power of these structural models to track the short-term movements of the economy, variables were added to the various functions on a pragmatic basis, i.e. what worked best in explaining the data in hand was used as a basis for the equations used in forecasting. Each variable so added required either the addition of an equation to explain the new variable or the new variable was added to the list of predetermined or exogenous variables. As a result the pragmatic choices of the structural forecasting models began to represent no consistent economic logic. Equations were there and took the form they did because they satisfied the needs of the forecasters, not of economic logic (Brainard and Tobin, 1968; Lucas, 1976). When the economy ceased to behave in the tranquil manner of the first two decades after the second world war (which the pragmatic equations were designed to track), the predictive and policy-suggestive powers of the IS–LM based models broke down. During the stagflation of the 1970s the Phillips curve trade off between inflation and unemployment no longer worked: notions of a natural rate of unemployment, that in time made monetary and fiscal policies ineffective in reducing unemployment, became dominant determinants of research programmes (Friedman, 1968; Phelps, 1970).

It should have been evident as early as the 1960s that the "Keynesian" structural approach lacked a satisfactory modelling of the monetary and banking system. Such models would have required a deep analysis of how investment and finance were related. The IS–LM formulation did not offer a basis for modelling investment in a manner that made financing a principal variable.[8]

In Friedman's presidential address to the American Economic Association and in his prior work on the consumption function, arguments were put forth that the data of the economy could be interpreted as if they were ground out by a moving Walrasian general equilibrium system.[9] Lucas seized the idea of the economy being represented by such a Walrasian structure to posit that the economy is in market clearing equilibrium at all times: this market clearing equilibrium is enforced because rational agents know or quickly learn their place in equilibrium and behave accordingly. This happens because the market forces losses upon them if they deviate from this equilibrium dependent behaviour. Units knowing their place in the economy and acting so as to maximize their wellbeing under these constraints underlies the results obtained under the rubric of rational expectations. Rational expectations is the analytic equivalent to Walras's auctioneer.

The strong equilibrium-seeking and sustaining character of the economy posited by the new classical economics proves too much. It leaves no room for business cycles. Lucas recognized this when he cited Jack Gurley's review of Friedman's Fordham lectures.[10] Friedman (1961), Lucas and his followers, following the lead of Friedman, created a variety of ingenious constructs in which exogenously imposed monetary disturbances led to price and output changes. In the key Lucas contribution, agents did not know whether changes in the prices they confronted reflected changes in price levels or in relative prices (Lucas, 1981). Cycles were transitory phenomena as agents learned the true nature of disturbances. Generating business cycles as the result of lagged adjustments to innovations and shocks is old hat, this characterized the pre-second world war cycle theories of Slutsky (1937) and Frisch (1933). Lucas's innovations spawned a variety of monetary, institutional rigidity and real business cycle theories.[11]

In the 1970s the post-Friedman monetarists made strong claims that a properly announced disinflation would be rather painless as far as recession and unemployment were concerned.[12] In the early 1980s disinflation took place accompanied by the greatest and longest recession and highest levels of unemployment since the second world war. In the USA in the 1980s a combination of union-weakening government interventions, sustained unemployment and a flood of imports led to the stabilization of money wages and even declines in "real" wages. As the 1980s proceeded, evidence accumulated that the movement of money wages, which reflected both unemployment rates and structural characteristics of the labour market, rather than the behaviour of money supply, was the main determinant of price level changes.

Even as the logical weakness of the Lucas-led monetarism mark two became evident (the strong results were due to assumptions made, not propositions demonstrated), the behaviour of the economy contradicted their views. The rapid expansion of the money supply in the late 1980s did not breed inflation.[13] A Keynesian fiscal posture in the form of massive deficits led, with a lag, to a large-scale reduction of unemployment.

As the end of the century nears, both the IS–LM model of the 1950s and 1960s and the new classical theories of the 1970s and early 1980s are of questionable legitimacy. In this vacuum a new Keynesian economics has emerged. To the new Keynesians, Keynesian results are defined as:

1) the creation and persistence of unemployment even though all units are maximizing,
2) the possibility that the dynamics are chaos inducing, and
3) the effectiveness of monetary and fiscal policies.

These results are to be derived within models in which expectations are model-consistent and outcomes with unemployment and financial disruptions are consistent with maximizing behaviour by the various decision-making units.

The new Keynesians are advancing propositions that have been part of the post-Keynesian canon through the years. The question is whether this "coincidence of maintained propositions" reflects some deeper agreement of what Schumpeter called "vision", or whether it reflects the "power" of technically able economists to force results that are consistent with the priors they hold as to how the world behaves.

4.   EXPECTATIONS

The treatment of expectations in the large-scale econometric models had a specially weak theoretical basis. Given the detailed treatment of expectation formation in *The general theory* and the emphasis that Keynes had placed upon decisions under uncertainty in the *Treatise on probability* (Keynes, 1921) the rational expectation would be that Keynesian economics and economists would be strong on the expectations front. However, the IS–LM theorists and econometric model builders handled expectations as *ad hoc* extrapolative or adaptive transformations of observations. Expectations did not reflect, as they did in Keynes, the result of rational agents trying to behave in a sensible way in a world they really did not understand. In particular, Keynes's distinction between short-term expectations (sales or profit expectations), which guide the use of existing facilities (employment), and long-term expectations, which guide investment, was lost.[14]

Mark two monetarists under the leadership of Lucas, building upon a seminal article by Muth (Muth, 1961), argued that decision makers would use all available information, including a maintained theory about the structure and behaviour of the economy, in deciding upon actions. If an agent's theory mis-specified the behaviour of the economy, the agent would be punished by avoidable losses. These losses concentrate the agents' minds so that they soon learn what they need to know about the true behaviour of the economy. As a result, systematic losses disappear.

If we add a further precept to monetarism mark two, that the economy is a strong equilibrium-seeking and maintaining system, which is well represented by a Walrasian general equilibrium structure, then loss-containing actions of individual units reinforce the equilibrium. Strong theorems such as policy irrelevance and the equivalence of debt and tax-financed government expenditures follow.

The post-Keynesians maintain that an essential aspect of Keynes's work was the treatment of investment decisions, which depend upon currently held expectations of future profit flows. Furthermore, investment and the building of capital assets are financed, at least in part, by debts. Therefore both investment and capital-asset prices depended upon the expectations and interactions of bankers and businessmen. In a capitalist economy, bets in the form of investments, capital asset acquisitions, and financing agreements, are placed every day on the basis of imperfect, private and therefore asymmetric information, i.e. in conditions of uncertainty.

The result of negotiations and deals among households, businessmen and bankers (both as agents managing the money of others, and as principals hazarding their own and their bank's equity) is a price system of financial and real assets. To post-Keynesians, who emphasize the structure of financial arrangements, "the interest rate", as used in IS–LM formulations, is of secondary importance. The financial variables of central importance are:

1) the actual cash flows from economic activities,
2) the internal finance cash flows provide, and
3) the success or failure of actual cash flows to validate, first prior commitments to pay that are embodied in the complex structure of financial interrelations and instruments and, secondly, the prices that were paid for capital assets and investment output.

These fundamental financial variables are inputs to the determination of current expectations of future profits: i.e. current long-term expectations.

To Keynes (and the post-Keynesians), the grounds for holding particular long-term expectations are often flimsy. Crises, epidemics of losses in asset values, and declines of profit flows are common events whose timing is uncertain. A decline of the prices of real capital assets relative to that of investment output, because of a combination of a change in portfolio preference towards "secure" assets and adverse current expectations of future profit flows, can cause a collapse of investment that triggers a depression.

To post-Keynesians the critical market failure in a capitalist economy is that once current expectations of future profits are insufficient to induce enough investment to sustain full employment, households, bankers and firms are likely to behave so as to worsen rather than improve profit expectations and thus to increase the shortfall of investment. A critical Keynesian precept is that downward wage and price flexibility in times of unemployment is likely to make unemployment worse rather than better. This is so because deflation, with an accompanying decline in current and near term expected profits, has an adverse effect upon investment by adversely affecting margins of safety in current liability structures and current expectations of profits in the long run. Recent work tends to support this post-Keynesian view.[15]

5.   THE TREATMENT OF ASSET PRICES

Kregel (1982; 1983; 1984; 1987) has drawn attention to Keynes's experience with the behaviour of spot and futures foreign-exchange markets in 1914 and Sraffa's (1932a; 1932b) discussion of own rates of interest (his refutation of the natural rate of interest argument of Hayek) as fundamental inputs to the development of Keynes's position that the critical missing link in the orthodox economics of his time was a theory of the determination of asset prices. That is a theory of how, in a modern economy, the price system connects the past, the present and the future. This link is still missing in today's theories that start from a neoclassical base.

Kregel holds that experience with future markets for currencies and Sraffa's argument led Keynes to conclude that asset prices provide the essential links among the past, the present and the future in a capitalist economy. As agents adjust their portfolios in the light of different expected rates of return on traded assets, asset prices adjust so that their rates of return become equivalent. As the returns on asset holdings are multidimensional, a simple tendency towards equality of the ratios between expected monetary returns and the monetary prices of capital assets is not observed: equivalent returns are not equal returns. This leads to the question "What are the dimensions of these equivalent returns?"

Rational agents maximizing their portfolio's returns are interested in the profit flows from their assets (whether retained or paid-out), the assurance of these profit flows, the commitments they have to make in order to finance their holdings of assets, and the ability to change their portfolio's composition as their needs and views about the future change.

The prices of capital assets and liabilities of firms reflect the views of agents that deal in such assets of how gross profits are determined. To the agents that manage wealth, assets are debts of other agents or equities, real or financial: they are either protected or residual claims on profit flows.[16] If asset managers believe that profit flows to capital assets as collected in firms are always known with certainty, and equal to the marginal product of the capital assets times the quantity of the capital asset, then the cash flows available to fulfil the commitment on each financial instrument based upon these profit flows are known with certainty. If this is true, claims to the earnings of capital assets and firms, whether debts or equities, will be priced as if they were Treasury securities.

The economy needs to be in a perpetual full equilibrium for the return on capital assets always to be the marginal product of capital times capital. If excess capacity exists because of either aggregate demand failures or structural inconsistencies, if the pursuit of maximum portfolio returns takes place in the context of the total of profits being determined by the economy's macroeconomic performance or the structure of demands, if the competition among capitals that counts is for profits, and if portfolio managers value the ability to change their portfolio, then present prices of capital assets and financial instruments summarize conjectures of market participants about the future of the economy, the future efficiency of various actors and the future performance of financial markets. Actual asset prices, given the price of the asset money is always one, reflect the different margins of safety that various portfolio managers require as well as their views about the future course of aggregate profits.

Three fundamental propositions of post-Keynesian theory follow from this construction:

1) the price level of capital assets is not tied down in any precise way to the current production costs of investment output.
2) the endogenously determined course of aggregate profits is a critical variable in determining the viability of any liability structure.
3) changing market valuations of the "virtue of liquidity" (the ability to change the assets of a portfolio into cash without changing price concessions) will change both the relative prices of assets and the price level of assets that are mainly valued for the income they yield relative to the price level of current output and the money wage rate.

The third proposition is due to the special nature of money as an asset that follows from the institutional arrangement that debts are denominated in money: the subjective yield of money (value of an insurance policy) sets a floor to the yields that assets which do not possess the properties of money can earn. In particular, if circumstances arise in which the subjective yield of money increases (what Keynes called an increase in liquidity preference) then the money prices of assets that are mainly valued for the money income they are expected to earn will fall. Such a fall in the price of assets mainly valued for the money returns (income) they are expected to yield relative to the price of money, which is always one, will also be a fall in the prices of capital assets relative to those of investment outputs. As the money prices of assets relative to the current supply price of investment outputs are, along with the availability of finance, a main determinant of investment output, a shift in portfolio preferences towards greater holdings of money will lead to a fall in investment output and therefore in income and profits.

Liquidity preference is in the first instance a theory of asset prices and of how present effective demand is linked to present expectations of what the future will bring, but it is ultimately an explanation of why instability is a natural characteristic of financially sophisticated economies. This is so because financial intermediaries are vulnerable to being in a position where they need to make position by selling out position.[17] Keynes's theory of liquidity preference rationalizes the need and function of the central banks in capitalist economies and also explains how central bank intervention can be effective in containing downside instability.

The actions of rational maximizing agents, who are not sure how the world in which they must act behaves, determines not just the allocation of existing employed resources among alternative uses, but also the volume of resources that will be employed and the conditions under which resources will be created, i.e. investment will be undertaken. In the argument of *The general theory*, the proximate determinant of effective demand is investment output. The guts of Keynesian economics is a theory of capital asset prices based upon decisions of individuals under uncertainty. It shows how precarious the quantity of investment and therefore the level of effective demand can be.

In the macroeconomic and econometric work of the era during which IS–LM was dominant, the emphasis was not on investment demand but on the more amenable consumption demand. The research programme that followed the IS–LM view emphasized the determinants of consumption (which was easy) rather than the understanding of investment (which is hard). As a result of work mainly under the guidance of Jorgenson (1963), models that ignored the importance of financial relations became the basis for macroeconomic views of investment. Only recently, mainly in the work of Steve Fazzari (1987, 1988) with various colleagues, have models which take financial variables into account been shown to have significant explanatory power for investment.

The treatment of money and profit flows as generating the price level of assets whereas the price level of output is determined by money wage rates and markups remains a characteristic which distinguishes post-Keynesian from other variants of Keynesian economics. Tobin's q is analogous to this ratio, but, in the literature it has spawned, the analytical relations that determine the two price levels are not linked to liquidity preference and the market processes that determine wage rates and output prices.

6. THE FUNDAMENTAL POSITION OF POST-KEYNESIAN ECONOMICS

Post-Keynesian theory is not about abstract economies. It is about capitalist economies in which long-lived capital assets as well as business firms earn incomes and are bought and sold.[18] That firms can be bought and sold in whole or in part implies that there are prices for such assets and firms, and these prices are not simple transformations of their historic cost of production, "today's" production costs or of known future profits.

Post-Keynesian economics deviates from orthodox neoclassical and Keynesian economics in the specific recognition that there are two sets of prices in capitalist economies: one of capital assets and the second of current output. Capital assets are different from tools in that they are expensive; sophisticated and ever-evolving techniques for financing ownership or control over capital assets and businesses are intrinsic characteristics of modern capitalist economies. Banks, bankers and other specialists in the financing of investments and of positions in capital assets are essential players in the processes that propel capitalist economies through time. There can be no economic theory of capitalist economies that does not allow for profit-seeking bankers and financiers to play an essential role in the determination of system behaviour through calendar time.[19] In financing investment and positions in capital assets, the units doing the financing receive claims to the incomes to be earned by capital assets and firms.

No one doubts that in modern economies money is mainly the liability of banks.[20] Post-Keynesian theory stresses that its quantity is determined by the profit-seeking behaviour of the financing agencies and firms that operate the economy's capital assets. Post-Keynesian theory is as rooted in the analysis of individual behaviour as is neoclassical theory. The difference is that post-Keynesian theory focuses upon the profit-seeking activities of banks, businessmen and bankers. Post-Keynesian theory recognizes that the decisions of businessmen and bankers are more significant in determining the growth, cyclical performance and evolution of the economy than those of households: profit seeking drives capitalist economies.[21]

Post-Keynesian theory links the price level of capital assets and the availability of financing for investment output to banks and through them to the quantity of money. The price levels of investment output and labour are not directly linked to money, but are determined through the interactions between demand and supply for output and labour in the context of particular institutional arrangements. Post-Keynesian theory of the determination of output prices is guided by the idea that prices are both mechanisms for recovering costs and carriers of profits. In the aggregate, the main out-of-pocket costs that need to be recovered are wage costs, so that, as a first approximation, the price level of current output is determined by money wage rates. A more complete explanation of prices adds markups, as determined by the aggregate of profits, to wage costs.

In the IS–LM synthesis and the various monetarisms, labour supply and demand are stated in real terms: in the determination of output prices the labour market is decoupled from other markets. In a monetary-production economy, labour is paid in nominal terms and the cash flows that have to be generated by product prices (if debts and asset prices are to be validated) are in nominal terms. But the cash flows that outputs generate are determined by the composition of aggregate demand, in particular in the simplest versions gross profits are determined by gross investment (Kalecki, 1971). Gross investment in turn depends upon the relation between profit expectations in the long run, current financing conditions for investment, and the nominal supply price of investment outputs.

A well-established tradition in economic argumentation is to treat the labour market with real variables as the overriding determinant of equilibrium employment: Keynes took exception to this in chapter 2 of *The general theory*. The labour market augmented IS–LM models conform to this tradition. The new classical economists generalize the dominant labour-market equilibrium to a moving Walrasian general equilibrium, and add "rational expectations" to constrain behaviour to be equilibrium-enhancing. Rational expectations assume each agent knows where it fits into the economy at equilibrium and acts accordingly.

The treatment of the labour market in both the IS–LM and new classical economics resurrects the "money is a veil" proposition of pre-Keynesian economics. In the post-Keynesian perspective, nominal money wages are determined as a result of market processes in which aggregate demand, product-market institutions, the income objectives and power of labour-market organizations, and the monetary fiscal policy regime interact to determine the supply prices of output. Aggregate money demand may or may not sustain these supply prices at acceptable employment levels: if the result is that they do not, then the policy reaction determines whether deflation, stagflation or inflation results.

There is a post-Keynesian "dichotomization". In post-Keynesian theory nominal investment determines nominal aggregate demand and labour-market dynamics determines the course of money wages and the supply price of outputs. This dichotomization is a first step towards recognizing the interdependence between the processes determining aggregate demand and profits and the institutional structures that affect the course of prices and wages. As a result the course of the economy can be modelled as the outcome of market processes that force consistency between two systems of dynamic interactions, each of which can be said to "march to its own drummer" (Minsky and Ferri, 1984).

7. THE ROLE OF INSTITUTIONS

In post-Keynesian theory the endogenous dynamics of market economies are not necessarily nice: monotonic explosive, explosive amplitude cycles and even chaotic cycles are possible paths through time. The interactions described by Irving Fisher in *The debt deflation theory of business cycles* are readily incorporated into post-Keynesian frameworks (Fisher, 1933; Tobin, 1980; Minsky, 1975; 1982). Such awkward endogenous dynamics need to be contained and constrained if the economy is to approximate orderly behaviour for substantial periods of time.

A dynamic process of a set of structural equations through time can be transformed into a set of polynomial equations of the form:

$$x(t) = A_1 u_1^t + A_2 u_2^t + A_3 u_3^t \ldots \tag{6.1}$$

In this polynomial the u's are transformations of the parameters of underlying structural equations and the A's are transformations of the initial conditions. In an economy that tends to fly off into chaotic or other unsatisfactory states, interventions and constraints are necessary if even a semblance of order is to result. Such interventions and constraints impose new initial conditions that bring about a transitory reign of nice behaviour out of otherwise nasty dynamics. Business cycles can result either from the values of the "u's" being complex, from regular interventions that contain the economy between "floors and ceilings" if the "u's" are greater than 1, and from introductions of energy from outside if the "u's" are less than 1[22] (Minsky, 1957; 1959; Frisch, 1933; Hicks, 1950).

The fact that the normal path of an economy is cyclical implies that the various markets and institutions are subject to stresses and strains (Mitchell, 1913). As a result the opportunities open to agents change as such an economy transits through time. But stresses and strains and changing opportunities imply that there are profits to be earned from institutional innovations: profit seeking drives institutional evolution. Institutional evolution makes economic processes irreversible: economies exist in historical time. Post-Keynesian theory rejects the notion of economic theory as a study that derives theorems about the behaviour of an economy that are not conditioned by a particular historical, social and institutional context.

From the above it follows that:

1) political processes generate and sustain an economy's structure of intervention and containment: the path through time of an economy is a "political economy phenomenon";
2) the effectiveness of an in-place institutional structure to achieve tolerable outcomes is likely to attenuate through time as agents learn how to evade, avoid and exploit the constraints, and as the incentives to behave "well" diminish;
3) new institutional structures of containment and intervention become necessary from time to time.

The post-Keynesian proposition that "a big-government interventionist capitalism" is more stable and efficient than a small-government capitalism reflects the difference in the performance of the capitalist economies since the second world war when compared with earlier periods (Minsky, 1986a). The crisis of the 1930s, together with the lessons from the second world war, led to the development of a regime of intervention and regulation that has proven to be effective in sustaining income and employment. In the USA this regime included a structure of labour relations and a model of industrial policy, as well as contracyclical monetary and fiscal policies.

This regime was effective through the mid-1960s. After 1968, while stagflation, inflation, cost-push excesses, OPEC exercise of market power and a return of financial instability took place, this regime's effectiveness declined. Since 1968 the policy regime inherited from the post-second world war period has been under pressure, the "crises" have involved unemployment, shifting economic power among nations, and finances. However, big-government capitalism has been sufficiently resilient so that a major depression has not occurred. The continued effectiveness of this regime is evident by the way the impact of the stock market crash of October 1987 has been contained.

8.   SOME CONCLUDING REMARKS

Macroeconomics has been a dynamic discipline over the past 20 years. The undermining of the orthodox labour market-augmented neoclassical Keynesianism of the late 1960s by a combination of logical criticisms, empirical shortcomings and developments in the economy has not been followed by the emergence of a successor consensus macroeconomics. During the twenty years that followed an orthodox monetarism and a new classical economics had short reigns, but each in turn gave way to logical criticism and the apparent failure of its policy precepts. Today there may be a mainstream consensus on modelling techniques, but there is no mainstream consensus view of the substance of macroeconomics, on a body of maintained propositions.

At present a new view – often called a new Keynesian economics – is making its presence felt in mainstream economics. By emphasizing private asymmetric information, by rejecting glib assertions about universal market clearing, and by recognizing the essential importance of contracts and money, the new Keynesian economists are resurrecting persistent unemployment, potentially perverse dynamics and policy effectiveness as system characteristics. The new Keynesians take these to be the essential properties of a Keynesian economy.

These new Keynesian economists have only peripherally focused upon the financing structure of capitalist economies. As they extend their vision to include the role of imperfect and asymmetric information in the negotiations that lead to the liability structures that finance investment and positions in capital assets, then, we are willing to venture, a convergence between the new Keynesian economists and a technically proficient new generation of post-Keynesian will take place. Post-Keynesian economics, born in the 1960s out of a dissatisfaction with what was perceived to be a trivialization of Keynes in the IS–LM synthesis and the econometric forecasting models, will, we are confident, find its fulfilment in the 1990s and even onto the twenty-first century as the problems of managing a financial capitalism that is inherently endogenously unstable move centre stage.

The easy times of capitalism after Keynes may be over. Hard times, in which the development of programmes to constrain and control the forces making for incoherence in market economies is the central issue, may be beginning.[23] Formulating such policies requires a deeper understanding of capitalist dynamics than is offered by either the IS–LM or the new classical models. Economics once again promises to be an exciting discipline and macroeconomics the central concern of engaged economists. It is in this spirit that there are fields to be conquered that the emergence of the *Review of Political Economy* is welcomed.

ACKNOWLEDGEMENTS

The authors thank Steven Fazzari and an anonymous referee for comments and help. The usual disclaimer applies: what virtues this paper has owes much to them, the faults obvious and obscure are ours.

NOTES

*   This is a reprint of the article: Piero Ferri and Hyman P. Minsky (1989), "The breakdown of the IS–LM synthesis: implications for post-Keynesian economic theory", *Review of Political Economy*, 1 (2), 123–43. The authors gratefully acknowledge the publisher Taylor & Francis for giving permission to reprint this article.

1.   We concentrate on the work of the financial and labour market post-Keynesians. The important work of J. Robinson (1956) and Kaldor (1961) among others, which endeavours to draw the implications of *The general theory's* way of looking at the economy for longer-run developments, largely ignores the monetary and financial relations that become the LM part of the IS–LM orthodoxy. Therefore their work is only of peripheral interest to our subject: the implications of the breakdown of the IS–LM synthesis for post-Keynesian theory.

2.   The last sentence of the first chapter of *The general theory* is relevant: "Moreover, the characteristics of the special case assumed by the classical theory happen not to be those of the economic society in which we actually live, with the result that its teaching is misleading and disastrous if we attempt to apply it to the facts of experience" (Keynes, 1936:3). The operative phrase that emphasizes the institutional characteristics of the analysis is "the characteristics . . . of the economic society in which we actually live . . .".

3.   "At some schools, the IS–LM model is not even taught at the graduate level; it is thought to be the relic of a bygone age." Mankiw (1987).

4.   Labelled monetarism mark two by Tobin (1980).

5.   Bibliographies of the fast growing new Keynesian literature can be found in Mankiw (1987), Leijonhufvud (1987), Hahn and Solow (1986), and Greenwald and Stiglitz (1987). The economists spotlighted in the *Economist's* (Dec 24, 1988) survey of rising stars of American economics can be characterized as new Keynesians.

6.   The policy synthesis that emerged out of the great depression in the USA had two main macroeconomic facets: the maintenance of aggregate demand by means of fiscal and monetary policy and the containment of potential debt deflations by means of "lender of last resort interventions" by the Federal Reserve. After the credit crunch of 1968 the Federal Reserve was forced to act as lender of the last resort at regular intervals over the following two decades. Minsky (1986a), Giordano (1987).

7.   Duesenberry, *et al.* (1965) is an introduction to the state of the art macroeconomic model that was subject to the criticisms of the 1970s.

8.   The structural forecasting models often used the McGraw Hill survey of investment intentions for their forecasts. Monetary variables appeared to determine some prime interest rates and other interest rates were derived from these rates. Interest rates mainly impacted the economy through their effect upon housing.

9.   "The natural rate of unemployment, in other words, is the level that would be ground out by the Walrasian system of general equilibrium equations, provided there is imbedded in them the actual structural characteristics of the labour and commodity markets, including market imperfections, stochastic variability in demands and supplies, the costs of gathering information about job vacancies and labour availabilities, the cost of mobility, and so on" (Friedman, 1968:8). As the Walrasian system grinds out the natural rate of unemployment it will simultaneously grind out relative prices and outputs.

10.   Lucas concludes his paper "Expectations and neutrality of money" noting that "this paper has been an attempt to resolve the paradox posed by Gurley (1961) in his mild but accurate parody of Friedmanian monetary theory: 'money is a veil, but when it flutters, real output sputters'".

11.   Leijonhufvud (1987) reviews the after-Lucas business cycle literature, including various attempts to derive real business cycles.

12.   Given the new classical economists' assumption that the Walrasian equations ground out the natural rate of unemployment level, and all other real variables along with the

natural rate, the result is trivial in theory and irrelevant to what happens in the economy in which we live.

13. Financial innovations, such as money market funds and the securitization of hitherto bankable assets, made the definition of money problematical as the 1980s progressed.

14. How chapters 12 and 17 of *The general theory* were lost to the pre-1968 "Keynesian" mainstream is a mystery. The new Keynesian economists are picking up the imperfect competition, and imprecise, private or asymmetric information aspects of Keynes's thought. They are not as yet integrating Keynesian uncertainty into their models, although the modelling of information structures can come close to Keynesian thinking.

15. Recent work that supports this post-Keyenesian perspective includes Caskey and Fazzari (1987), Delong and Summers (1986) and Hahn and Solow (1986).

16. Household and government debts, which are of great importance in the world of the 1980s, are put aside in this argument for they were substantially less important at the time Keynes was setting up Keynesian theory.

17. The position of a financial institution (and by extension any organization) consists of those assets that are held because of the income they are expected to yield. "Making position by selling out position" takes place when an organization needs cash and the ordinary sources of cash are not available for one reason or another. Central banks and other refinancing arrangements are designed to forestall the need "to make position by selling out position".

18. Long-lived capital assets are plant and equipment, i.e. produced means of production. Business firms are profit-seeking organizations which control and operate produced means of production that have some domain of increasing returns.

19. Schumpeter's vision in Chapter 3, Credit and capital, of the *Theory of Economic Development* (Schumpeter, 1934) is fully consistent with a Keynesian perspective on growth and development.

20. Fanciful views of money that enters the economy by being dropped from helicopters ignores the elementary fact that money always enters the economy in an exchange in which the recipient of money promises to pay money back at some later date. Financing and refinancing are the basic concepts, money is an outgrowth of financing and refinancing. The development of money-market funds and the securitization of primary financial claims indicates that money does not need to be a liability of a financial institution that holds financial assets and manages a fund which includes monetary assets among the liabilities.

21. The emergence of the leveraged buyouts and other speculative financial market developments in the 1980s reflects the increased weight of managed money due to the growth of pension and mutual funds. The assimilation of these developments to the analysis of the behaviour of capitalist economies through time is beyond the scope of this paper.

22. The solution equation to a linear second-order difference equation (such as the accelerator multiplier interactions) give rise to:

$$x(t) = A_1 u_1^t + A_2 u_2^t$$

If both roots, u_1 and u_2, are greater than 1 and the initial conditions lead to a growth rate that is less than the smaller root, u_2, but the growth rate of the initial conditions is of the same order of magnitude as the smaller root (1.03 may be the initial conditions growth rate and 1.05 the smaller root), then the A_2 will be large and positive and A_1 will be small and negative. The endogenous dynamics that the solution equation will generate will be of decreasing positive growth followed by explosive negative contraction, i.e. the system will degenerate from behaving in a nice manner to behaving in a nasty manner. A floor, or a policy intervention that constrains the rate of decline, will lead to a nice and then to a nasty explosive expansion. Once again intervention can lead to constraining the explosive (inflationary) expansion, repeating the constrained growth that degenerates into an explosive decline.

23.   As this paper was being revised for publication the first weeks of the Bush administration
      were being taken up by the problems of the Federal Savings and Loan Insurance
      Corporation; in particular its inability to finance the insurance commitment to
      depositors of savings and loan associations which have negative net worths.

7. Market processes and thwarting systems

Piero Ferri and Hyman P. Minsky*

1. INTRODUCTION[1,2]

In this paper we argue that the current state of economic theory as well as the performance of capitalist economies in recent years support the view that the path through time of a capitalist economy is best described as the result of the interaction between the system's endogenous dynamics, which if unconstrained would lead to complex paths that include periods of apparent growth, business cycles and economic instability, and the impact of institutions and interventions which, if apt, constrain the outcomes of capitalist market processes to viable or acceptable outcomes. We call these institutions and interventions *thwarting systems*.

We deviate from the conventions of orthodox economic theory by assuming that in capitalistic economies the core decision makers are profit seeking businessmen and bankers.[3] Even though their key actions are forward looking, these agents are constrained by legacies of the past in the form of capital assets and financial commitments. Furthermore, they do this within an institutional structure which they know is changing even as they act. Every day the actions of businessmen and bankers determine "tomorrow's" capital asset and financial structure. In capitalistic economies, yesterday and tomorrow are present today.

The agents' expectations of how the economy will perform is one way in which tomorrow is present today. Each day contracts are entered upon on the basis of tenuously held beliefs and imprecise information: our bankers and businessmen act and decide under conditions of uncertainty in the sense of Keynes.[4] Because businessmen and their bankers have liabilities, the relevant uncertainty is mainly about future profits (cash flows). The emphasis on businessmen and bankers and on financial commitments and decisions based upon expectations that respond to events (and are thus endogenously determined) and that are often tenuously held, makes our argument a Keynesian one.[5] It is a Keynesian precept that the performance

of the economy affects the model of the economy that agents use in forming expectations.[6]

Intertemporal linkages, financing, and the endogenous determination of
the model that agents use in guiding the formation of expectations mean
that the appropriate mathematical formulation of the economics we are
investigating will be complex time-dependent systems. The mathematics
of such systems leads to the proposition that capitalist economies should,
from time to time, exhibit economic instability.[7] However, instability rarely
becomes explosive. We need to understand why.

We use the ceiling-and-floor version of the accelerator-multiplier interactions that were developed in the 1950s as a simple prototype model
which endogenously can generate unsatisfactory states, but which can be
constrained by interventions to generate satisfactory states. We postulate
that institutions and interventions thwart the instability breeding dynamics that are natural to market economies by interrupting the endogenous
process and "starting" the economy again with non-market determined
values as "initial conditions".[8] It follows that the observed behaviour of the
economy is not the result of market mechanisms in isolation, but is due to
a combination of market behaviour and the ability of institutions, conventions and policy interventions to contain and dominate the endogenous
economic reactions that, if left alone, breed instability.[9]

In Section 2 we contrast the endogenous stability plus shocks view
of business cycles with the view based on endogenous instability with
thwarting or containing mechanisms. In Section 3 we consider how these
two views of the dynamics of the capitalist economy imply different
policy perspectives. In Section 4 we take up examples of thwarting forces
within the endogenous instability view. Section 5 states and interprets two
theorems – an anti-laissez faire theorem and a limitation upon performance theorem – that are implicit in the argument. The last section presents
our concluding remarks.

2.   TWO VIEWS ON DYNAMICS

There have long been "two views" of business cycle dynamics: one is that
the endogenous process of the economy generates an equilibrium which
may be static but now is usually taken to be a "growth equilibrium",
and the other is that endogenous processes lead to business cycles and
instability.[10]

The first view leaves business cycles to be explained. In the work of
Slutsky (1937) and Frisch (1933) – as well as Friedman (1968) and Lucas
(1972) – the economy is a mechanism that transforms exogenous shocks,

which are either random or unanticipated policy interventions, into business cycles. The important difference between Slutsky and Frisch, on the one hand, and Friedman and Lucas, on the other, is that the former explore the consequence of treating the economy as an agent that averages shocks, whereas the latter accept the economy as an averaging agent but ground their shocks in the difficulty of maximizing agents to interpret changes in the environment. In Friedman and Lucas, environmental changes are initiated by money supply changes.[11]

The second tradition views business cycles – and economic instability – as the natural and inherent consequence of self interest motivated behaviour in complex economies with sophisticated financial institutions. The most important economists working within such a tradition are Marx, Mitchell, Schumpeter, Kalecki and Keynes.

A "Keynesian" endogenous explanation of business cycles received a mathematical statement in the formalization of the interaction of the accelerator and multiplier as a second-order linear difference equation (Samuelson, 1939). As it could generate only four types of time paths (oscillatory and damped, oscillatory and explosive, non-oscillatory and damped, and non-oscillatory and explosive), none of which would do for business cycle analysis, this simple form was unsatisfactory except as an expository device.

Starting with a Samuelson-type multiplier–accelerator interaction and assuming that the parameter values lead to explosive (monotonic or cyclical) paths, Hicks (1950) added ceilings and floors that had the effect of constraining the economy to acceptable paths. This model was extended by Minsky (1957, 1959), who motivated the ceilings and floors by referring to the behaviour of monetary and financing relations and interpreted the ceilings and floors as the imposition of new initial conditions.[12] This allowed the endogenous dynamics to be such that unsatisfactory performance would be generated by the unconstrained economy even as the constrained behaviour is acceptable. As policy can be interpreted as the imposition of new initial conditions in Minsky's formulation, policy can play a positive role.

Interest in these models of endogenous cycles waned after the 1950s: strong business cycles did not appear and the rather steady growth made it plausible to assume that the (moderate) fluctuations of experience can best be interpreted as transformations of stochastically or systematically determined deviations from a growth path, i.e. that the Frisch–Slutsky approach was valid.[13] In the work of Lucas (1972, 1981, 1987) and others, business cycle analyses that claimed to be consistent with the equilibrium-seeking and sustaining character of microeconomic theory were advanced.

In more recent years, the breakdown of the Bretton Woods system, serious recessions, and chilling episodes in financial markets have cast doubt on the endogenous stability of capitalist economies. At the same time, knowledge that simple deterministic non-linear relations can generate time series that are chaotic, together with the results of computer simulations which explored the properties of mathematically intractable dynamics models (see Day, 1982, 1986), have shown economists that fully endogenous economic processes can generate complex patterns.[14] These non-linear models are not vulnerable to the criticism that endogenous business cycle models generate time series that are too regular. At the same time, these series are not necessarily explosive.[15]

3.   ECONOMIC THEORY AND LAISSEZ FAIRE

Adam Smith's "invisible hand" conjecture that each agent ". . . intends only his own gain, and he is in this, as in many other cases, led by an invisible hand to promote an end which was no part of his intention" (Smith, 1776, book IV, chap. 2) is the foundation upon which exogenous shock models of business cycle rest. The Smithian conjecture has been transformed into the theorem that competitive equilibrium is a Pareto optimum. The "invisible hand" proposition leads to laissez faire as a policy position.[16]

The formal demonstration that a competitive equilibrium is a Pareto optimum theorem was achieved in the 1950s by Arrow and Debreu (1954) and McKenzie (1959). This achievement fulfilled only one part – the proof of the existence of a competitive equilibrium – of the research program of general equilibrium theory. The full research program included the demonstration of the uniqueness and stability of competitive equilibrium. It is now known that the second and third part cannot be achieved: the competitive equilibrium is not unique and it is not stable. Even at the most abstract levels, it is not possible to claim that if left to its own device, a competitive economy would achieve and sustain an equilibrium.[17]

The formal model for which the existence theorem has been demonstrated abstracts from innovations in technology, institutions and policy interventions. There is no money as liabilities of banks. The financing of investment in resources that are expected to produce profits is not considered. Arrow and Hahn (1971) cite Yeats, "the center does hold", when they briefly examine extensions of the General Equilibrium model to Keynesian concerns.

Once the domain of what economists must explain is broadened to include such economic activities as resource creation, finance, innovation, market power, and the creation and modifications of institutions, then Adam Smith's proposition that each agent promotes ". . . an end which was no part of his intention. . ." need include among the ends promoted not only the effective working of markets, economic progress, and growth but also instability. Agents each intending ". . . only his own gain . . ." contribute to market relations that make breakdowns of the economy, such as that which occurred over the period 1929–33, endogenous phenomena.

Technical change, innovations, capital assets, institutional behaviour, and ever evolving financing relations are features of the economy that were ignored when the theorem that competitive equilibrium exists and is an optimum was derived. When these elements are taken into account, the theory needs to link yesterday, today and tomorrow. The models become complex, the problems even more difficult to deal with, and policy conclusions less straightforward.

4. THWARTING SYSTEMS

Once it is recognized that the endogenous interactions of the economy are important elements in determining its dynamical pattern, there is a need to explain why frequent bouts of instability are not observed. The answer put forth here is that the economy has evolved usages and institutions, including agencies of government, whose economic impact is to thwart the instability generating tendencies of the economy. This is so, especially when the conjectural nature of the model of the economy that agents use as they form the expectations that guide their behaviour is taken into account: the belief that "they won't let it happen" with regard to serious depressions is by itself stability enhancing.[18]

The piecewise linear model of business cycles based upon ceilings and floors can be constructed as a metaphor for the interplay between market valuations and outcomes, on the one hand, and the impact of the thwarting forces, on the other. The ceiling and floor models, as extended by Minsky (1957, 1959), allow for policy determined variables – such as the money supply or the government's budget deficit – to set new initial conditions or to contain the time series that can be generated.

The thwarting forces change in time.[19] They differ among economic systems. The thwarting systems are analogous to homeostatic mechanisms which may prevent a system from exploding. However, they are not mechanical. Policy agents and law makers need to interpret what is happening and need to understand how their actions can affect the behaviour of endogenous agents and thus the economy. Peter Albin remarked that "Agents in the model have a model of the model". Among the agents who need to have a model are policy "agents". If the economy is endogenously unstable, then policy based upon the assumption that the economy is endogenously stable is likely to be inept.

A transitory semblance of stability can be achieved by policy interventions and institutionally constrained behaviour. However, units learn how policies and institutions affect the outcomes that result from their actions, and try to adjust their behaviour in the light of what they think they know.

The study of complex systems is incomplete without the examination of specific thwarting systems. The theory tells us what we have to look for: we have to look for customs, institutions, or policy interventions that make observed values of variables different from what they would have been if each economic agent pursued "only his own gain".

Three examples from the US economy will be examined to illustrate how institutional structures and systems of interventions affect the behaviour of the economy: the Piore–Sabel conjecture with respect to labour markets, the uses of market power, and lender-of-last resort interventions by central bank mechanisms. These, of course, do not exhaust the list of thwarting mechanisms.

4.1.   Labour Market Institutions

Piore and Sable (1985) argue that the US post-World War II wage policy consensus was a significant factor in creating the era of apparently tranquil progress that ruled for the first two decades after World War II. The wage policy consensus was that hourly wages should increase each year by a factor that reflected productivity gains plus realized inflation, i.e. the purchasing power of wages was to increase by about 3% each year. This consensus made for tranquil progress because it held "underconsumption" in check, which Piore and Sabel hold to be one of the causes of serious depressions. Buoyant worker demand resulted from this wage policy consensus. Piore and Sabel also suggested that this trade union settlement forced the banking system to be properly accommodating: the wage consensus dominated the monetary mechanism.

Underlying the productivity plus inflation rule for nominal wage changes was the view that competitive market forces could not be depended upon to transform falling unit labour costs into lower prices. If product markets were competitive and money wages were constant, then productivity increases would be translated into falling money prices. The argument for the post-war settlement has to draw on a proposition that market prices do not adjust to decreasing unit labour costs or that if such adjustments took place there would be adverse consequences.

In practice, the wage consensus led to a rule that would transform a shortfall of productivity increases into rising product prices. If, for any reason, wage increases exceed the rate given by productivity and inflation, then supply conditions would make for further inflation. The consensus rule assumed that if inflation takes place the banking system would be accommodative. This meant that "next" year the realized inflation plus productivity wage increase would increase.

However, after a burst of wage increases in excess of the productivity plus inflation rule in 1968–69, the wage setting process became an engine of inflation. Escalator clauses, together with a banking system that accommodates the demand for financing, either because of a consensus view of what the banking system should do, or because the authorities feared unemployment more than inflation, tend to amplify the dangers of inflationary instability. Thus, the rule of monetary accommodation which was stabilizing in one set of circumstances, became destabilizing in another.

4.2. Market Power and Financial Structures

In our modern world successful production, administration, communication, distribution, and transportation processes often use very expensive and long-lived capital assets.[20]

Expensive, long-lived capital assets require financing. In some capitalist economies – such as Italy – many of the industries that require such assets are publicly owned and externally financed by means of debts of government agencies. In the US, almost all such industries are private, and in many cases there are alternative suppliers of the services or goods.

When J.P. Morgan was riding high, it was discovered that for such capital intensive industries as the railways, intense competition, which forces price to marginal cost, will not yield enough cash to validate bonds or the cost of building the asset. This intense competition would result either from "overinvestment" in a regime of decentralized markets for financing or from recessions that cut the demand for the industry's output.

The banker's interest in business is that the cash flows must be large enough to validate the debts that were assumed to pay for the capital assets when they were acquired. Such debt validation and validation of prices paid for assets is possible for production with constant or diminishing marginal costs, if, and only if, price exceeds marginal costs. Intense competition, in periods of excess supply, must not be allowed to push price down to marginal cost. Bankers who take seriously their responsibilities to the holders of instruments they put out or sell, will not finance industries that require expensive capital assets unless there is some believable guarantee that price will not fall to marginal cost.

Such guarantee can take two forms: one is to guarantee that aggregate demand will be adequate, and the second is for the owners of the capital to possess market power, either because of the non-competitive nature of the market(monopoly, oligopoly) or because government regulates the industry to prevent strong competition from emerging. Since individual units, even Wall Street bankers, cannot guarantee that aggregate demand will be adequate, bankers will favour clients that possess market power.

Both monopoly and the regulation of industry that constrains competition satisfy the need of bankers for devices that limit the exposure of clients to downside profit risks. The question is whether the financing efficiency thus gained – which facilitates capital intensive investment – offsets or fails to offset the allocational inefficiency of non-competitive industries and regulated monopolies. In Schumpeter's vision of accumulation and innovation, technical dynamism requires that bankers and businessmen cooperate in forcing the economy out of the path that leads to simple reproduction. In the view that ignores the processes by which accumulation is financed, regulation and oligopoly lead only to allocational inefficiency.

The market power solution to the problem of protecting lenders against downsize exposure – whether through oligopoly or regulation – loses some of its force when fiscal and monetary intervention succeeds in maintaining aggregate demand and aggregate profits. With demand maintained and prices stabilized through the exercise of market power by way of regulation or oligopolistic interactions, profits are higher than anticipated even though unused market power can exist. As a result of the unused market power, rising costs will not bring profits down but will be translated into rising prices. If the problem is formalized in terms of wage rounds and price rounds, a situation in which the use of previously unused market power becomes a basis for subsequent wage increases is brought into being.

Prior to the import boom, the US automobile and steel industries were examples of shared monopolies in which unused market power was translated into worker wages and benefits. This led to a cost structure which became untenable once trade underdetermined the product market monopoly. The problem of how to meet competition that erodes market power may require a reconsideration of the standard argument for free trade. The institutional structure that emerged when the issue was the financing of capital intensive productions in a world where finance required protection through market structures against aggregate demand failures can be counterproductive in a world where such demand failures do not occur and the monopoly power that supported favourable wages is eroded.

4.3.   Lender-of-Last-Resort Intervention

Both monetarism and the orthodox Keynesianism that ignores the historical period in which *The General Theory* was written are alike in that they emphasize the Central Bank as the creator of money rather than the Central Bank as the lender-of-last-resort. In the 1990s, with the recent experience of bank and thrift institution failures that have led to a Government refinancing, it is not necessary to go into any abstract discussion of a lender-of-last-resort intervention; we need only point to what happened in Mexico, Argentina, Continental Illinois, Maryland, Ohio, the Savings and Loan industry, etc.

The internal dynamics and interactions with business that needs to finance control over capital assets, and with households that prefer to hold indirect or protected assets, lead to situations in which a collapse of asset values and financing of activity, and therefore of income and employment, seems likely. Over the years the Central Banks have developed interventions which do not permit realized values to represent the unconstrained dynamics of the system.[21]

Situations where lending of last resort occurs are definitively instances when overt intervention which overrules the operation of market processes is generally accepted. Even though Central Banks and lender-of-last-resort interventions are common to capitalist economies, the institutions and the form of the interventions vary. In particular, the existence of government "holding companies" means that intervention in a country such as Italy is often at the firm level, whereas in the US the intervention is almost always at the financial institution level. (Chrysler and the Railroads of the Northeast are the major exceptions.) Whereas interventions at the firm level may not have any monetary policy implications, interventions at the financial institution or financial market level affect the reserve base of banks and the interest rate structure. At times, the Federal Reserve's reactions to what it interpreted as an incipient financial crisis led to both a refinancing of threatened organizations and a significant easing in monetary policy.

5.   TWO THEOREMS

Two theorems which differ from accepted views emerge from the proposition that the internal dynamics of a capitalist economy will in time lead to unacceptable system states. The first is an anti-laissez faire theorem and the second is a "limitation upon the attainable" theorem.

The anti-laissez faire theorem states: In a world where the internal dynamics imply instability, a semblance of stability can be achieved or sustained by introducing conventions, constraints, and interventions into the environment. The conventions imply that variables take on values other than those which market forces would have generated; the constraints and interventions impose new initial conditions or affect parameters so that individual and market behaviour change.

The second theorem, relative to limitations upon performance, follows from the first. If the pursuit of individual gains or well being in the market leads the system to rush off into inflation, deflation, or rapid oscillations, which throw off signals that exceed computational capabilities, then the economy will from time to time be moving rapidly away from any reasonably defined notion of "allocation" or "stabilization" efficiency. If there is an observation lag, and less than perfect adjustment by interventions, the system can never be in an optimal allocation alignment. This implies that the "practical best" for an economy falls short of the abstract best.

There is a corollary to the limitation upon performance theorem. Each agent maximizes within the system of interventions and institutions that constrain the performance of the economy to tolerable outcomes. To agents for whom the constraints are binding the attainable maxima are deemed to be inferior to the unconstrained maximum.

Effective constraints imply both the expectations of gain and the objective possibilities of gains are smaller than the agent believes they would be if the constraints were removed. In the laissez faire world, each agent's maximizing behaviour is consistent with the system's achieving and sustaining its "best". In the complex world in which we live, each agent seeking only its own gain under unconstrained conditions, i.e. maximizing under market constraints as the only conditions, contributes to instability. Intermittent instability, not order, results from each agent behaving in the Smithian manner in an unconstrained environment. Individualistic decision making leads to instability in an unconstrained world, whereas individualistic decision making leads to a tolerable outcome if appropriate institutions and interventions are included.

As agents learn the effects of constraints, institutions and interventions, they will modify their behaviour, and this will in turn change the systemic effect of the interventions. A system of intervention put in place in one environment can be effective for a while, but as agents acquire knowledge of how this system affects their outcomes they will adapt their behaviour and this will change the effectiveness of the interventions. The system of intervention cannot be put in place once and for all. Policy makers must be aware that there are always incentives to evade and avoid the interventions, and they must adjust their interventions accordingly.

Our two theorems imply that any success in sustaining stable growth depends upon the institutional structure. Furthermore, because the institutional structure and the sources of instability change, due in part to the effects of units seeking only their own gain, the success of any policy structure will be transitory. "Revolutions" such as the one associated with

Roosevelt in the 1930s or the "Age of Keynes" from 1946 to the late 1960s will lead to successful performance of the economy even as the seeds of future failures are ripening as structural relations, conventions, and institutions change. There is no automatic pilot for an economy.

Because in each epoch the practical best falls short of a theoretical best, there always seems room for improvement. However, improvement takes on a variety of meanings in an economy that both allocates given resources and uses resources to create resources, in which technologies embodied in capital assets are given even as agents strive to change technology, and in which institutions and tastes are themselves economic variables. Economists are given to talking about efficiency, and in models of the invisible hand tradition, efficiency means allocative efficiency. However, in a dynamic view of the economy, a variety of "efficiencies" can be defined. Improvement in one type of "efficiency" may lead to deterioration in another. All too often the "room for improvement" will be along "one" of the efficiency dimensions, but success may mean that one or more of the others are compromised.

6.   SOME CONCLUSIONS

This paper has developed the endogenous instability view of the economy, in which institutional structures and interventions stabilize the unstable,[22] an approach which literally reverses Lucas's conception. Apt intervention and institutional structures are necessary for market economies to be successful.

This view is consistent with history: laissez faire capitalist economies were failures almost everywhere in the 1930s, whereas the post-World War II capitalist economies that have been successful are government interventionist economies.

The emphasis in discussing policy must be upon "apt". The proposition that apt policy and institutions thwart the endogenous development of instability does not mean either that any policy regime will do the job or that there is a unique effective policy regime. We can hazard the view that a policy and institutional regime is more likely to be apt if it reflects an understanding of what there is about the economy that leads to unstable dynamics. We recognize, of course, that there is no serious reason to believe that those who developed the institutions and interventions that make up the welfare state, which has enjoyed (transitory?) success in the post-war period, had any deep understanding of the potentially perverse dynamics of capitalist economies. The political leadership and the public in the 1930s were sceptical of the claims that were advanced for laissez faire. Trial and error led to the structure of interventions and institutions that survived.[23]

The statement that complex systems will from time to time generate unstable movements through time is a mathematical proposition. However, mathematics is not economics. Economists need to identify the economics that lead to unstable dynamics. One aspect of the economy that may do this is the way successful performance transforms market power from a factor that facilitates investment to a factor that supports inflation. The expectations induced by stability and regular growth of profits changes the economic role of marker power.

The economics of the "neo-classical" synthesis accepted that market economies were flawed in that there are no adequate market processes to guarantee the achievement and maintenance of a close approximation to full employment.[24] The political economy problem in the world after Thatcher and Reagan is to recognize once again that the market way of doing things is flawed, not only in its ability to maintain adequate aggregate demand, but also as a device for assuring productive investment and a tolerable distribution of income.

NOTES

* This is a reprint of the article: Piero Ferri and Hyman P. Minsky (1992), "Market processes and thwarting systems", *Structural Change and Economic Dynamics*, 3 (1), 79–91. The authors gratefully acknowledge the publisher Elsevier for giving permission to reprint this article.

1. University of Bergamo and Jerome Levy Economics Institute (NY).

2. We wish to thank E. Greenberg for helpful comments and anonymous referees for stimulating suggestions.

3. The conventional view is that "Any economic model is going to have as its center a collection of hypothetical consumers whose decisions, together with the technology and market structure, determine the operating characteristics of the system . . ." (Lucas, 1987, p. 20).

4. See Keynes (1937, pp. 213–4).

5. It is a problem in the intellectual history of economics to explain how Keynes's treatment of expectations formation under conditions of uncertainty, which is central to an understanding of the General Theory, disappeared from the orthodox Keynesianism of the post-war period (*General Theory*, chaps XII and XVII; and Minsky, 1975).

6. In the rational expectation school's view the model of the economy that guides agents' behaviour is invariant with respect to unfolding economic experience.

7. We define dynamic instability in a rather informal way. Essentially, we mean the irregular pattern and the persistence in time of the most common macroeconomic diseases, such as unemployment and inflation. This instability can give rise to runaway situations such as deep depressions or hyperinflation phenomena.

8. Central bank interventions, both as they affect money market conditions and as a lender of last resort, which have been in place over the centuries, are one form that interventions and constraints take. The lender-of-last resort function of central banks developed out of the experience with intermittent endogenously determined instability.

9. This view harks back to Minsky's 1957 article.

10. In his memorial of Wesley Mitchell, Schumpeter distinguishes between those economists who hold that ". . . the economic process is essentially non-oscillatory and that

the explanation of cyclical as well as other fluctuations must be sought in particular circumstances (monetary or other) which disturb that even flow" and those holding that "the economic process itself is essentially wavelike – that cycles are the form of capitalist evolution" (Schumpeter, 1951, p.252). Schumpeter maintained that Mitchell, Keynes and himself held the view that "cycles are inherent in the capitalistic process".

11. Lucas concludes his 1976 paper by noting that "This paper has been an attempt to resolve the paradox posed by Gurley (1961) in his mild but accurate parody of Friedmanian monetary theory: money is a veil, but when the veil flutters, real output sputters." (Reprinted in Lucas, 1981, p.84.)

12. For an interpretation of new initial conditions as changes in regime, see Ferri and Greenberg (1989).

13. Goodwin maintained an interest in endogenous cycles throughout this period (see, for instance, Goodwin, 1967).

14. Chaotic behaviour is defined as ". . . a time path that will pass most tests for randomness" (Baumol and Benhabib, 1989, p.77). It can be generated by simple deterministic models: "In essence, chaos theory shows that a simple relationship that is deterministic but non-linear, such as a first order non-linear equation, can yield an extremely complex time path. Intertemporal behaviour can acquire an appearance of disturbance by random shocks and can undergo violent, abrupt qualitative changes, either with the passage of time or with small changes in the values of the parameters" (p. 79).

15. It is worth stressing that modern analysis of non-linear models allows for the presence of instability which does not degenerate into runaway situations. However, in such models small changes in parameters can be responsible for large changes in the dynamics. Thus, various innovations that might change parameters might have the effect of setting up entirely new dynamics such that people lose the ability to interpret the future and this affects their behaviour. In this context, thwarting mechanisms try to control outcomes and keep them more stable.

16. The assumption underlying this view is that laissez faire does not unleash predators motivated by greed who acquire and exploit market power, but that market conditions force powerless agents to serve a "social good".

17. The argument that claim of the power of the "Walrasian system of general equilibrium equations" made by many economists goes beyond the proven properties of the Walrasian system is to be found in Ingrao and Israel (1987), Arrow and Hahn (1971) and Duffie and Sonnenschein (1989).

18. We shall see below how this kind of attitude can become destabilizing in other situations.

19. Boyer and Mistral, along with other French economists, write about "regulation" (see Boyer and Mistral, 1984).

20. Often does not mean always. What has been called the "Emilian Way" can coexist with and prosper alongside operations that require expensive capital because of technology, or the scale of operations. For a discussion of this model, see Brusco (1982).

21. Fisher's (1933) description of a debt-deflation process leads to the perception that central banks intervene to short circuit the process and therefore to avoid extreme consequences.

22. Minsky (1986a) makes the same points without reference to the mathematical properties of non-linear systems and within a specific model of profit generation, in which profits are determined by the structure of demand.

23. The above is a myopic US based view. Sweden, which had a particularly sophisticated group of economists in the 1930s and a knowledgeable political leadership in their Social Democratic Party, may have knowingly introduced the welfare state.

24. For a discussion of these models, see Ferri and Minsky (1989).

PART III

Deepening the methodology

8. Micro and macro in Minsky's models

1. METHODOLOGICAL ISSUES

There are three characteristics of the three co-authored papers that are worth stressing. First, they are closely linked to Minsky's three main books (1975, 1982 and 1986a) and so help to reveal particular aspects of these works along with their relations. Second, they stimulate some methodological considerations that lead to deepening the analysis. Finally, they induce the search for new developments to face the challenges deriving from the evolution of both the theory and the economy. While this last characteristic will be covered in Part V, in what follows we start deepening the methodological aspects which concern, according to the usual triad, the following:

1. aggregation;
2. the foundations of dynamics;
3. the nature of the transactions.

Contrary to our expectations expressed in the 1989 paper, there has not been any process of convergence between the new-Keynesian and the post-Keynesian economics. In fact, the former tried to reach a new compromise with the new classical theorists on two grounds: microfoundations and dynamics. The so-called DSGE (discrete stochastic general equilibrium) models sanction this new compromise.

While dynamics will be dealt with in Chapter 9, the microfoundation of the analysis is considered in what follows. It needs deepening for the simple reason that the DSGE models had not been developed at the time we wrote both the 1989 and the 1992 papers.

2. A VARIETY OF SOLUTIONS

There is a widespread view that Minsky did not trouble himself to explain methodology in detail in his publications. The posthumous publication of his PhD dissertation (see Minsky, 1954/2004) has certainly contributed to challenging the view of a supposed neglect of methodological problems, and this has stirred further discussions (see Toporowski, 2008, p.726).

As is stated in the 1989 co-authored paper, the core of Minsky's analysis is "to understand the dynamics of accumulating capitalist economy, with complex and evolving financial, product and labor markets, where the dynamics may lead to explosive growth, implosive decline or complex business cycles rather than sustained exponential growth" (Ferri and Minsky, 1989, p.124). The financial instability hypothesis, his most well-known theory, is better understood within this perspective.

In fact, Minsky always tried to blend his early research on the business cycle with various macroeconomic theories, ranging from Keynes's analysis of investment under conditions of uncertainty to the Kaleckian theory of profits, using them as backgrounds to his theory.

In the present chapter, the successive steps of this complex theory will be examined from a methodological point of view. In doing this, two guidelines will be followed. First, the emphasis will be put on micro–macro relationships. Second, these methodological problems will be faced within a dynamic perspective.

The thesis put forward is that Minsky suggested different solutions for dealing with these problems. This richness of approaches is not a limitation. On the contrary, it is in keeping with Chick's (2016) conclusion, according to which micro–macro studies are based upon compromises, which are therefore changeable. Minsky identified three principles underlying these micro–macro studies. First, microeconomics must be macrofounded. Second, micro and macro approaches are to be reconciled. Finally, macro instability is not a mechanical necessity because it is challenged by thwarting forces of different natures (see Ferri and Minsky, 1992).

These solutions have different properties and are worth considering because they can contribute to enlightening a debate that is still on the agenda (see Toporowski and Denis, 2016).

3.   THREE DIVIDING LINES

During the so-called neoclassical synthesis period, micro and macro were considered separately. As Hicks (1983, p. 349) wrote, reviewing Weintraub's (1979) book:

> The student goes to "micro" lectures on Mondays and to "macro" lectures on Thursdays, and they just do not fit. Not because the Monday lectures were concerned with the firm and the individual, the Thursday lectures with the

Table 8.1   Two lines of division

	Micro (A)	Macro (B)
I. Neoclassical	X	
II. Keynesian		X

whole economy, as the micro–macro distinction apparently implies. If that were all, there would be no problem. The trouble is that the approach is different, the Monday lectures being in some sense classical, the Thursday lectures being Keynesian.

For these reasons, Hicks reached the conclusion that there are two lines of division and this is at the origin of the troubles. My suggestion is that there are in fact three lines of division, and this further distinction, even if it makes things more complicated, allows a better understanding of the evolution of the literature on the subject. Table 8.1 summarizes the Hicksian two-division approach.

Table 8.1 shows the state of the art prevailing during the period of the so-called neoclassical synthesis. At the same time, it illustrates possible extensions, which then took place in subsequent periods. For instance, the new neoclassical synthesis (see Goodfriend and King, 1997 for a definition), which tries to bridge the divide separating the new classical economists referring to "real business cycles" from those called "new Keynesians" (see Mankiw and Romer, 1991), has closed the gap existing in line I. Minsky, on the contrary, tried to fill the gap in line II.

However, to understand the properties of these developments, it is essential to introduce a third line of division into the analysis. This is strictly methodological and refers to the way in which macro results are generated starting from micro observations. Table 8.2 identifies two possibilities, isomorphism and complex relations, to be discussed later on.

The new neoclassical synthesis is deeply characterized by its methodological approach based upon the representative agent (see Kirman, 1992 and Gallegati and Kirman, 1999). Even though these contributions pay lip

Table 8.2   A third line of division

III. Micro–macro	Properties		Foundation
(A)	Isomorphism		Representative agent
(B)		Complex	Interaction

service to the general equilibrium theory, they actually consider macroeconomics as its factual counterpart. In this perspective, simplifications are allowed. One of these is the use of the representative agent, a methodological cornerstone that eventually prevailed in this kind of literature.

This choice is also shared by the so-called new Keynesians (see Farmer, 1999), who introduce some market frictions that are justified by the presence of a monetary economy. There seem to be two contradictions in this new-Keynesian paradigm. On the one hand, the presence of these frictions can hardly be justified by the same microfoundation process that is at the root of the main equations, and so this school of thought cannot escape from the infamous accusation of "ad hockery". On the other, new Keynesians and new classical synthesis share the "representative agent" approach, and so generate results that look like those obtained by partial equilibrium analysis and therefore are subject to the same fallacies of composition that characterize those kinds of analysis (see Ferri, 2011).[1]

4. A TWO-WAY PROCESS

Neither Keynes nor Minsky can be associated with line I of Table 8.1. Rather, they belong to line II and put different weights on the two cells IIA and IIB. In fact, Hicks (1983, p.352) wrote about the necessity of filling cell IIA of Table 8.1:

> Monetary institutions, certainly; but also a look at other markets, labour markets, and product markets to see how they really work, and can work. Not in the same way in all times and places; so it will widen the mind to turn to some of the older economists, to see how they thought that markets worked, in their time.

The microeconomics of both Keynes (1936) and Minsky (1975) imply the presence of an environment characterized by a monetary economy of production, the presence of uncertainty, bounded rationality and divergent evaluations by entrepreneurs and bankers. All these elements have a double implication. On the one hand, the micro units tend to operate in an environment that is radically different with respect to that hypothesized by the new neoclassical synthesis. On the other, the process of reaching a macro conclusion starting from micro considerations becomes complex. As Chick (2016, p.110) stressed: "This can be a two-way process, with a notion of relevant grouping at the macro level guiding decision theory at the micro level, and the theory of individual behavior shaping macroeconomic aggregates."

This two-way process, where interdependence of decisions and actions between agents are admitted, generates outcomes that differ from the sum of those decisions and actions. Micro and macro are irreducible phenomena, and this implies compromises in moving between the two levels. But as Chick (2016, p. 110) added, "some compromises are better than others, and theorizing needs to include justification of the compromises made".

5. THE FINANCIAL INSTABILITY HYPOTHESIS AND THE FALLACY OF COMPOSITION

The strategy followed by Minsky to fill the IIA cell in Table 8.1 can be named the macrofoundation of microeconomics. In this context, the micro units have to take decisions that depend on the presence of a complex environment. In this sense they are macrofounded, while the macro environment is characterized by unemployment, uncertainty and financial intermediation.

This is not the point at issue. The debatable point is how this behavior contributes to shaping the macro results, closing a two-way process started from these macrofounded units.

This difficulty is exactly the point raised by Lavoie and Seccareccia (2001), who detect a fallacy of composition in Minsky's financial instability hypothesis. In fact, looking at Diagram 5.4[2] in Minsky's *John Maynard Keynes* (1975), one realizes that the title is "The financing behavior of a representative firm". This representative firm, or agent, although different from its neoclassical counterpart, seems to lead to an isomorphism between micro and macro. Furthermore, it would tend to generate fallacies of composition. Specifically, Lavoie and Seccareccia (2001) claim that an increase in debt that allows an increase in investment stimulates profits and this leads to an invariant financial position. This is the so-called debt paradox. In this perspective, the financial instability hypothesis, which implies an increasing debt, simply cannot hold. The methodological weakness of that diagram is the missing link tying profits to investment that has a typical macro dimension.

At least two problems arise at this stage of the analysis. One is analytical and refers to the theoretical incompatibility between a Kaleckian theory of profits and the financial instability hypothesis. Another is methodological and refers to the possibility of understanding this phenomenon through the lens of Diagram 5.4.

As far as the first is concerned, Fazzari et al. (2008) have obtained macro results that are in keeping with Minsky's theory of financial instability in spite of assuming endogenous cash flows (see also Charles, 2016). The result is important not only because it allows the possibility of generating the financial instability hypothesis, but also because it helps illustrate the analytical and methodological evolutions characterizing Minsky's approach.

6.   THE MACROFOUNDATION OF MICROECONOMICS

There is no doubt that when Minsky wrote his *John Maynard Keynes* (1975), the Kaleckian theory of profits was not among his tools of analysis. It was considered just after (and collected with other essays in his 1986 volume).

If this is the theory that generates the macro results, one must face the problem of what is the meaning of Diagram 5.4. This diagram must be understood to represent the macrofounded behavior of an agent in a complex financial world. It does not generate the macro results but rather reflects the impact of a macro environment on a firm's situation, characterized by a fixed level of internal funds. It refers to a process rather than to a representative (balance sheet) structure.

The approach is top-down, from macro to micro, and therefore there is no fallacy of composition because it is the macro aspects that drive the system. This happens in a static environment, from which Minsky tried to escape on several occasions, and it is just one example of the richness of approaches he referred to.

As far as the macro level is concerned, one has to stress that the results underlined by Lavoie and Seccareccia (2001) depend very much on the assumptions made about the Kaleckian mechanism at work. In fact, if debt increases only by the gap between investment and profit, then the Kaleckian mechanism is the only one at work and so the financial instability hypothesis cannot materialize. However, this is not Minsky's world, which is characterized by tensions in the financial markets. These tensions have an impact on the rate of interest and therefore on the dynamics of both investment and debts. In this case, the financial instability hypothesis can be generated (see also Charles, 2016). It is not an iron law, but it depends on the values of the parameters and can manifest in different ways, as the Great Recession has shown (see Ferri, 2016). Furthermore, it can be thwarted by a complex set of forces, as suggested by Ferri and Minsky (1992).

7.   INDUCED INVESTMENT AND BUSINESS CYCLES

Chapter 5 has shown that this is not the only way Minsky faced the micro–macro problem. However, before going back to that approach contained in

"Prices, employment, and profits" which we co-authored, it is important to consider other attempts.

One of these is his dissertation at Harvard that gives the title to this section. He wrote the dissertation initially under the supervision of Schumpeter, who passed away in the meantime, and then under Leontief. It was published posthumously in 2004, edited by Papadimitriou at the Levy Economics Institute.

Minsky describes the objective of his dissertation as the formulation of a model of product markets that will establish the foundation of aggregate analysis, enabling him to consider a number of public policies that are relevant to crafting an effective business cycle theory. The dissertation is based upon three pillars.

The first is a review of the most important contributions in the literature, ranging from linear (Samuelson, 1939) and piecewise linear (Hicks, 1950) to nonlinear models (Goodwin, 1950). The second pillar is the criticism of these models, which although different, are too mechanical in the sense that they do not "analyze both the interrelations among a few broad aggregates and the behaviour of individual units of particular markets" (Papadimitriou, 2004, p.1). The third pillar is the link between economics and finance. As investments are functions of financial conditions reflected in balance sheets and cash flow projections, a firm's survival constraint becomes important. In this context, liquidity (i.e. the ability to meet cash commitments) and solvency (i.e. the ability to maintain some level of net worth) characterize the various firms, and the risk of surviving is differentiated by the balance sheet position (Minsky, 1954/2004, p. 202).

According to Papadimitriou, Minsky considered his approach in the dissertation to be the microfoundation for determining macro performance. This will be explored in more detail later. The same holds true for the financial instability hypothesis, which, according to Delli Gatti and Gallegati (1997), is present "in nuce" in this dissertation.

What makes Minsky's dissertation particularly interesting is the methodological considerations put forward. In particular, they deal with the micro–macro problems within a dynamic context, represented by business cycles.

In dealing with the foundations of business cycles, Minsky emphasized the theory of investment based upon the accelerator principle. According to Minsky, the parameters of the functions which are included in the aggregative model are to be interpreted as shorthand symbols for the more complex processes: "In contrast to the mathematical pendulum business cycle models (including the non-linear theories) a theory of the business cycle which considers the generation of the values of the coefficients in such accelerator models as the meaningful economic problem must investigate the relevant market process" (Minsky, 1954/2004, p.75).

In particular, Minsky stresses that this coefficient can have three meanings (see Toporowski, 2008):

1. it may represent a structural parameter linking statistical aggregates;
2. it can be a coefficient of "induced investment", as opposed to realized investment;
3. it can refer to a coefficient of realized investment.

According to Minsky, it is this last meaning that deserves to be interrogated further by means of a process of complex disaggregation, which almost certainly leads to "mathematical complexity". According to Toporowski (2008, p.728): "This can be overcome by adding supplementary sets of relationships to a 'core model'. These supplementary relationships determine the parameters of the core model."

In other words, one has to construct a model consisting of an inner circle of relationships between the most important macroeconomic variables and a series of supplementary relationships directed at studying these macro variables.

In this perspective, the accelerator equation can be written in the following way (see Minsky, 1954/2004, p.213):

$$I = \beta \Delta Y \tag{8.1}$$

where I is investment, ΔY represents the increase in income, and β is the accelerator coefficient. Suppose that consumption of a particular good can be expressed in the following way:

$$\Delta C_\mu = \alpha_{\mu, t} \, \Delta Y_\mu \tag{8.2}$$

where α_μ is the marginal propensity to consume the particular good μ. In a parallel way, investment in the same good can be expressed as:

$$I_\mu = \beta_\mu \Delta C_\mu \tag{8.3}$$

Since aggregate investment is given by:

$$\sum I_\mu = I \tag{8.4}$$

it turns out that the accelerator coefficient is equal to:

$$\beta = \sum \beta_\mu \alpha_\mu \tag{8.5}$$

There are two main consequences of this approach. On the one hand, the macro coefficient is the result of the sum of disaggregated levels. On the other, these values are the results of a complex micro analysis reflecting the behavior of firms, functioning of the markets and financial conditions.

To summarize the results, one can say that this Minskyan approach is characterized by a double level of analysis where the specification of the equation is determined at the macro level while the values of the parameters are determined by a bottom-up procedure.

It follows that macro parameters can change, and this generates more complex dynamics with respect to traditional business cycle models based upon mechanical relationships. Changes in expectations could be a source of parameter instability long before Lucas advanced his famous critique.

It is legitimate to wonder whether these results are related to the financial instability hypothesis. The answer is affirmative. This theory is already "in nuce" in these early writings. It is cast in dynamic terms and can be expressed through changes in the values of the macro parameters. These in turn reflect the real, financial and institutional complexities of the various markets.

8.   THE MINSKY–FERRI APPROACH

The methodology in the dissertation is further refined by the approach followed by Minsky and Ferri (1984) shown in Chapter 5. It is worth reconsidering this paper for two main reasons. On the one hand, it allows the deepening of the relationships between micro and macro in a dynamic context (see also Ferri, 2013). On the other, it deals with some macro aspects that constitute the dimension within which the financial instability hypothesis must be studied.

When the 1984 paper was written, the Kaleckian theory of profits was fully accepted by Minsky, and it is at the root of the analysis which considers both micro and macro aspects and their dynamic relationships. The approach starts from firms setting prices according to a markup formula. This is in keeping with the macrofoundation of microeconomics since the behavior of firms depends on the particular state of the economy.

This markup determined at the micro level is to be reconciled with a macro function of profits determined à la Kalecki through changes in employment. Given a dynamic theory of wage determination, a general equation of price dynamics is generated that looks like the reduced form of the accelerator–multiplier trade cycle models (see Minsky, 1959).

Like that equation, this price equation also presents a variety of dynamic possibilities. Minsky has shown that changes in the initial conditions can check the process of instability. In other words, the so-called thwarting forces checking instability (see Ferri and Minsky, 1992) are materialized by changes in the initial conditions that make the dynamic process re-start.

In the present model, this process is set in motion when the markup fixed at the micro level becomes incompatible with the macro determination. In this case there is a feedback from macro to micro and therefore new initial conditions are generated. In this model prices are vehicles for profits. The model can be extended in order to introduce financial considerations. From a methodological point of view, the approach implies a two-way process from bottom-up to top-down that tries to reconcile the two dimensions.

9.   A SYNOPTIC VIEW

Before continuing the analysis, it is a good idea to summarize the different approaches examined so far. Table 8.3 may help. It classifies the different analytical approaches according to a double criterion based on both micro–macro relationships and dynamic devices conceived to check instability.

Some considerations are worth stressing. In the first place, explicit dynamic solutions are more present in the earlier stages of Minsky's research. In the second place, the financial instability hypothesis is always present even though in different forms and with different methodological approaches. Finally, some of these different approaches have the property of isomorphism between micro and macro. One way to break this is to introduce heterogeneity.

Table 8.3   Different methodological solutions

Analysis		Time profile		Micro−macro	
Chronology	Theme	Nature	Devices	Methodology	Properties
Minsky (1986a) vis-à-vis (1975)	Financial instability	Statics		Macrofoundation of micro	Isomorphism
Minsky (1954/2004)	Business cycle	Dynamics	Changes in parameters	Top-down Bottom-up	Complexity
Minsky and Ferri (1984)	Prices income distribution	Dynamics	Changes in initial conditions	Bottom-up Top-down	Reconciliation

10. HETEROGENEITY AND STATISTICAL PHYSICS

Heterogeneity has three functions. First, it is more appropriate to capture Minsky's division between hedgers, speculators and Ponzi agents. Second, it breaks the isomorphism between micro and macro. Finally, it requires a new technique to deal with the micro–macro relationship. Statistical physics (see Aoki, 1996 and Aoki and Yoshikawa, 2007) and the so-called agent-based model (ABM) (see Judd and Tesfatsion, 2006, Delli Gatti et al., 2011 and Chiarella and Di Guilmi, 2011) could become very important research tools. In this chapter, the focus will be on the first alternative, while the second approach will be considered later on (see chapters 13 and 16).

If heterogeneity is introduced into the analysis along with the structural presence of stochastic components, then statistical physics becomes a privileged tool of analysis.

> In standard economic theory, which ignores microeconomic fluctuations, the outcome of optimization by an economic agent is given by a "point" in some set or space; typically, a point is supported by a price vector. . . we explain that this approach is not valid because of microeconomic fluctuations. Given the complexity of the macro-economy, we must explicitly consider stochastic deviations of microeconomic behavior from its mean. . .[The] micro behaviors of individual households and firms are very diverse. Thus we have *distribution* of responses by microeconomic agents as an equilibrium rather than a unique response by a representative agent. (Aoki and Yoshikawa, 2007, p. 58)

Once the concept of the stochastic equilibrium distribution has been accepted, a top-down approach can be developed.

The objective of the top-down approach is to identify the micro distribution starting from some macro information. It describes macro phenomena by means of changes in the structure of the population, being represented either by consumers or firms. Following this approach, Aoki and Yoshikawa (2007) obtain results that support the role of aggregate demand in the labor market, business cycles and growth by virtue of it impacting on the micro distribution.

These results are very interesting and really promising. However, one could argue that the actual strategy followed by agents is more complex compared to that implied by this version of statistical physics (see Foley, 2008).

11. AN ALTERNATIVE STRATEGY

In what follows, we try to suggest an alternative strategy to those followed by statistical physics in order to carry out dynamic analyses. It is essentially bottom-up and in this sense produces macro results through the interaction of structurally heterogeneous agents by means of the so-called master equations. It is called the mean field approach (see Aoki, 1996). One limitation of the analysis is that the macro results do not feed back on the behavior of the micro heterogeneous units.

Our alternative suggestion is to consider the concept of stochastic equilibrium distribution and insert it into a dynamic context to obtain a two-way approach.

As is well known, Minsky (1986a) identified three fundamental types of agents according to their financial position: hedge, speculative and Ponzi finance. In this perspective, the financial instability hypothesis implies the endogenous tendency to an increasing share of the ultra-speculative component, that is, Ponzi finance, where the prospect of a positive cash flow is uncertain and situated far into the future. Minsky (1986a), however, also stressed that the number of cases increases if stochastic elements are inserted into the analysis. In this case, the economy consists of S kinds of firms characterized by their financial structures.

In what follows we suppose that

$$\sum_{i}^{s} f_i = F \tag{8.6}$$

where f_i represents the number of firms having the financial position i, while F is the total number of firms, which is supposed to be given.

Assume that the financial status of the various firms is measured by their net cash flows (π_i) and that, without loss of generality, the following inequalities hold:

$$\pi_1 < \pi_2 < ... < \pi_s$$

where the Ponzi units are set at the beginning of the series.

Total net cash flow is given by:

$$\sum_{i}^{s} \pi_i f_i = \pi \tag{8.7}$$

where p is total (net) profit in the system.

In a Kaleckian environment, one can suppose that net profits are generated by investment (I) so that equation (8.2) can be written as (see Fazzari, Ferri and Greenberg, 2008 and Charles, 2016):

$$\sum_{i}^{s} \pi_i f_i = I \qquad (8.8)$$

Given macro information on the value of I, the distribution of firms across the different financial types can be generated. As shown by Aoki and Yoshikawa (2007, p. 79), it turns out that the solution is given by:

$$\frac{f_i}{F} = \frac{e^{-\frac{F\pi_i}{I}}}{\sum_{i}^{s} e^{-\frac{F\pi_i}{I^i}}} \qquad (8.9)$$

This equilibrium solution is called the "Boltzmann–Gibbs" distribution.

If the different macro conditions determining net cash flow change, new stochastic equilibria are reached. For instance, in the case of an increase of total (net) profits, the curve becomes flatter, which means that the weight of the worse firms diminishes, while the average cash flow increases. In fact, the average cash flow (per firm) is given by the following expression:

$$\bar{\pi} = \frac{\pi}{F} \qquad (8.10)$$

where a bar on the variables stands for average.

Given a macro average, the micro stochastic distribution is obtained by means of a top-down procedure. However, this result cannot be the end of the story for our analysis. In fact, the result is static while our analysis intends to be essentially dynamic. To reach this goal, the new equilibrium distribution obtained when the macro conditions change can be interpreted as imposing new initial conditions on the macro model, a strategy well known to Minsky. In this case, therefore, there are also bottom-up forces that impact on the dynamics and a two-way process is set in motion.

12. CONCLUDING REMARKS

The core of Minsky's analysis is the dynamics of an accumulating capitalist economy, with complex and evolving financial, product and labor markets, where complex patterns can be generated. The financial instability hypothesis, his well-known theory, is better understood within this perspective.

In fact, Minsky always tried to blend his early research on the dynamics of the business cycle with various macroeconomic theories, ranging from Keynes's analysis of investment under conditions of uncertainty to the Kaleckian theory of profits, which represent the macro support to his theory.

In the present chapter, the successive steps of this complex theory have been examined from a particular methodological point of view, centered on the micro–macro relationships considered in a dynamic perspective.

Minsky has offered different solutions to these methodological problems arising from the presence of heterogeneous agents interacting within a dynamic system. These solutions range from top-down to bottom-up methods, some of them characterized by a two-way process, and others much simpler. All these attempts seem to be in keeping with Victoria Chick's thesis, according to which these solutions can only represent compromises that are not valid under any circumstance.

In this perspective, this variety of approaches is a sign of richness, characterized, however, by two unifying principles. On the one hand, microeconomics tend to be macrofounded. In other words, micro behavior reflects the state of the economy, which is characterized by complex real and financial interrelationships coupled by the presence of particular institutions. On the other hand, macro dynamics are dominated by a complex set of forces that can thwart instability.

From both micro and macro perspectives, new compromises can be reached, while new justifications must be looked for.

NOTES

1. It is worth stressing that the general equilibrium with heterogeneous agents can also produce isomorphism (see Stiglitz, 2011).
2. Diagram 5.4 determines investment as a function of its price, the price of capital assets, the marginal lender's risk, the borrower's risk and the internal funds, which are assumed to be fixed. It is this assumption that creates difficulties in interpreting the diagram.

9. The foundations of medium-run dynamics

1. THE DYNAMICAL TENET

Differently from the old neoclassical synthesis, the dynamic stochastic general equilibrium (DSGE) models are rooted in a dynamic environment. The challenge is to understand what kind of dynamics they refer to. In fact, the DSGE models are mainly driven by exogenous shocks, which are the *deus ex machina* of dynamics.

According to Woodford (2009) the debate about the nature of macroeconomics seems to be dominated by the presence of a substantial methodological similarity between the various paradigms so that the exogeneity of the dynamics is not questioned. In fact, this similarity is centered around the maximizing role of agents in a dynamic environment, where the driving forces are exogenous shocks while the main mechanisms of transmission are based upon the concept of intertemporal substitution.

This methodological monism must be put into historical perspective. In fact, according to Hicks (1965), there is not a unique way of studying dynamics. On the contrary, there are different methods. If one considers the classical authors, the Swedish school, Keynes, Harrod, von Neumann and Ramsey, one discovers a plurality of approaches. Within this historical perspective, one realizes that the different methods are not necessarily focused around the problem of microfoundation. They strictly concern the way dynamics are generated. The dynamical tenet remains strategic and deserves to be deepened.

2. STEADY STATES

A central element in dynamics is the concept of steady state, which is the dynamic equivalent to the equilibrium concept in a static theory. If these points of steady state are attractors, then two consequences follow. On the one hand, they reflect the long-run forces of the system and therefore one can neglect temporary dynamics that just have a secondary role to play. On the other, one can apply so-called growth accounting. This technique, originated by Solow (1956), accounts for growth according to some identities based upon the production function (see Hicks, 1965). The famous Kaldorian stylized facts could also be derived within the same methodology (Kaldor, 1961).

This technique has been recently expanded in such a way so as to include the role of human capital, and therefore new stylized facts have been introduced into the analysis (Jones and Romer, 2009).

Although these approaches are undoubtedly interesting, they tend to hide the most interesting part of the story. Growth is a dynamical phenomenon, characterized by drivers and adapters. Furthermore, dynamics face constraints that must be identified. In other words, growth is a much more complex phenomenon than is usually recognized by that part of the literature ignoring the unfolding of disequilibria in time.

3.   THE NEWCLASSICAL APPROACH

Abandoning steady state is not enough to generate meaningful dynamics. In fact, if one considers the so-called real business cycle (RBC for short) literature (see Cooley, 1995), one realizes that other limitations arise. RBC has fundamentally reconsidered intertemporal maximization put forward by Ramsey (1928). It is based upon three pillars:

1.   infinite horizon;
2.   perfect foresight;
3.   intertemporal substitution.

Much emphasis has been put on the intertemporal mechanism that is the true *deus ex machina* of the various models. There are two examples that are worth mentioning. The first concerns intertemporal consumption allocation and the concept of intertemporal elasticity. The second concerns labor supply and its intertemporal mechanism.

Both examples deserve particular attention, partly because consumption and labor supply will be dealt with in a totally different way in parts IV and V. However, only the first example will be considered in some detail at this stage of the analysis. The second one is more complex because, apart from the intertemporal mechanism, it implies other important aspects that are not central in this book.

To illustrate the intertemporal mechanism in the consumption function, let us consider the following life-cycle/permanent-income hypothesis (PIH) as developed by Romer (1996).

Consider an individual who lives for T periods, whose lifetime utility is

$$U = \sum_{t=1}^{T} u(C_t) \quad u'(*)>0, \, u''(*)< 0 \tag{9.1}$$

Suppose that the individual's budget constraint is

$$\sum_{t=1}^{T} C_t \leq A_0 + \sum_{t=1}^{T} Y_t \tag{9.2}$$

where A_0 is the initial wealth, while Y is labor income. In this framework, if one forms the Lagrangian and takes the first order conditions, one obtains:

$$u'(C_t) = \lambda \tag{9.3}$$

where λ is the shadow price of the constraint. Since (9.3) holds for every period, the marginal utility of consumption is constant, and this implies that consumption is also constant and equal to (through the budget constraint):

$$C_t = \frac{1}{T}\left(A_0 + \sum_{\tau=1}^{T} Y_\tau\right) \text{ for all } t \tag{9.4}$$

This theory has many implications. First, since consumption is determined by permanent income, it follows that the time pattern of income is critical to saving. In fact, since saving can be defined as

$$S_t = Y_t - C_t$$

one obtains

$$S_t = \left(Y_t - \frac{1}{T}\sum_{\tau=1}^{T} Y_\tau\right) - \frac{1}{T}A_0 \tag{9.5}$$

This formula implies that saving is high when income is high relative to its average. "Thus the individual uses saving and borrowing to smooth the path of consumption. This is the key idea of the life-cycle/permanent-income hypothesis" (Romer, 1996, p. 311).

The second implication is that the presence of an interest rate is bound to strengthen the presence of an intertemporal mechanism. To this end, let us specialize the utility function in the following way:

$$U = \sum_{t=1}^{T} \frac{1}{(1+\rho)^t} \frac{C_t^{1-\theta}}{1-\theta} \tag{9.1} \text{ bis}$$

where θ is the coefficient of relative risk aversion (i.e. the inverse of the elasticity of substitution between consumption at different dates). In this case, the Euler equation produces the following result:

$$\frac{C_{t+1}}{C_t} = \left(\frac{1+r}{1+\rho}\right)^{1/\theta} \tag{9.6}$$

Consumption is rising over time if r exceeds ρ, given the value of θ.

In empirical applications, the neoclassical general equilibrium approach boils down to representative agent modeling. Furthermore, two further aspects are considered:

1. a weak form of uncertainty is introduced;
2. log-linearization is implemented.

The consequence of the first assumption is that perfect foresight models become models based upon rational expectations. In general, however, the certainty equivalent results are obtained if particular utility functions are introduced. The consequence of the second hypothesis is that one only moves around the steady state. Outside this simplified world, a problem of computability arises (see Howitt and Ozak, 2009). Finally, dynamics are driven by exogenous shocks that only work locally around the steady state.

It follows that the so-called DSGE models not only ignore fundamental uncertainty but generate pseudo dynamics.

4.   MINSKY'S THREE BASIC CONCEPTS

For an alternative conception of dynamics, the benchmark is Minsky's article "The integration of simple growth and cycles models", reprinted in his 1982 volume as Chapter 12. The choice of this article is strategic because it stresses three basic concepts – the time horizon, one-sidedness and incompleteness – that will be taken into consideration in the present book. According to Minsky (1982, p.258):

> In many ways, the most interesting analytical and forecasting range is neither the very short run nor the very long run. An intermediate horizon, of ten to fifteen years, is of great practical interest for economic policy, for this is the time span that encompasses the possibility of major or deep depression cycles.

This intermediate period is often called the "medium run" (see Ferri, 2011, Solow, 2000 and Blanchard, 1997), where very short-run vibrations are ignored, but where the impact of investment on the productive capacity cannot be neglected, while institutional changes are left for long-run analyses. This is the main difference with long-run growth models, also called growth models *tout court*, where the role of institutional elements, human capital and ecological aspects cannot be ignored. One of the consequences of considering a medium-run perspective is that the explanations of the dynamics must be endogenous. In fact, the role of exogenous shocks cannot bear the burden of explanation for such a long period.

The second concept is the one-sidedness of the approach, which needs to be overcome. According to Minsky: "Both the short-run and the long-run models are one-sided, in that they are concerned with either aggregate demand or aggregate supply" (1982, p.259). The strategic choice is to consider both, which, however, need to be reconciled. To this end, many strategies can be followed.

Finally, most models are incomplete, in that they do not include other markets apart from the product market, that is, the labor market and the monetary and financial ones are usually ignored.

In Part IV the labor market will be considered, and this will allow us not only to deepen the dynamic and methodological aspects of this relationship but also to consider the policy implications contained in Minsky's posthumous book *Ending Poverty: Jobs, Not Welfare* (2013).

5. MEDIUM RUN AND DISEQUILIBRIUM

In a medium-run perspective, two considerations are relevant. The first is that an explanation based upon exogenous shocks becomes particularly unsatisfactory, and this is particularly so the longer the time span considered.

As expected, Minsky referred to an "intermediate model".

> Although it is legitimate in constructing short-run forecasting models to ignore the impact of investment upon productive capacity and of finance upon the stock of financial instruments outstanding, over a ten-or fifteen-year period these small changes will cumulate and be of decisive importance in determining system behavior. On the other hand, the standard strategy in constructing long-run models is to assume that the impact of financial variables can wash out. Thus, both practical and theoretical possibilities open up when an intermediate horizon is adopted. (Minsky, 1982, p. 259)

The other consideration is that disequilibrium is present because the markets do not have enough time to clear. There are four kinds of disequilibrium that must be considered. The first is led by expectations. In this case, even though expectations can be consistent with data in the long run, they can generate dynamics in the medium run. This is the approach suggested by Fazzari et al. (2013) in order to consider dynamics within a Harrodian perspective.

The second one is based upon the disequilibrium between investment and saving. This kind of disequilibrium was the subject of much work by Minsky and has also been studied in detail by Aghion and Banerjee (2005), who stress the role of finance in bridging the gap between the two.

The third is based upon a regime switching model (see Ferri, 2011). In the medium run, agents know that there can be bad states and good states, even though they do not know the probability of switching. Behavior is different. One can further assume that in the bad state the chances of being liquidity constrained become bigger. In this case, disequilibrium manifests itself as an adjustment of reality to changing optima. Furthermore, agents are not only bounded rational, but they are also learning.

The fourth kind of disequilibrium refers to the structural changes in the production side under the combined pressure of technical changes and changes in the composition of demand (see Pasinetti, 1993).

Inserted into a medium-run growth model, these disequilibria contribute to create a dynamic process that is different from that depicted by steady state. Growth becomes a dynamical phenomenon, characterized by drivers and adapters, as will be shown in Chapter 11. Furthermore, dynamics face constraints that must be identified. In other words, growth is a much more complex phenomenon than is usually recognized in the literature.

6.   MINSKY'S LEXICON

As has been said, Minsky (1982) underlines the role of the disequilibrium between saving and investment in order to feed the process of growth in a medium-run perspective. Consider a consumption function of the type:

$$C_t = (1 - s)Y_{t-1} \qquad (9.7)$$

where s is the propensity to save. In this case, the following difference represents the ex-ante saving:

$$Y_{t-1} - C_t = S_t^* \qquad (9.8)$$

The equilibrium conditions imply that:

$$Y_t = C_t + I_t \qquad (9.9)$$

which defines ex-post saving as:

$$S_t = Y_t - C_t \qquad (9.10)$$

or

$$S_t = I_t \qquad\qquad\text{(9.9) bis}$$

Dividing through (9.9) by last year's income, the following result is obtained:

$$g_t = i_t - s - 1 \qquad\qquad\text{(9.11)}$$

where i_t stands for the ratio between investment and last year's output. It follows that growth is a function of the discrepancy between investment and the desired rate of saving.

This dynamic setting has two implications. The first is that a necessary condition for the realization of the investment ratio during an expansion "is that a source of financing of investment in addition to ex-ante saving should exist" (Minsky, 1982, p.236). This reference indicates the way to overcome the incompleteness of the various models, ignoring financial aspects.

The second implication is that aggregate supply aspects are to be introduced into the analysis. This tries to overcome the one-sidedness discussed earlier. In fact, investment increases capacity, and this brings about new production that has to face aggregate demand. In other words, the rate of growth of aggregate demand must be reconciled with that deriving from aggregate supply.

Two further aspects are worth stressing at this stage of the analysis. The first is methodological and refers to the role of ceilings and floors that has been advocated in order to guarantee this reconciliation (see Hicks, 1950). Minsky preferred to refer to changes in the initial conditions that do not necessarily imply the presence of physical constraints, and therefore are less mechanical.

The second is analytical. Minsky, although he considered the dual role of investment on both demand and supply, ignored what Harrod called the natural rate of growth. In this case, the labor market must be explicitly considered and a specific reconciliation process must be identified. This will be considered in Part IV, when the Minskyan black box will be further investigated.

Before doing this, some further general considerations need to be addressed.

7.   EXPECTATIONS FOR THE MEDIUM RUN

There has been a renewed interest in the debate on information (see, Arthur, 1994). However, in the case of a turbulent environment, it is very important to face the problem of uncertainty (see also Basili and Zappia, 2010). In particular, in considering the bearings of these models, one has to deal with the relationship between risk and uncertainty. To this end, one can assume different situations.

1.   Long run with certainty. In this case, Ramsey's model is perfectly rea-
     sonable from a logical point of view, even though it is hard to reconcile
     with facts.
2.   Short run with noises. Also in this case, what has been done in the
     RBC literature is legitimate. One refers to the linearized version of
     the model in equilibrium and considers the role of the various shocks.
     However, in all other contexts this method does not work.
3.   Medium run.

According to Preston (2005), if one refers to subjective expectations, which are different from rational expectations, one is supposed to consider not just the Euler equation, which implies one period ahead, but also expectations referring to other periods.

Within this medium-run perspective, where uncertainty is present, there are three main challenges that the analysis must face. The first refers to the relationships between uncertainty and the length of time to be considered. In this case, one might have the following situations:

1.   Perfect foresight within an infinite horizon. This boils down to a series
     of Euler equations that are paradoxical because they imply an amount
     of exact information that is not available in a period of turbulence.
2.   Learning accompanied by the presence of long-run expectations.
3.   Learning with uncertainty, where, probably, the horizon must be
     shortened because information is simply not available.

Some of these different situations will be considered in Part V.

The second challenge refers to market clearing. If this hypothesis holds, then the distinction between points 1 and 2 disappears. However, if this does not happen then complications must be considered. Liquidity constraints, for instance, must be taken into account, while quantity adjustments cannot be excluded.

The third one is aggregation. Uncertainty may stimulate heterogeneity. The presence of heterogeneity might have important consequences on the consumption theory in particular (see Eusepi and Preston, 2009), and on the representative agent models in general.

8. A LEARNING PROCESS

In a world of uncertainty, agents do not have enough information to take unchangeable decisions, but they might have some learning mechanisms. The number of learning devices is really numerous, so one cannot pretend to be exhaustive. However, in what follows, a learning technique will be presented because it will be used later on in Chapter 15.

Assume that agents do not have a complete knowledge of the model and therefore use simple rules to forecast the future output growth and inflation. Suppose, as is done in De Grauwe (2008), that the agents can be either optimistic or pessimistic.[1]

The optimists' forecast is given by the following relationship:

$$\bar{E}_t^{opt} g_{t+1} = f(g_{02})$$

That is, they expect that a bigger rate of growth is always prevailing, according to some function to be specified. On the other hand, the pessimists' forecast is the opposite:

$$\bar{E}_t^{pess} g_{t+1} = f(g_{01})$$

The market forecast is obtained as a weighted average of these two forecasts, that is:

$$\bar{E}_t g_{t+1} = \alpha_{opt,t} \, \bar{E}_t^{opt} g_{t+1} + \alpha_{pess,t} \, \bar{E}_t^{pess} g_{t+1}$$

$$\alpha_{opt,t} + \alpha_{pess,t} = 1 \tag{9.12}$$

Following Brock and Hommes (1997), a selection mechanism is introduced. In fact, agents compute the forecast performance by referring to the mean squared forecasting error:

$$U_{opt,t} = -\sum_{k=1}^{\infty} \chi_k \left[g_{t-k} - \bar{E}_{opt,t-k-1} g_{t-k} \right]^2 \tag{9.13}$$

$$U_{pess,t} = -\sum_{k=1}^{\infty} \chi_k \left[g_{t-k} - \bar{E}_{pess,t-k-1} g_{t-k} \right]^2 \tag{9.14}$$

where χ represents geometrically declining weights. The proportion of agents is determined à la Brock and Hommes (1997):

$$\alpha_{opt,t} = \frac{\exp(\gamma U_{opt,t})}{\exp(\gamma U_{opt,t}) + \exp(\gamma U_{pess,t})} \tag{9.15}$$

$$\alpha_{pess,t} = \frac{\exp(\gamma U_{pess,t})}{\exp(\gamma U_{opt,t}) + \exp(\gamma U_{pess,t})} \tag{9.16}$$

where γ measures the intensity of choice.

These formulae indicate that those that had a success in the past will convince more people to follow them in the future. (This selection mechanism is named evolutionary by De Grauwe, 2008). *Mutatis mutandis*, the same formulae can also be applied for inflation expectations.

When considering the various hypotheses on how to model adaptive learning, one realizes that the possibilities are numerous. This does not mean that one necessarily enters the wilderness as feared by some literature. In fact, what is important to stress is that, according to Hommes and Sorger (1998), expectations must be consistent with data.

This consistency criterion implies two things. First, it implies that agents do not make systematic errors. Second, it implies that, at least, the forecasts and the data should have similar means and autocorrelations.

This does not mean that there are no problems. For instance, the hypothesis that all agents have the same expectations makes the aggregation problem much easier, as stressed by De Grauwe (2008). However, the problem of the coordination of expectations remains an unchallenged one.

9. IMPLICATIONS FOR GROWTH

The observations made so far can be extended to the whole system. In considering the whole system, one must get acquainted to the fact that, from the supply side, the presence of uncertainty implies the presence of imperfect competition. This is for three main reasons:

1. there can be both a price and a quantity strategy;
2. capacity cannot necessarily be fully employed;
3. the rate of profit cannot necessarily be equal.

Once the whole system is taken into consideration, two questions become relevant:

1. What are the interrelationships between medium-run events and longer-term growth?
2. What mechanisms, apart from intertemporal substitution, are operating in shaping these consequences?

As far as the first question is concerned, one has to mention the cleansing effect of recession on growth underlined by the Schumpeterian approach (see Aghion and Howitt, 1998). However, there is also a Keynesian effect via aggregate demand that must be taken into consideration and that, when considered, is confined to the short run.

The answer to the second question is bound to lead to some other mechanism for growth emerging. Disequilibrium is the most important.

10. THE LESSONS

This chapter has tried to show how the departure from the neoclassical mechanism of intertemporal substitution as the main engine of growth can allow a different vision of the process of growth, characterized by uncertainty and disequilibrium.

They are both important engines. The former can be contained by the existence of particular institutions, while the latter, which can be specified in different ways, may unify the domain of fluctuations with that of growth, ensuring that the interdependence between aggregate demand and aggregate supply plays a decisive role.

One may wonder what benefits are obtained through following this alternative strategy. There are at least three. One benefit is that dynamics in general, and the process of growth in particular, can be led by aggregate demand, something that, apart from Harrod's original paper, has been neglected in the growth literature (see Aoki and Yoshikawa, 2007).

A second is that finance is something that can be imported into this domain. In this case, not only can one reconsider the role of finance in the consumption function alone, but it can be extended to the whole system. Furthermore, it is worth stressing that in this framework the disequilibrium forces driving the dynamics can be on the supply side, with finance helping the aggregate.

A third benefit is that there can be a relationship between aggregate demand and aggregate supply that can go beyond the medium run. For instance, stagnation episodes would not only be cleansing periods where the fittest tend to prevail and so enhance long-run productivity, but also lapses of time resulting in missed opportunities that impact on growth.

This is the context where the labour market is brought into the picture and where the financial instability hypothesis faces a new challenge.

NOTE

1. This formulation is well known in finance. Dieci and He (2018) name it "HAM" (i.e. heterogeneous agent model). They also compare this approach with the more general agent-based models (ABM).

10. New tools for dynamics

1. THE DYNAMICS OF PRICES, PROFIT AND EMPLOYMENT REVISITED

The central message of the paper "Prices, employment, and profits" is the necessity of endogenizing profit share, and therefore cash flow, within a dynamic context. It can be seen as an attempt to bridge the analysis of profit determination contained in Minsky's financial instability hypothesis with his dynamic contributions contained in his *Can "It" Happen Again?* In other words, the basic analytical aspect of the paper is that of linking prices, profits and investment in a double feedback relationship so that one of the pillars of the financial instability analysis, that is, cash flow, would be made endogenous.

However, along with this leading theme, there are other aspects that deserve to be stressed because they make it clear why the analysis can be at the same time updated, deepened and broadened. Apart from the methodological contribution regarding the reconciliation between micro aspects and macro results, considered in Chapter 8, two further aspects of the paper deserve to be considered. First, the paper was conceived in a period of stagflation, a relatively new phenomenon which challenged the neoclassical synthesis. It is important to stress that in the paper this phenomenon is generated without referring to supply shocks. However, since this was a typical phenomenon of the 1980s, there is the necessity of dealing with new stylized facts, characterized by moderate inflation or even deflation. To update the analysis, the structure of transactions underlying the model has to be considered. It will be shown how these transactions rooted in a monetary economy of production can generate Phillips curves as system results, as the agent-based models (ABMs) have tried to do (see Delli Gatti et al., 2015).

The second aspect to be considered is that the device used to generate dynamics, which was taken from *Can "It" Happen Again?* and was based upon changes in the initial conditions, can be generalized so that new tools for dynamics become available to the analysis. The dynamical background consisted in reproducing a reduced form similar to that obtained for the accelerator–multiplier model studied by Minsky in his early studies. In this case, no new technicalities had to be put forward because most of the philosophy underlying the change in initial conditions has already been clearly stated. These changes allow endogenous dynamics which, however, can be obtained in different manners with different tools of analysis, as will be shown in this chapter. The analysis itself can be broadened, but that will be the task of the following chapters.

2.   A NEW SPECIFICATION OF THE MODEL

The priority is to generalize the analysis in order to be able to cover situations other than stagflation that, on the contrary, was the dominant stylized fact in the 1980s. In the present situation, mild inflation or even deflation seem to be the new stylized facts. To pursue this aim, both analytical and methodological changes are put forward.

The specification of the model presented in Chapter 5 has been modified in two ways. First, the investment function has been made explicit and dependent on both income distribution and the acceleration principle. The latter assumption underlines the role of quantity adjustments, while the former represents the limitations that finance can imply for the accumulation process. The second change refers to productivity, which is made dependent on capacity utilization, a variable that was lacking before. The role of this variable has been particularly stressed by the so-called Kaleckian strand in the post-Keynesian tradition (see Lavoie, 2014), where the investment function can assume different specifications implying different results. The differences, however, have more the nature of nuances than of deep disagreements.

The institutional setting is different. The epoch of big government, big firms and big unions is over. The last protagonist underwent the biggest changes. In this perspective, the hypothesis of given money wages is reasonable because it takes the new situation into account. Also, the role of government has changed, with monetary policy prevailing over fiscal policy. This, however, is not analyzed in the model and remains in the background. It will be considered later on.

It follows that the model can be represented in the following concise way:

$$P_t = k \frac{W^*}{A^*} \tag{10.1}$$

$$I_t = \eta_0 + \eta_1 (Y_{t-1} - Y_0) + \eta_2 (\alpha_{t-1} - \alpha_0) \tag{10.2}$$

$$Y_t = \frac{w^*}{P_{t-1}} N_{t-1} + I_t \qquad (10.3)$$

$$h_t = \frac{Y_t}{Y^*} \qquad (10.4)$$

$$A_t = A^* + \beta(h_t - h_0) \qquad (10.5)$$

$$N_t = \frac{Y_t}{A_t} \qquad (10.6)$$

$$\alpha_t = 1 - \frac{w^*}{P_t A_t} \qquad (10.7)$$

Variables with an asterisk represent exogenous variables, while variables marked by 0 refer to steady state values. The first equation is the same as in Minsky and Ferri (1984). The investment function has been modified along the lines previously discussed (see also Fazzari et al., 2008). The third equation represents aggregate demand. Capacity utilization is represented by the variable h_t, that is, the ratio between actual output and the optimal one. A_t represents the actual output per man. It is important to stress that while this is the variable that is important for the labor demand determination (see equation 10.6), it is its (exogenous) steady state value that enters the price equation. Finally, α represents the profit share.

The system is nonlinear and includes seven equations in seven unknowns, P, I, Y, h, A, N and α all expressed in a time dimension (t).

3. A MENU OF NONLINEARITIES

The dynamics of the model are studied by a regime switching technique that replaces the device used by Minsky and Ferri (1984), which in turn is an innovation with respect to ceiling and floor barriers. As is well known, regime switching is a particular case of a piecewise linear technique capable of generating complex dynamics (see Ferri, 1997, 2000, 2001, 2008 and 2011).

In economics, the first example of a piecewise linear technique is found in the literature about ceilings and floors, introduced by Hicks (1950) in a slightly altered version of the Samuelson accelerator–multiplier model. Ceilings and floors are theoretical constructs postulated to check explosive patterns that are otherwise implied by linear difference equations. Because they introduce a particular case of nonlinearity, they imply a richer menu of dynamic paths than do simple linear models. These paths are more consistent with historical experience than those implied by linear models in which instability implies an explosive dynamic path or where harmonic oscillations can be obtained only in an Occam razor kind of situation. The ceiling and floor theory of the business cycle also contrasts with a view that attributes cycles to exogenous (stochastic) shocks. The apparently greater econometric support for the latter theory discouraged the development of endogenous explanations. However, enough contrary evidence to the thesis of the obsolescence of the business cycle has been presented recently to revive interest in nonlinear models and hence in an endogenous explanation. Ceiling and floor models are piecewise linear models within the nonlinear world. On dynamical mathematical grounds, Hicks's model is only sketched and lacks important details. Minsky (1959) interpreted such floors and ceilings as imposing new initial conditions, so that the dynamic process could start anew whenever they become effective.

The concepts of ceilings and floors have been questioned on several grounds (e.g. by Matthews, 1959). On empirical grounds, ceilings have been questioned because upper cyclical turning points often occur before full employment is reached. The floor concept is even more debatable, both empirically and theoretically. To overcome some of these objections, two different research strategies have been pursued. The first alternative consisted in developing nonlinear models whose parameters vary with system behavior. Goodwin (1967), for instance, developed models that could generate closed orbits and, under more restrictive hypotheses, limit cycles towards which all possible paths of the variables converge. The other alternative consists in maintaining the piecewise approach but introducing changes in the interpretation of ceilings and floors. The overall results depend on the cocktail of assumptions made and the analytical devices put forward. For instance, Hicks himself thought that ceiling and floor could be interpreted along financial lines, and these were particularly useful in interpreting the old cycle, when the Bank of England had to convert notes and deposits into gold at a fixed parity and this provided a firm ceiling for expansion. "But this old style of financial cycle . . . thus came to an end" (Hicks, 1989, p.101) when the Federal Reserve started operating on a different basis. A different strand of literature has insisted that if one abandons the "fixprice" economy, the limitations to booms can derive more from inflation than from physical constraints. In this perspective, the concept of ceilings as a physical "barrier" is replaced by that of "threshold", which imparts a piecewise change in the difference equation that governs the dynamics (see also Minsky and Ferri, 1984). Ferri and Greenberg (1989) present a regime switching mechanism in the Phillips curve capable of generating business cycles. In this case, the piecewise character of the analysis is preserved, while the possibility of generating cycles is maintained (see Ferri et al., 2001). Finally, Ferri and Minsky's (1992) interpretation of the ceiling and floor model is that of a metaphor for the interplay between the structural economic forces represented by the model and the role of institutions in checking their dynamics, which is explained by the presence of external barriers.

Recently, Pesaran and Potter (1997) placed the "ceiling and floor" model in a time series perspective. This means that "ceilings and floors" are just statistical phenomena. Their results suggest that the turning points of the business cycle provide new initial conditions for the ensuing growth process à la Minsky (1959), and they also show important asymmetries in response to shocks. However, as the authors themselves recognize, ". . .we have left open the economic explanation of the nonlinear phenomena found" (Pesaran and Potter, 1997, p. 692).

In a time series perspective, it is well known that regime switching devices are a genus that covers the first two approaches. Regime switching can be either deterministic (Ferri and Greenberg, 1989) or stochastic. Furthermore, they can be classified as endogenous and exogenous. The endogenous variety includes the so-called threshold autoregressive (TAR) models, where regime switching is endogenous but is generated by a fixed lag. In the case of Pesaran and Potter, the lag is endogenous. In contrast, the Hamilton (1989) model, based upon Markov regime switching, is one of the most important examples of the exogenous category.

4. A REGIME SWITCHING DEVICE

In the present case, the regime switching strategy has been implemented in the following way. For a level of employment smaller than a certain threshold (N_{th}), where

$$N_{t-1} < N_{th}$$

the price equation is that specified in the model, that is:

$$P_t = k \frac{W^*}{A^*}$$

If the level of employment trespasses this threshold, then the price equation is specified in the following way:

$$P_t = k_2 \frac{W^*}{A^*} \qquad \text{(10.1) bis}$$

where k_2 is different than k. In this case, it is supposed to be bigger. This means that the markup increases with the state of the economy, given the correspondence between employment and production. Since the share of profits can also be expressed in the following way:

$$\alpha_0 = \frac{\kappa - 1}{\kappa}$$

it follows that the hypothesis made about the markup behavior implies a pro-cyclical behavior of the profit share. Of course, the opposite hypothesis can also be put forward (for a discussion, see Ferri et al., 2015 and Bils et al., 2018).

5. DYNAMIC PATTERNS

The regime switching model has been simulated. The dynamics are represented in Figure 10.1, while the values of the parameters used in the simulations are given in Table 10.1.

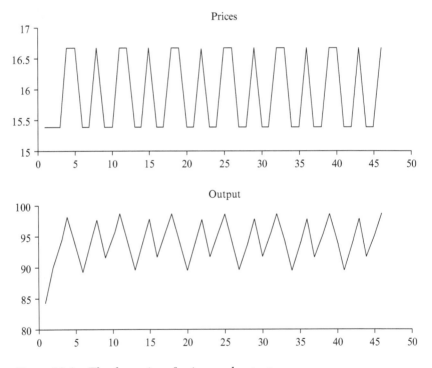

Figure 10.1   The dynamics of prices and output

Given these values of the parameters, the steady state investment equation undergoes a shock lasting only one period in order to trigger dynamics. The ensuing dynamics are shown in Figure 10.1.

Two major results emerge from Figure 10.1. The first is that fluctuations are persistent and generated in an endogenous way. The second is that there is a positive correlation between prices and output, contrary to the stagflation results obtained in the Minsky–Ferri (1984) model.

The fate of this Phillips curve (though it would be more correct to call it a "trade-off" curve) depends on the overall structure of the model and not only on the nature of the labor and the product markets. In this perspective, it is not surprising that it can change in time. The globalization of the present period and the intense technological change, accompanied by the weaker power of unions, are at the root of the present flatness of the curve.

Table 10.1 The values of the parameters

η_0	0.35
η_1	0.16
η_2	0.6
β	0.3
k	1.5385
k_2	1.6667

6. REDUCING THE DIMENSION

The 7-D nature of the model (for each regime) can be reduced. By substituting the various equations, one can obtain the following pair of equations:

$$Y_t^{(1)} = (\eta_0 - \eta_2 \alpha^{(1)}) + \eta_1 Y_{t-1}^{(2)} + \frac{w^*}{P_t^{(1)}\left(A^* + \beta\left(\frac{Y_{t-1}^{(1)}}{Y^{(1)*}} - 1\right)\right)} Y_{t-1}^{(1)} +$$

$$\eta_2 \left(1 - \frac{w^*}{P_t^{(1)}\left(A^* + \beta\left(\frac{Y_{t-1}^{(1)}}{Y^{*(1)}} - 1\right)\right)}\right)$$

$$Y_t^{(2)} = (\eta_0 - \eta_2 \alpha^{(2)}) + \eta_1 Y_{t-1}^{(2)} + \frac{w^*}{P_t^{(2)}\left(A^* + \beta\left(\frac{Y_{t-1}^{(2)}}{Y^{(2)*}} - 1\right)\right)} Y_{t-1}^{(2)} +$$

$$\eta_2 \left(1 - \frac{w^*}{P_t^{(2)} \left(A^* + \beta \left(\frac{Y_{t-1}^{(2)}}{Y^{(2)*}} - 1 \right) \right)} \right)$$

where the different values of α^j separate the two regimes.

These equations can be expressed in terms of Figure 10.2. There are two driving forces of the models. One depends on the dynamics built inside the models. The other depends on the regime switching mechanism. In turn, this latter depends on the value of the threshold, as said before, and on other forces that deserve some more attention. Special attention must be placed on the relative values of the respective steady state values of the two regimes. In the present case, they lie in the opposite regimes. In other words, Regime 1 has a steady state that lies in Regime 2 (see point a), and vice versa (see point b). It is these contradictions that drive the dynamics of the model. In Chapter 15 it will be shown how this hypothesis can be changed.

This 2-D model replicates the cycle. Furthermore, the results are robust to changes in the values of the parameters and to the value of the threshold.

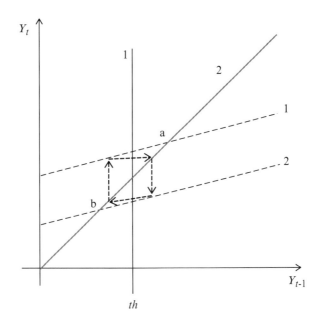

Figure 10.2   The dynamics of 1-D maps

7.   THE STOCHASTIC COMPONENT

In order to generalize the model, one can imagine that the threshold is given by the following expression:

$$N_{th, t} = N_{th} + e_t$$

where the error term is a stochastic variable with a normal distribution $(0, \sigma)$.

This change does not modify the endogenous nature of the fluctuations. It rather changes their dynamic patterns in the sense that they become more persistent. An economic justification for this modification can be found in the heterogeneity of the economy. In this environment, the threshold cannot be an exact number.

In this stochastic case, the dynamics of the model are represented in Figure 10.3.

In this case, the dynamics are more persistent, and at the same time they remain robust to changes in the values of both the parameters and the threshold.

8.   GENERATING A TRADE-OFF CURVE

There is an underlying result common to all these simulations that deserves to be stressed. In fact, if one transforms the price dynamics into their acceleration in order to consider inflation, then a positive correlation with employment (and output) is obtained.

This curve has been labeled the trade-off by Samuelson and Solow (1960). The trade-off emerges if the employment rate is replaced by the rate of unemployment. (This change can be easily made in the present model because labor supply is supposed to be given.) In the empirical literature, this curve is sometimes confused with the Phillips curve, even though the latter relates wage changes to unemployment. Although related, the two curves are different.

Two observations are worth making. The first is that the empirical counterpart of these curves reflects the working of the whole system and not only the specificity of the labor and the product market (see Ferri, 2000). The second is that this trade-off is generated in spite of the assumption of given money wages. If wages were supposed to be a function of employment, then the trade-off curve would have been more marked.

Prices

Output

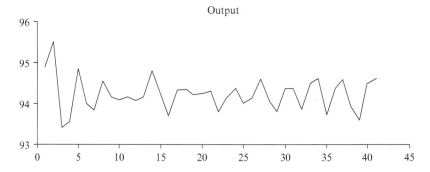

Figure 10.3   The dynamics with a stochastic threshold

9.   SOME CONCLUDING REMARKS

The analytical results depend on the premise that money wages are the relevant assumption in a monetary economy of production, as Keynes taught a long time ago. This assumption, which reflects important institutional aspects, can generate Phillips curve relationships as a system result and are a fundamental determinant of labor share.

The methodology used in this chapter has been studied intensively elsewhere and with the collaboration of many authors.[1] These works contain generalizations of the methodology employed in this chapter. While the first works with Greenberg were based on the same set of assumptions, and in particular on the hypothesis that the steady state of the two regimes lied in the opposite regime and this constitutes the mechanism of dynamics, in development, this assumption has been dropped (see Tramontana et al., 2010). The same happens in Part IV. Furthermore, the dynamics could also become chaotic (see Ferri et al., 2001).

As far as the analytical aspects of the present model are concerned, they should be generalized in order to verify the implications generated by a countercyclical assumption on the profit share.

The exercise shown in this chapter has not only tried to deepen the analysis in the original paper written with Minsky but also allows the putting forward of a methodological device particularly useful for dealing with the complex dynamics of a system where real and financial aspects are connected in an uncertain environment. Within this environment, the financial instability hypothesis can also be better understood. This will be done in steps. In Chapter 14 the financial instability hypothesis will be generalized so that it applies also to the household sector, while in Chapter 15 an analysis based upon a regime switching technique will try to encapsulate the hypothesis within a meta-model where different policies and institutions can be envisaged. Furthermore, the results of the present chapter will be further generalized because the steady state of each regime would lie inside the regime and the dynamics can only be generated by different values of the parameters. In this context, both counter- and pro-cyclical markup behaviors are allowed.

NOTE

1. Including Greenberg, Day, Gardini, Tramontana.

PART IV

Entering the black box

11. Drivers, adapters and constraints

1. BROADENING THE ANALYSIS

Part III, which revised the co-authored papers, had two priorities: on the one hand, to generalize the analysis in order to be able to cover new stylized facts; on the other, to deepen the methodological aspects concerning the dynamic, transaction and aggregative structure of the various models.

To achieve this, analytic changes were introduced. These efforts try to enter the black box of tools that Minsky used. According to Dymsky and Pollin (1992), Minsky's analysis would have been much richer were the black box of his analytical tools enriched. In particular, they ask "what emerges when one opens the black box? To begin with, Minsky's approach implies that distributional questions, as reflected in the determination of wage rates and mark-ups, do not have major macroeconomic implications. But this is incorrect, even within the confines of Minsky's model" (1992, p. 51).

However, this is not true, as the paper "Prices, employment, and profits" has shown and its revision contained in Chapter 10 has tried to reinforce. Even though the revision's relationship with the financial instability hypothesis is still remote, it is true that important steps in that direction have been made. The dynamics of cash flows are an essential part of that hypothesis.

The financial instability hypothesis will be further considered, in detail, in Chapter 14, where its ability to explain the Great Recession will be discussed, while in Chapter 15 a meta-model, based upon the regime switching technique, tries to encapsulate the financial instability hypothesis in a broader context. All these contributions constitute an attempt to generalize Minsky's formulation in order to meet the new challenges deriving from a changeable environment.

However, before dealing specifically with the financial instability hypothesis, it is important to revisit Minsky's dynamics that are contained in his 1982 volume. Some technical developments have been suggested in the previous chapter, while the foundations of dynamics were considered in Chapter 9. New analytical aspects can now be introduced.

2. ENRICHING THE BLACK BOX

In Chapter 9 we saw how the foundation of Minsky's analysis is rooted in the following:

1. it refers to a medium-run period;
2. it tries to overcome the one-sidedness of the approaches by considering both aggregate demand and aggregate supply;
3. it considers financial aspects in order to get over the incompleteness characterizing most of the literature.

The essays "The integration of simple growth and cycle models" and "Monetary systems and accelerator models" contained in his 1982 volume, as Chapter 12 and Chapter 11 respectively, try to cover all the points just mentioned, with the former focusing on the first two and the latter on the third.

In Chapter 12 Minsky tries to reconcile two rates of growth that are generated by the dual nature of investment. Investment is a component of aggregate demand and therefore has an impact on growth. It also feeds accumulation and therefore capacity, and hence impacts on a growth rate based upon capacity.

In this context, productivity is endogenous and depends on investment. Furthermore, the two rates of growth must somehow be reconciled: a reconciliation "which states that actual income equals aggregate demand unless aggregate demand exceeds the maximum aggregate supply or falls below the minimum aggregate supply, in which case actual income will equal the appropriate aggregate supply" (Minsky, 1982, p. 260).

In other words, one can write

$$g_t = g_t^d < g_t^s$$

If this inequality is violated, a rationing process is set in motion.

One limitation of this analysis is that it does not consider the labor market. In fact, if it were considered, the analysis would become much more complex.

3. GROWTH AND THE LABOR MARKET

If the labor market were to be included in the analysis, then the rate of growth of supply would be equal to:

$$g_t^s = \tau_t + gN_t^s$$

where τ_t is the rate of growth of productivity, while gN_t^s represents the rate of growth of labor supply. In other words, it would be equal to what Harrod (1939) called the "natural rate of growth".[1]

Unlike Harrod (1939), one can suppose that the system is characterized by unemployment. The introduction of this variable has important consequences on the working of the system. It allows the enrichment of both Harrod's and Minsky's analysis. On the one hand, unemployment is the most important source of inequality in the economic system.[2] On the other, it can act as a buffer in the system, and this can impact on growth. This relationship between growth and unemployment is made complex by the presence of an endogenous supply of labor, the role of technical change (see Chapter 12) and the existence of mismatches that this process implies (see Chapter 13).

Both aspects of unemployment have an impact on the reconciliation process and on the stability of model. Furthermore, by considering unemployment within a medium-run perspective, we will be in a better position to comment on Minsky's work on poverty (Minsky, 2013).

4.   THE TWO HARRODIAN CHALLENGES

If, as suggested by Minsky (1982), one is to consider growth in a medium-run perspective (i.e. a span of time where investment feeds back on capital accumulation but the role of institutions can be assumed to be given), one has to face two fundamental problems:

1.   the instability of the dynamic process (see Ferri et al., 2011);
2.   the reconciliation, to use Harrod's (1939) terminology, between the warranted rate of growth prevailing in the product market and the natural rate of growth generated in the labor market.

One peculiarity of the literature on the subject is that these two problems have been tackled separately, the second one being more deeply examined than the first one. The result is that growth has been mainly studied within a steady state framework. Here, the neoclassical analysis, starting from Solow (1956), has stressed the role of supply factors in determining growth, with aggregate demand playing no active role. The situation is no different in the so-called new growth theory (see Romer, 1986), nor even in the Schumpeterian approach (see Aghion and Howitt, 1998).

On the contrary, the so-called Cambridge school (see Robinson, 1956 and Kaldor, 1957) has insisted that aggregate demand plays a role, while supply fully accommodates to its dynamics. In a sense, supply is assumed to be perfectly elastic. Efforts to consider supply aspects in post-Keynesian models in a more complex way are becoming numerous (see Dutt, 2010, Lavoie, 2014, Setterfield, 2010 and Skott, 2010). However, in these contributions the first fundamental problem, that is, the possible instability of the model, is also either ignored or dealt with using traditional comparative statics devices.

In a recent contribution, Fazzari et al. (2018) tackled the two problems together. They found that while autonomous demand plays the role of the driver of the growth process, aggregate supply accommodates to aggregate demand at a finite speed and this contributes to create a complex dynamics, where unemployment is a persistent phenomenon.

The aim of the present chapter is to enrich this integrated approach by deepening the relationship between growth and unemployment.[3] In the present framework, unemployment has a dual role: it makes the adaptation of labor supply to the needs of growth easier and, since it cannot assume a negative value, it can change the constraints limiting the growth process. At the same time unemployment can affect consumption, because it creates heterogeneity among people. This dual role contributes to making the dynamics of growth bounded and unemployment a persistent phenomenon. In this perspective, two analytical aspects will be considered. First, the role of the various parameters in making the reconciliation process feasible will be examined vis-à-vis their role in maintaining the system bounded. Second, the robustness of the model to changes in the values of the parameters will be considered.

5.   DRIVERS, ADAPTERS AND CONSTRAINTS IN THE MEDIUM RUN

Since the analysis extends to a medium-run period, where the markets are in disequilibrium, the thesis put forward is that growth must be considered as a dynamic process, where drivers, adapters and constraints coexist to generate persistent and bounded unemployment. At the same time, the presence of unemployment makes the reconciliation process easier and can inhibit instability processes. Finally, the presence of unemployment justifies the assumption of given wages and prices.

In this context, the role of driver is often assigned to autonomous demand in the literature (see Lavoie, 2014 for a survey). Autonomous demand can be studied in relation to public expenditures (see Allain, 2015) or to consumer expenditure (see Serrano, 1995). Furthermore, there are a variety of analytical approaches, ranging from that of Harrod to that of Kalecki.[4]

Three main results emerge from this literature. The first is that the rate of growth of autonomous demand dominates the dynamics of the model. The second is that the average propensity to consume and hence to save becomes endogenous and this helps introduce a degree of flexibility into the model. Finally, a distinction between the levels of income and rates of growth reveals differences between the various models.

All these results are present in a previous model of ours (see Fazzari et al., 2013). One limitation of this model is that the natural rate of growth is simply postulated to be equal to the warranted rate of growth driven by autonomous demand. In the present model, we extend our analysis and study the impact of an endogenous supply (see also Dutt, 2006 and 2010).

This integrated approach, carried out in an intermediate horizon, allows specification of the conditions under which autonomous demand can play a strategic role for growth. In this context, the impact of recession on growth can also be considered. It is not uncommon to find analyses that stress the role that the Great Recession may have on future growth (see Delong and Summers, 2012), as will be discussed in the next chapter. Furthermore, the presence of an endogenous ceiling makes the interaction between aggregate demand and aggregate supply operate in a particular way.

The thesis put forward is that this model can unify the two Harrodian problems, namely instability and the reconciliation process. In fact, on the one hand, the model shows how the interaction between aggregate demand and aggregate supply can prevent runaway dynamics, without necessarily referring to an exogenous ceiling. On the other, it shows that the presence of unemployment is a structural feature of the model, where it plays two fundamental roles: it justifies the hypothesis of given wages and prices and it offers resources for growth.

By endogenizing the Harrodian natural rate of growth, supply reacts by changing capacity and not only its utilization rate. In this framework, the impact of autonomous components on growth is conditioned not only by the endogenous reaction of supply but also by the capability of operating at potential.

There is a double constraint in the system. On the one hand, autonomous demand, the driver of the system, is constrained by the availability of resources. On the other, supply expansion, based upon dynamic increasing returns, is limited by the presence of insufficient aggregate demand. Their interaction creates interesting results. The presence of autonomous demand protects growth from downward runaway situations because it sets up a floor. At the same time, instability matters for growth, and since the former is driven by aggregate demand, this implies that aggregate demand plays a decisive role. This hypothesis does not exclude supply from the analysis. On the contrary, it argues that growth is constrained only in particular circumstances, when the ceiling is hit. Otherwise, the actual rate of growth is maintained in the presence of slack resources. It is the integral of these growth rates that shapes the process of growth in a medium to long-run perspective where the ceiling is also endogenous.

In this perspective, Minsky's contribution can be strengthened and a new dynamic setting for his financial instability hypothesis can be found, as will be shown in Part V.

6.   UNEMPLOYMENT, HETEROGENEITY AND INEQUALITY

Unemployment is one of the major sources of inequality in the system. In addition to ethical aspects, inequality can have important economic consequences (see Ferri, 2016). A convenient starting point in our analysis is to consider the impact of unemployment on consumption, the most important driver of aggregate demand, at least from a quantitative point of view. In this context, where wages and prices are given and income distribution does not change, unemployment matters.

Even though it does not appear frequently, it is possible to find in the literature studies where unemployment affects consumption.[5] The mechanisms behind this are, however, different. First, there are those who, like Palley (2012), insist on the role that unemployment can have on uncertainty, which stimulates precautionary saving (see also Carrol, 1992). Second, there are those who stress the role that heterogeneity in employment status can have on the pattern of overall consumption (see Eusepi and Preston, 2015). Finally, there are studies that underlie the negative correlation between level of income (with respect to the average) and the propensity to consume (see Alichi et al., 2016).

In what follows, unemployment will be used as a proxy for poverty in a heterogeneous model of consumption based upon the polarization, rich and poor people (see Ferri et al., 2018). Consider the following equation:

$$C_t = C_t^n + C_t^u \tag{11.1}$$

That is, total consumption is the sum of the consumption from employment (n) and from unemployment (u). Dividing through by income, one obtains the overall propensity to consume:

$$c_t = c_t^e + c_t^u \frac{Y_t^u}{Y_t} \qquad (11.2)$$

where Y_t^u represents income from unemployment[6] and the following inequality holds:

$$c^u > c^n$$

Put in words, both propensities are considered given, but the propensity to consume for unemployed people is supposed to be bigger than that of other people. In this perspective, the behavior of the overall propensity to consume depends on the relative incomes (Y^u/Y).

The assumption is that inequality increases as unemployment rises, with respect to steady state (u_0), and therefore this ratio is negatively related to the rate of unemployment (u_t). As done in Ferri (2016), a macro variable is used to proxy the degree of inequality.

In mathematical terms, one can write:

$$c_t = c_{11}[1 - \eta_1(u_t - u_0)] + c_{22}[\eta_2 - \eta_3(u_t - u_0)] \qquad (11.3)$$

where the propensity to consume of the employed (c_{11}) is affected by precautionary saving that increases with the rate of unemployment (the terms within the first set of square brackets), while the propensity to consume of the unemployed (c_{22}) is affected negatively by inequality that rises with unemployment (the terms within the second set of square brackets).

Re-writing (11.3), one obtains:

$$c_t = c_{11} + c_{22}\eta_2 - (c_{11}\eta_1 + c_{22}\eta_3)(u_t - u_0)_t \qquad (11.4)$$

An increase in u_t decreases the propensity to consume, and this depends on both the presence of precautionary saving and the inequality effect that shrinks unemployed income in the presence of a greater rate of unemployment.[7]

7. A NONLINEAR INTEGRATED MODEL

This consumption function based upon heterogeneous agents is to be inserted within the tenets of a nonlinear model. To this end, a preliminary aspect to be considered is the information structure. In particular, suppose that expectations of the rate of growth (g_t) are formed according to the following adaptive rule:

$$E_{t-1}g_t = (1-\alpha)g_{t-1} + aE_{t-2}g_{t-1} \qquad (11.5)$$

where E_{t-1} is the expectation operator at time $t-1$ (henceforth, this temporal notation will be omitted).[8]

Given this hypothesis, the consumption function can be specified in the following way:

$$C_t = [Y_{t-1}(1 + Eg_t)][c_1 - c_3(u_{t-1} - u_0)] \qquad (11.6)$$

where the term inside the first pair of square brackets represents expected income, given by the last period level of income increased by the expected rate of growth. The term in the second set of square brackets expresses both the heterogeneity and inequality aspects discussed in the previous section.[9]

To determine investment, consider the following equation that states that the evolution of aggregate demand stimulates the following desired capacity:

$$K_{t+1} = v^* EY_{t+1} = v^*(1 + Eg_t)^2 Y_{t-1}$$

where K is capital, while v^* is the optimal capital output coefficient.

In this context, investment tries to close the gap between actual and desired capacity, as appears in the following equation:

$$I_t = [v^*(1 + Eg_t)^2 Y_{t-1} - (1 - \delta_t)K_t] \qquad (11.7)$$

while the capital dynamics are given by:

$$K_t = K_{t-1}(1 - \delta) + I_{t-1} \qquad (11.8)$$

In this context, aggregate demand is represented by:

$$Y_t = C_t + I_t + F_t \qquad (11.9)$$

where F_t represents the presence of an autonomous component that varies according to the following formula:

$$F_t = F_{t-1}(1 + g^*) \qquad (11.10)$$

where g^* is an exogenous rate of growth. This rate plays a driving role not only in the dynamic analysis but also in the determination of the steady state values.

8.   ENDOGENOUS SUPPLY

Consider first labor supply, which can be expressed by the following equations:

$$L_t = (1 + \sigma_t)L_{t-1} \tag{11.11}$$

$$\sigma_t = \rho_0 - \rho_1 u_{t-1} \tag{11.12}$$

These equations imply that the dynamics of labor supply are endogenous and their rates of change depend negatively on the rate of unemployment, as recent experience has shown (see Delong and Summers, 2013 and IMF, 2018).

The other variable, A_t, that is, output per person, also needs to be endogenized. The following specification is suggested:

$$A_t = (1 + \tau_t)A_{t-1} \tag{11.13}$$

$$\tau_t = \theta_0 + \theta_1 \frac{i_{t-1}}{v_{t-1}} \tag{11.14}$$

$$i_t = \frac{I_t}{Y_t} \tag{11.15}$$

$$v_t = \frac{K_t}{Y_t} \tag{11.16}$$

One of the most important determinants of the rate of growth of productivity is investment, as Kaldor (1978) stressed a long time ago and as the recent literature on investment in research and development (R&D) has shown. The specification (11.14) is in line with the Kaldor–Verdoorn law. As McCombie (2002, p.99) stresses: "the basis of the Verdoorn Law would seem to be a linear Kaldorian technical progress function with an allowance for increasing returns."

In the present perspective, the gross rate of accumulation, which includes depreciation, becomes the strategic factor. It is simply equal to the investment ratio divided by the capital/output ratio, which is defined by equation (11.16), while (11.15) defines the investment ratio.

In this context, the demand for labor is represented by the following equation:

$$N_t = \frac{Y_t}{A_t} \tag{11.17}$$

while the rate of unemployment is defined as:

$$u_t = 1 - \frac{N_t}{L_t} \geq 0 \qquad (11.18)$$

Finally, the rate of growth is defined in the canonical way:

$$g_t = \frac{Y_t}{Y_{t-1}} - 1 \qquad (11.19)$$

Given an exogenous rate of autonomous demand growth g^* and the expected/optimal capital output ratio v^*, the system refers to 15 unknowns – I_t, K_t, C_t, F_t, Y_t, u_t, N_t, L_t, g_t, v_t, τ_t, A_t, σ_t, i_t and $E_{t-1}g_t$ – inserted in 15 equations.

9. STEADY STATE AND THE RECONCILIATION PROCESS

In steady state all rates of growth must be set equal. In this perspective, it is convenient to express the definition of potential supply in terms of rates of growth as:

$$g_t^s = (1 + \tau_t)(1 + \sigma_t) - 1 \qquad (11.20)$$

This is the Harrodian natural rate of growth. By substituting equations (11.12) and (11.14) the following equation is obtained:

$$g_t^s = (\rho_0 + \theta_0 + \rho_0\theta_0) + \theta_1\frac{i_{t-1}}{v_{t-1}} + \rho_0\theta_1\frac{i_{t-1}}{v_{t-1}} - \left(\rho_1 + \rho_1\theta_0 + \rho_1\theta_1\frac{i_{t-1}}{v_{t-1}}\right)u_{t-1}$$

A fixed natural rate of growth is represented by the terms included in the first parentheses, which is simply the compounding of a fixed rate of growth for labor supply (ρ_0) and productivity (τ_0). Another aspect to be considered is the presence of the rate of unemployment.

The presence of unemployment in the model serves two purposes. First, it can justify the assumption of given wages and prices. Second, it can facilitate the process of reconciliation between aggregate demand and aggregate supply, as will be shown shortly.

Steady state for demand (0 used as a subscript refers to a steady state situation) implies that:

$$g_t = g^*$$

and

$$i_0 = v^*(g^* + \delta)$$

In other words, demand must grow at the same rate as autonomous demand and the investment ratio must correspond to the "warranted" rate. Furthermore, f_0, that is, the steady state share of autonomous demand, is endogenously given by:

$$f_0 = (1 - c_0) - v^*(g^* + \delta)$$

where c_0 is defined by the consumption function and is equal to c_1.

These equations underline the Keynesian nature of the model because investment drives saving. In fact, both the marginal propensity to save (s) and the average propensity are endogenous because of the presence of f_0 and u_0.

In Fazzari et al. (2013), g^* and g_0^s were equal by hypothesis. If this hypothesis is dropped, g_0^s must in some way be reconciled with g^*, the warranted rate of growth generated by autonomous demand.

In the present case

$$g_0 = g_0^s$$

implies (from 11.20) that

$$g^* = \rho_0 + \theta_0 + \rho_0\theta_0 + \theta_1(g^* + \delta)/v^* + \rho_0\theta_1(g^* + \delta)/v^*$$

$$- [\rho_1 + \rho_1\theta_0 + \rho_1\theta_1(g^* + \delta)/v^*]u_0$$

and that

$$u_0 = \frac{[\rho_0 + \tau_0(1 + \rho_0)] - g^*}{\rho_1(1 + \tau_0)}$$

Two observations are worth making at this stage of the analysis. The first is that unemployment depends on both demand and supply aspects, and this is the difference from Malinvaud's (1977) model where the different sources of unemployment were not present in a simultaneous way. The second is that the values of the variables and the parameters must be such so as to generate the usual inequality

$$u_0 \geq 0$$

which can have important dynamic implications.

One might ask why it is not possible to get endogenous supply accommodating demand growth from the productivity process alone. Mechanically, the reason is that this approach specifies endogenous productivity growth as a function of the investment ratio (i_{t-1}). In steady state, i_0 is determined by the condition for steady state demand growth. There is no variable that can be adjusted to create equilibrium between demand growth and supply growth if unemployment is eliminated from the equations by setting $\rho_1 = 0$.

10. BOUNDED UNEMPLOYMENT

The nonlinear system has been simulated. The values of the parameters are shown in Table 11.1. These are within the range of the values found in the literature (see also Fazzari et al., 2018).

Given the values of the parameters, the steady state of the model has been shocked for one period. The ensuing dynamics are illustrated in Figure 11.1.

Three observations are worth stressing at this stage of the analysis. The first is that the model presents persistent fluctuations. The second is that fluctuations are always bounded, and this is the result of the interplay between aggregate demand and aggregate supply. Finally, the dynamics of the rate of unemployment depend, inter alia, on the specification of the productivity and labor supply equations. Within this framework, an increase in ρ_1 and θ_1 may stabilize the system, depending on the specification of the model in general and of the heterogeneity hypothesis in particular. In this sense, the reconciliation process, facilitated by the endogeneity of supply, helps in checking instability.

The mechanisms behind these results are quite simple and straightforward. The driving force of the model is a super-multiplier (see Hicks, 1950 for a definition) accompanied by the presence of an accelerator. When the steady state of the system is shocked, for example by events that affect expectations, aggregate demand depresses the rate of growth and causes unemployment to increase. However, the presence of a growing autonomous demand can stop this process and transform it into a virtuous circle.

Table 11.1   The values of the parameters

$c_1 = 0.608$	$\delta = 0.12$	$v^* = 0.655$
$c_3 = 0.20$	$g^* = 0.04$	
	$\rho_0 = 0.042$	$\rho_1 = 0.30$
$\theta_0 = 0.0001$	$\theta_1 = 0.2$	$\alpha = 0.8$

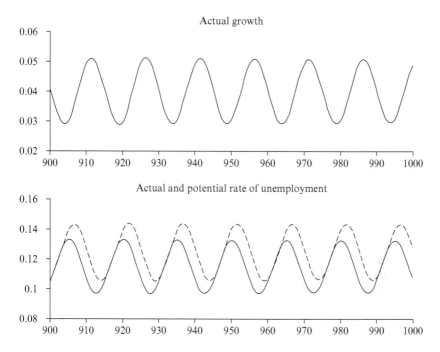

Figure 11.1   The dynamics of the nonlinear model

In turn, this ascending phase is checked by the presence of two feedbacks: the supply feedback and inequality feedback.

It is the presence of these feedbacks that makes the correlation between growth and unemployment complex. In fact, if it is true that an increase in *g* causes the rate of unemployment to decrease, it is also true that an increase in the rate of growth stimulates productivity and affects the labor supply. The relative weight of these two forces can cause an increase in the rate of unemployment that, via the inequality feedback, can negatively affect consumption.

As usual, it is the co-presence of positive and negative feedbacks that guarantees the presence of bounded fluctuations.

11.   CONSTRAINED DYNAMICS

The values of the previous parameters were such so as to guarantee that aggregate demand was always less than aggregate supply. At this stage of the analysis, this assumption is dropped so that the model is simulated with the following inequality:

$$Y_t = \min(Y_t, Y_t^s) \tag{11.21}$$

Two points are worth stressing at this stage. The first is that this inequality is different from that put forward by Minsky (1982), where

$$Y_t^s = \frac{K_t}{v_t}$$

In the present context supply is equal to:

$$Y_t^s = A_t L_t^s$$

In what follows we assume that only the latter can be constraining.

The second point to be stressed is that inequality (11.21) implies the following inequality:

$$u_t = 1 - \frac{N_t}{L_t} \geq 0$$

Given these inequalities, the dynamics of the model are illustrated in Figure 11.2.

To generate this new simulation, the value of v^* has been increased (v^* has become 0.7). This change would cause the dynamics to become unstable. However, the presence of the constraint prevents this from happening. In this environment, two points are worth stressing. The first is that there is a gap between the average value of the actual rates of growth and the steady state value. Actually, it is significant, with a high degree of volatility. The second is that the constraint on production also creates a constraint on unemployment in the sense that it guarantees a positive value for u_t.

12. SOME CAVEATS

The results discussed so far must come with two caveats. The first refers to the driving role of autonomous demand g^*. In a medium-run perspective, the assumption that autonomous demand plays a driving role may be considered reasonable, but this does not necessarily imply that it cannot be amended.

The second refers to the presence of physical constraints. Minsky (1982) has criticized this assumption. As has been said already, in his opinion

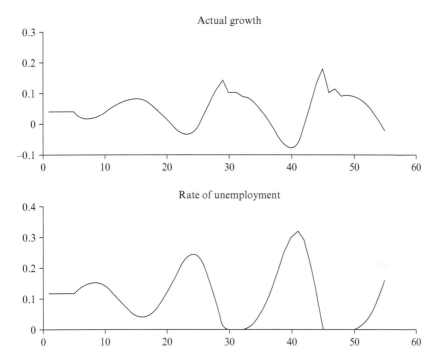

Figure 11.2   The dynamics of the constrained model

ceilings and floors referred to policy variables or to the role of institutions that could change the initial conditions of the process. In other words, the dynamics set by the market process were discontinued by the presence of these thwarting forces that made the process start from a new basis.

In the next chapter, a step towards abandoning the physical dimension will be made by assuming a greater role of prices, which could accelerate when these bottlenecks take place. Later, in Part V, the philosophy of the interaction between market forces processes and thwarting forces will be reconsidered within a regime switching setting in order to present a meta-model of the financial instability hypothesis.

NOTES

1. This formula ignores interactions.
2. The impact of inequality on aggregate demand is studied by Auclert and Rognlie (2018).
3. In the literature, this relationship is mainly considered from a supply perspective, as in Goodwin (1967) and Aghion and Howitt (1998). An exception is Dosi et al. (2012).

4. On the differences between the two approaches, see Skott (2010) and Lavoie (2014).
5. Hsu et al. (2018) have studied the impact of unemployment insurance on the housing market.
6. According to Eusepi and Preston (2015) the income differential between families belonging to the labor force with respect to those outside is about 20 percent. For Hall (2009) the difference is between employed and unemployed and in this case amounts to 15 percent. It is worth stressing that these figures were calculated before the Great Recession when unemployment was lower and had a smaller duration.
7. From a mathematical point of view, this implies that income per unemployed diminishes as unemployment rises and this offsets the increase of their share in total income due to an increase in u.
8. See Ferri and Variato (2010a) and Ferri (2011) for more sophisticated formulae, along with Chapter 15.
9. Lagged unemployment increases the recursiveness of the model. It can be dropped in the linearized version. In this formula, $c_1 = c_{11} + c_{22}\eta_2$; $c_3 = (c_{11}\eta_1 + c_{22}\eta_3)$.

12. Growth, technical change and unemployment

1. UNEMPLOYMENT AND TECHNICAL CHANGE

In the previous chapter, the relationship between unemployment and growth was considered. It is a two-way relationship that depends on both aggregate demand and aggregate supply aspects. For a given rate of technical change, the supply aspects are dominated by the behavior of labor supply, which reacts endogenously to the level of unemployment.

As we have seen, the consequences of this endogeneity are twofold in the sense that it affects both the process of reconciliation between aggregate demand and aggregate supply and the instability of the model. In general, one can say that under this hypothesis the rate of unemployment remains an imperfect indicator of the state of the labor market. Labor supply matters, not only through its dependence on the rate of unemployment but also by means of migration processes and demographic aspects (see IMF, 2018).

In the literature, these phenomena are present, but they are usually confined to developing countries. However, these are aspects that are also relevant for advanced economies, in spite of the fact that there is no longer over-employment in agriculture.

At this stage of the analysis, it becomes important to study the role of technical change in more detail.[1] Even though it is already present in the analysis found in Chapter 11, it is important to deepen its role when it increases in intensity. In a world of globalization, where there has been an information technology revolution, it is vital to understand what technical change adds to the relationship between growth and unemployment studied in the previous chapter.

2. LINEARIZING THE MODEL

To better understand the role of technical change, the model in Chapter 11 has been linearized. All the variables are expressed as deviations from their steady state values. The multipliers are shown in the Appendix at the end of this chapter:

$$i_t = -I_1 v_t + I_2 Eg_t \tag{12.1}$$

$$Eg_t = (1 - \alpha)g_{t-1} + aEg_{t-1} \tag{12.2}$$

$$c_t = C_1 Eg_t - C_2 u_{t-1} \tag{12.3}$$

$$v_t = V_1 v_{t-1} + V_2 i_{t-1} - V_3 g_t \tag{12.4}$$

$$g_t = G_1 f_{t-1} - G_2 f_t \tag{12.5}$$

$$f_t = -i_t - c_t + g_t \tag{12.6}$$

$$\tau_t = P_1 i_{t-1} - P_2 v_{t-1} \tag{12.7}$$

$$\sigma_t = -\rho_1 u_{t-1} \tag{12.8}$$

$$gN_t = GN_1 g_t - GN_2 \tau_t \tag{12.9}$$

$$u_t = U_1 u_{t-1} + U_2 \sigma_t - U_3 gN_t \tag{12.10}$$

The system of linear equations can be shaped into a matrix form to generate the following expression:

$$x_t = A^{-1} B x_{t-1}$$

One can choose a parameter so that the modulus of the maximum eigenvalue, $|\lambda|$, is made equal to 1. This is a necessary condition to generate limit cycles, that is, a kind of non-exploding dynamics (see Ferri, 2016).

3.   THE SENSITIVITY ANALYSIS

To understand the role of the various parameters, let us start from Table 12.1, which contains the values of the parameters generating persistent fluctuations. Furthermore, it shows the impact of an increase in the values of the parameters on $|\lambda|$.

   The sign of the changes is in line with those obtained in the literature. Two points, however, are worth stressing. The first point to be considered concerns c_3, that is, the negative impact of unemployment on the consumption share. Its role is destabilizing. However, its absence will impact on the dynamic effect of the endogenous supply. In fact, and this is the second point, both ρ_0 and θ_0 are stabilizing, while the same is not true for ρ_1, the

Table 12.1 *The dynamic impact of a percentage increase in the values of the parameters on* $|\lambda|$

Benchmark values	Impact on $|\lambda|$ of an increase
$c_1 = 0.608$	+
$\delta = 0.10$	−
$v^* = 0.974$	+
$g^* = 0.04$	+
$\alpha = 0.9024$	−
$c_3 = 0.20$	+
$\theta_0 = 0.001$	−
$\theta_1 = 0.20$	−
$\rho_0 = 0.03$	−
$\rho_1 = 0.30$	+

parameter negatively linking the dynamics of labor supply to the rate of unemployment. On the contrary, a higher θ_1 is stabilizing. In other words, without referring to an exogenous ceiling, the endogeneity of supply can constrain the dynamics of aggregate demand. An increase in the values of these parameters makes the value of $|\lambda|$ smaller. In other words, the endogeneity of supply not only reconciles the various rates of growth but it also keeps the instability process under control.

4. THE DUAL ROLE OF TECHNICAL CHANGE

To deepen the role of technical change, it is convenient to re-propose the steady state value of unemployment:

$$u_0 = \frac{[\rho_0 + \tau_0(1 + \rho_0)] - g^*}{\rho_1(1 + \tau_0)}$$

Instead of presenting the impact by means of derivatives, the alternative route of using simulations has been followed. Table 12.2 includes increased values (with respect to Table 12.1) for various parameters, along with their impact on unemployment, the rate of growth of labor supply and productivity.

Three observations are worth making. The first concerns the robustness

Table 12.2   The impact of changes in the parameters on steady state
(in parentheses the benchmark values)

	u_0	σ_0	τ_0
(Benchmark)	(0.1064)	(0.0107)	(0.0293)
New values			
$\theta_0 = 0.02\ (0.001)$	0.1780	−0.0116	0.0520
$\theta_1 = 0.30\ (0.20)$	0.1658	−0.0077	0.0481
$\rho_0 = 0.05\ (0.03)$	0.1412	0.0077	0.0321
$\rho_1 = 0.40\ (0.30)$	0.0859	0.0077	0.0310

of the model. Changes in the values of the parameters do not affect the sign of their dynamic impact described in Table 12.1.

Second, the dual role of technical change is neatly described. In fact, an increase in both parameters θ_0 and θ_1 causes unemployment to increase but stabilizes the dynamics.

Finally, ρ_0 and ρ_1 have opposite effects on u_0, and this helps explain their different dynamic impact.

5.   A DEEPER INTEGRATION OF THE MODEL

To generalize the analysis, it is important to make the model more complete. As suggested at the end of the last chapter, if one has to examine the dynamics of the system near the ceiling, it is essential to introduce prices.

However, the introduction of prices implies a series of other adjustments necessary to integrate these monetary aspects into the model.

In the present model, the point of intersection of real and monetary aspects is represented by the investment function that is modified in the following way:

$$i_t = [1 - \xi(r_t - r_0)][v^*(1 + Eg_t) - (1 - \delta)v_t] \qquad (12.1)\text{ bis}$$

Two points are worth stressing. The first is that, in this case, the variables are expressed in an intensive form. In other words, both I_t and K_t have been divided by last year's output Y_{t-1}. This procedure makes the process of linearization around the steady state easier. The second point is that the investment function has been supplemented by the terms in the first set of square brackets. These imply that the adjustment between the target and the actual capital is made dependent on the gap between the actual rate of interest (r_t) and its steady state value (r_0).

The real rate of interest considered in the present model is defined in the following way:

$$r_t = \frac{(1 + R_t)}{(1 + E\pi_t)} - 1 \tag{12.11}$$

where $E\pi_t$ stands for some medium-run expectation of inflation made at time $t-1$. (This subscript is dropped, as usual.)

Inflationary expectations replicate the specification put forward for expected growth, and so:

$$E\pi_t = \beta E\pi_{t-1} + (1 - \beta)\pi_{t-1} \tag{12.12}$$

The nominal rate of interest is determined à la Taylor:

$$R_t = R^* + \gamma_1(E\pi_t - \pi^*) - \gamma_2(u_{t-1} - u_0) \tag{12.13}$$

where π^* is some target rate of inflation set by monetary authorities.

Inflation is determined à la Phillips:

$$\pi_t = \beta_1 E\pi_{t-1} - \psi_1(u_{t-1} - u_0) + (1 - \beta_1)\pi_{t-1} - \psi_2(\tau_{t-1} - \tau_0) \tag{12.14}$$

where Ψ_2 measures the impact of technical change on inflation.

6. THE DYNAMICS OF THE NONLINEAR MODEL

If one considers the nonlinear versions of the equations (12.2) to (12.10) (which are the same as those given in Chapter 11) and then appends the equations from (12.1) bis to (12.14), a different nonlinear system is obtained. For the values of the parameters given in Table 12.3, the dynamics of this extended system are shown in the Figure 12.1.

For this extended version of the model, fluctuations are also persistent. Unemployment remains bounded, while inflation is correlated and generates a Phillips curve relationship.

7. THE ROBUSTNESS OF THE INTEGRATED MODEL

The extended model has been linearized (see the Appendix for the values of the multipliers and the matrix form). It can generate persistent fluctua-

Table 12.3   The parameters of the extended nonlinear model

Benchmark values		
$c_1 = 0.608$		$c_3 = 0.20$
$\delta = 0.10$		
$v^* = 0.75$		
$g^* = 0.04$		
$\alpha = 0.9024$		$\beta = 0.80$
$\beta_1 = 0.90$	$\psi_1 = 0.05$	$\psi_2 = 0.1$
$\theta_0 = 0.001$		
$\theta_1 = 0.20$		
$\rho_0 = 0.04$		
$\rho_1 = 0.30$		
$\xi = 2$		

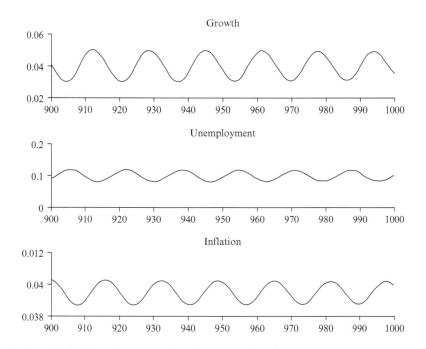

Figure 12.1   The dynamics of the integrated model

tions, as the nonlinear version suggested. The two versions of the model produce the same kinds of results in the vicinity of the steady state for almost the same values of the parameters.[2]

An analogue of Table 12.1 is replicated for values of $\xi \neq 0$ in Table 12.4.

The signs are in keeping with those shown in Table 12.1. Furthermore, they are in tune with the theoretical expectations. However, three points are worth stressing.

The first is the role of ξ, which represents the channel of transmission of the monetary aspects to the real side of the economy. Its increase is stabilizing. However, a too severe Taylor rule (i.e. an increase in γ_1) is destabilizing.

Second, the impact of v^* is extremely nonlinear. In fact, from a range of values from 0.5 to 1.4, its increase makes $|\lambda|$ larger. However, following a range of values when it creates non-cyclical explosion, its role changes, and it can become stabilizing.

Table 12.4 *The dynamic impact of a percentage increase in the values of the parameters on $|\lambda|$ for $\xi \neq 0$ in the extended model*

Benchmark values	Impact on $|\lambda|$ of an increase
$\xi = 1.5$	−
$c_1 = 0.608$	+
$\delta = 0.10$	−
$v^* = 1.0784$	+
$g^* = 0.04$	+
$\alpha = 0.9024$	−
$c_3 = 0.20$	+
$\theta_0 = 0.001$	−
$\theta_1 = 0.20$	−
$\rho_0 = 0.03$	−
$\rho_1 = 0.30$	+
$\gamma_1 = 2.8$	+
$\gamma_2 = 0.85$	−
$\beta = 0.8$	+
$\beta_1 = 0.90$	+
$\psi_1 = 0.01$	−
$\psi_2 = 0.5$	+

Finally, it is important to stress that a low value of Ψ_1 in the inflation curve is stabilizing, while an increase in Ψ_2, which measures the impact of technical change on inflation, is destabilizing.

8.   A STOCHASTIC COMPONENT

In most models focusing on the role of technical change, it is common to refer to a stochastic component. In the so-called real business cycle models, for instance, this is the only determinant of technical change. In more sophisticated models, like those put forward by Dosi et al. (2012), the stochastic component supplements the deterministic forces. The former represents either a sophisticated process of diffusion of technical change or the presence of heterogeneous agents.

In what follows, two different kinds of simulations are carried out. In the first one, productivity growth is shocked by a noise having a normal distribution.

Since there is a stochastic component, the simulations refer to a Monte Carlo technique and are repeated 100 times. The results are illustrated in Figure 12.2.

Three points are worth considering. The first is that the profile is less regular, but this is typical of the stochastic component. The second is that the rate of growth becomes bigger than the steady state value, while the rate of unemployment, and this is the third point, becomes smaller.

As will be shown in the next section, *mutatis mutandis*, these results hold for a slowdown of technical change.

9.   THE IMPACT OF CONSTRAINTS

The dynamics of the various models considered so far are such as to respect the constraints of the model. But as we did in Chapter 11, the constraint

$$Y_t = min(Y_t, Y_t^s)$$

can be made directly operative. To do so, g^* has been increased so that the likelihood of reaching a ceiling of capacity (or generating a negative rate of unemployment) becomes higher and the constraint becomes binding. The results of these operations are shown in Figure 12.3.

In this case, the rate of growth is higher, while unemployment is lower.

In other words, a more intense technical change accompanied by a more

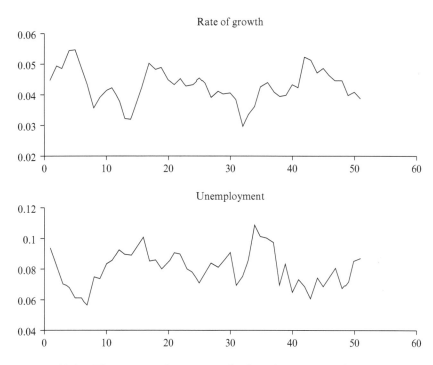

Figure 12.2   The impact of a positive shock with Monte Carlo simulations

expansive autonomous demand may produce higher growth and lower unemployment.

10.   THE SLOWDOWN OF TECHNICAL CHANGE

Much of the recent literature, however, has stressed a contrary hypothesis. It has insisted on the possibility of a slowdown in the rate of growth of productivity (see, for instance, Jorgenson et al., 2016). Some of the causes have been attributed to the long recession that, having hit the process of accumulation, will eventually slow down the dynamics of productivity. Other causes are instead attributed to the autonomous nature of technical change, reflecting the development of inventions and their applications. In this latter case, one can apply the same analysis as before with a change in sign. Still others refer back to Steindl (1952), who insisted on the role of concentration in constraining productivity.

Figure 12.4 shows the dynamics of the model when the rate of growth

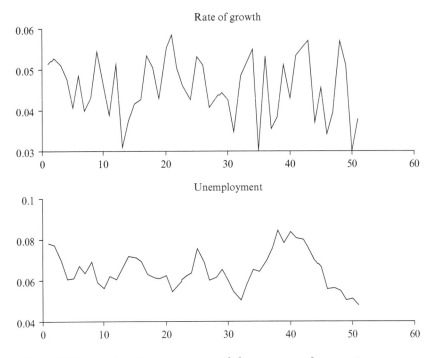

Figure 12.3   Stochastic component and the presence of constraints

of productivity is hit by a negative and permanent shock, distributed in a normal way, in the presence of operating constraints.

The mean of the actual growth rates is 0.0421, while the rate of unemployment is 0.0811. Given that the rate of growth of autonomous demand has not changed, a fall in the dynamics of technical change can be less damaging in the labor market, as underlined also by Carlin and Soskice (2018).

11. A SECULAR STAGNATION?

If one considers the literature more carefully, one realizes that the fear is not only a slowdown in the rate of growth of productivity, but rather a secular stagnation. Stagnation, that is, a persistent period of low growth, is not considered an unlikely event in the near future (see Eichengreen, 2015), and this constitutes a further stimulus to deepen the analysis of the chapter.

Stagnation is not at all a new hypothesis in the literature since it arises

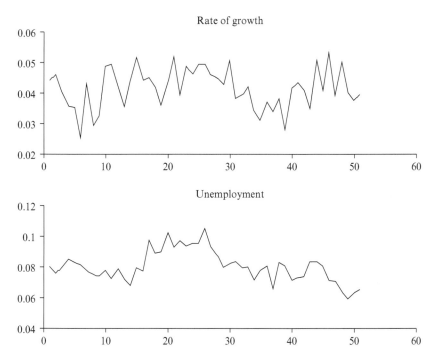

Figure 12.4 The impact of a slowdown in productivity

after every long recession. For instance, it was put forward after the Great Depression, with Alvin Hansen (1938) being one of the most prominent advocates. This phenomenon is attributed to different forces, ranging from productivity slowdown (see Gordon, 2015) to aggregate demand. In turn, aggregate demand can be affected via inequality (see Palley, 2016) or a world saving glut (see Bernanke, 2005). Furthermore, stagnation implies the use of a different policy (see Delong and Summers, 2012) and has a feedback effect on inequality (see Piketty, 2014). Ferrero et al. (2017) have insisted that demography plays a role.

In this context, g^* is also allowed to fall (=0.035). The results are shown in Figure 12.5.

When all these hypotheses are put forward, the average rate of growth becomes smaller, while the rate of unemployment is higher compared to the previous figure.

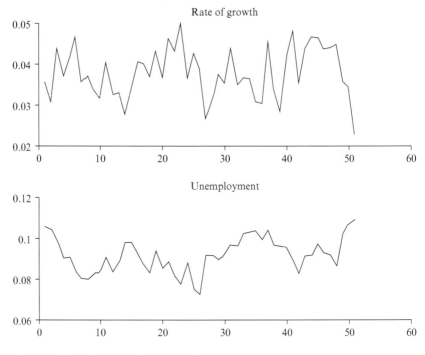

Figure 12.5   A stagnation scenario

12.   POSSIBLE EXTENSIONS

This chapter has analyzed the role that autonomous demand has in stimulating growth in a medium-run perspective within an economy with slack resources. Furthermore, by assuming that the two components of the Harrodian natural rate of growth, namely productivity and labor supply, are endogenously determined, it has linked the instability problem to the so-called reconciliation process, where the presence of a non-accelerating unemployment is maintained.

In the presence of a consumption function where heterogeneous agents have different propensities to consume and income inequality increases with the rate of unemployment, the labor market strengthens the feedback loop between aggregate demand and aggregate supply. In this context, the more flexible the supply response is to aggregate demand dynamics the more the system becomes stable and the dynamics of unemployment bounded. In this context, the complex role of stagnation on unemployment can also be reconsidered, where both supply and demand have a role.

The model, which can shed some light on the recent evolution of the economy, can be extended in several ways. First, the role of policies in reconciling effective demand to potential must be considered, along with the analytical complexity that this situation implies. Second, it would be stimulating to link the theme of technical change with the presence of financial aspects, as Minsky did in a conference organized jointly with the University of Bergamo at Washington University in the mid-1980s.[3] Finally, the perspective of the model can be extended. Beyond the medium run, there are situations where both structures (see Pasinetti, 1981) and institutions (Cynamon and Fazzari, 2016) change.

MATHEMATICAL APPENDIX

The two linearized models in the chapter differ for two fundamental reasons. The first is that the investment function is different. In fact, the specification of the reduced model is obtained by setting $I_3 = 0$ in the extended version

$$i_t = -I_1 v_t + I_2 E g_t - I_3 r_t \qquad (12.1) \text{ bis}$$

Furthermore, the extended version includes the linear equations ranging from (12.11) to (12.14) that are included in the matrices below but are absent in the reduced model.

On the contrary, the following multipliers are common to both versions:

$$C_1 = c_1 - c_3 u_0$$

$$C_2 = c_3 (1 + g_0)$$

$$I_1 = (1 - \delta)$$

$$I_2 = 2v^* (1 + g_0)$$

$$I_3 = (v^* (1 + g_0)^2 - (1 - \delta) v_0) \lambda$$

$$G_1 = G_2 = \frac{(1 + g_0)}{f_0}$$

$$P_1 = \frac{\theta_1}{v_0}$$

$$P_2 = \frac{\theta_1 v_0}{v_0^2}$$

$$GN_1 = \frac{1}{(1 + \tau_0)}$$

$$GN_2 = \frac{(1 + g_0)}{(1 + \tau_0)^2}$$

$$V_1 = \frac{(1 - \delta)}{(1 + g_0)}$$

$$V_2 = \frac{1}{(1 + g_0)}$$

$$V_3 = \left[\frac{v^*(1 - \delta)}{(1 + g_0)^2} + \frac{i_0}{(1 + g_0)^2} \right]$$

$$U_1 = 1$$

$$U_2 = \left[\frac{1 - u_0}{(1 + \sigma_0)^2} - \frac{(1 - u_0)(\sigma_0 - gN_0)}{(1 + \sigma_0)^2} \right]$$

$$U_3 = \frac{1 - u_0}{1 + \sigma_0}$$

$$r_1 = \frac{1}{1 + \pi_0}$$

$$r_2 = \frac{1 + R_0}{(1 + \pi_0)^2}$$

where the subscript 0 stands for the steady state value.

Given the values of these multipliers, the linear system is represented in the following matrix:

$$
\begin{pmatrix}
1 & 0 & 0 & 0 & 0 & 0 & 0 & 0 & 0 & 0 & 0 \\
-C1 & 1 & 0 & C2 & 0 & 0 & 0 & 0 & c3 & 0 & 0 \\
-I2 & 0 & 1 & I3 & 0 & 0 & 0 & 0 & 0 & -I1 & 0 \\
0 & 0 & 0 & 1 & G2 & 0 & 0 & 0 & 0 & 0 & 0 \\
0 & 1 & 1 & 0 & 1 & 0 & 0 & 0 & 0 & 0 & 0 \\
0 & 0 & 0 & 0 & 0 & 1 & 0 & 0 & 0 & 0 & 0 \\
0 & 0 & 0 & 0 & 0 & 0 & 1 & 0 & 0 & 0 & 0 \\
0 & 0 & 0 & -GN1 & 0 & GN2 & 0 & 1 & 0 & 0 & 0 \\
0 & 0 & 0 & 0 & 0 & 0 & -U2 & U3 & 1 & 0 & 0 \\
0 & 0 & 0 & V3 & 0 & 0 & 0 & 0 & 0 & 1 & 0 \\
0 & 0 & 0 & 0 & 0 & -GS2 & -GS1 & 0 & 0 & 0 & 1
\end{pmatrix}
\begin{pmatrix}
Eg_t \\ c_t \\ i_t \\ g_t \\ f_t \\ \tau \\ \sigma_t \\ gN_t \\ u_t \\ v_t \\ g_t^s
\end{pmatrix}
=
$$

$$
\begin{pmatrix}
\alpha & 0 & 0 & (1-\alpha) & 0 & 0 & 0 & 0 & 0 & 0 & 0 \\
0 & 0 & 0 & 0 & 0 & 0 & 0 & 0 & 0 & 0 & 0 \\
0 & 0 & 0 & 0 & 0 & 0 & 0 & 0 & 0 & 0 & 0 \\
0 & 0 & 0 & 0 & G1 & 0 & 0 & 0 & 0 & 0 & 0 \\
0 & 0 & 0 & 0 & 0 & 0 & 0 & 0 & 0 & 0 & 0 \\
0 & 0 & \theta1 & 0 & 0 & 0 & 0 & 0 & 0 & 0 & 0 \\
0 & 0 & 0 & 0 & 0 & 0 & 0 & 0 & -\rho_1 & 0 & 0 \\
0 & 0 & 0 & 0 & 0 & 0 & 0 & 0 & 0 & 0 & 0 \\
0 & 0 & 0 & 0 & 0 & 0 & 0 & 0 & U1 & 0 & 0 \\
0 & 0 & V2 & 0 & 0 & 0 & 0 & 0 & 0 & V1 & 0 \\
0 & 0 & 0 & 0 & 0 & 0 & 0 & 0 & 0 & 0 & 0
\end{pmatrix}
\begin{pmatrix}
Eg_{t-1} \\
c_{t-1} \\
i_{t-1} \\
g_{t-1} \\
f_{t-1} \\
\tau_{t-1} \\
\sigma_{t-1} \\
gN_t \\
u_{t-1} \\
v_{t-1} \\
g^s_{t-1}
\end{pmatrix}
$$

The system can be written in a matrix form:

$$Ax_t = Bx_{t-1}$$

In a more compact way, the system becomes:

$$x_t = Dx_{t-1}$$

where $D = A^{-1}B$.

Furthermore, if one chooses ρ_1 as a bifurcation parameter, the derivatives of the roots with respect to this parameter are not null and in general the conditions set by the Hopf (Neimark–Sacker) theorem are respected so that limit cycles are generated. The further conditions necessary to study their stability are discussed by Kuznetsov (2004).

NOTES

1. The theoretical impact of endogenous technical change on growth and distribution has been examined by Tavani and Zamparelli (2017).
2. The only exception is that $v^* = 0.75$ and $\xi = 2$ becomes $v^* = 1.07$ and $\xi = 1.7$.
3. The proceedings of this conference never got published; likewise, its off-springs did not get dispersed. Minsky later on went back to the necessity of linking the evolutionary ideas of Schumpeter with the state of aggregate demand and finance (1988). Also Dosi, one of the speakers, continued to work on the subject by referring to the so-called agent-based methodology (see Dosi et al., 2012).

13. Heterogeneity in the labor market

1. UNEMPLOYMENT AND HETEROGENEITY

In the previous chapters unemployment has been studied within a medium-run growth perspective. The double link underlying these two has been analyzed and an Okun's stylized fact has been generated, the relationship between the two variables being negative.

The benchmark growth model refers to work carried out by the following triad of authors: Harrod, for the dual presence of a warranted rate of growth and a natural rate one; Hicks, for the presence of ceiling and floors; and Minsky, for his reinterpretation of these constraints. Within this model, the role of an endogenous labor supply and of technical progress in influencing unemployment has been deepened.

In this model, the rate of unemployment plays the classical role of the Marxian reserve army that provides a resource for growth. In the above context, wages do not appear directly. They are incorporated into the price equations, which means that they fundamentally grow with productivity, while the markup in the price equation is sensitive to the economic conditions. In this sense, the neutral hypothesis on money wages is compatible with changing labor share.

This hypothesis is not only a technical assumption, but as Minsky stressed, implies the presence of a particular institutional environment where special rules are applied and certain conventions followed. These rules and conventions influence the impact of the thwarting forces on the working of the whole system.

These aspects deserve some more attention. However, before dealing with them, it is important to consider the implications that heterogeneity in the labor market can have on unemployment. Let us start from the literature.

2. A REVIEW OF THE LITERATURE

In reviewing the literature that studies the double link between growth and unemployment, on the one hand, and aggregate versus structural unemployment, on the other, Harrod's (1939) contribution remains the starting point. His analysis is important not so much because it tried to solve the problems we are dealing with, but because it helps in explaining the evolution of the various attempts that characterized the literature later on and offers hints at the solution of the problems.

Harrod's analysis both presents an interaction between aggregate demand and aggregate supply and contemplates the presence of unemployment. However, his analysis is beset by two problems: the interaction can generate instability, while unemployment can be unbounded because of the lack of reconciliation between the rate of growth of the product market (i.e. the so-called warranted rate of growth) and the one characterizing supply and the labor market, that is, the natural rate of growth.

The following literature has put more emphasis on the reconciliation problem. In this perspective, the neo-Keynesian school has tried to endogenize the saving rate via changes in income distribution (see Kaldor, 1957 and Pasinetti, 1962), while the neoclassical school has insisted on the adjusting role of technology driven by changes in relative prices (see Solow, 1956). In both cases, full employment is a basic characteristic of these models.

The strategy to introduce unemployment into growth followed different paths. On the one hand, Goodwin (1967) inserted unemployment into a classical growth cycle model, where changes in income distribution and the reserve army of unemployment played a crucial role. On the other, the new growth theories, and in particular those of Schumpeterian inspiration, have also introduced another kind of unemployment into the system. Aghion and Howitt (1998), for instance, use a search model of equilibrium unemployment where growth arises from the introduction of new technologies that require labor reallocation for their implementation. The working of the model is based upon two opposite mechanisms that can generate a bounded rate of unemployment: the capitalization effect, "whereby an increase in growth raises the capitalised returns from creating jobs and consequently reduces the equilibrium rate of unemployment", and the creative destruction effect, "whereby an increase in growth reduces the duration of a job match, thereby raising the equilibrium level of unemployment" (Aghion and Howitt, 1998, p.477).

However, both these theories, along with the many contributions that refined the original approaches, suffer from one-sidedness. In fact, the role of aggregate demand is almost totally absent. An exception is the contribution by Dosi et al. (2012), who innovate the Schumpeterian approach by introducing an explicit role for aggregate demand. Furthermore, they refer to a bottom-up methodology derived from an agent-based model (ABM). This convergence of results deserves special attention.

3. UNEMPLOYMENT IN AN AGENT-BASED MODEL (ABM)

Delli Gatti et al. (2015) have put forward a study of the labor market in general, and of unemployment in particular, based upon an ABM. The principles of the technique underlying these models are well known (see Delli Gatti et al., 2011). Some, however, are worth mentioning.

The first is that the aggregate economic system is more than the algebraic sum of the microeconomic decisions of rational agents. This statement constitutes a direct attack on the so-called microfoundation of macroeconomics.

The second principle states that microeconomic decentralized interactions take place out-of-equilibrium. In a sense, this is largely in the same vein as the approach suggested by Clower (1965) and Barro and Grossman (1971).

Third, market economies are interpreted as complex adaptive systems, where bounded-rational agents take decisions within an environment that they contribute to creating.

Finally, these micro decisions produce the emergence of unintended aggregate outcomes, which in turn feed back on the individual behavior (downward causation).

These principles have been applied to the labor market. This implies that "the stylised facts of the labour market have to be conceived as emergent properties of the system as a whole and must be explained at a higher level (the macroeconomic system) than that of individual purposive actions" (Delli Gatti et al., 2015, p.117).

Since search theory is applied to three interconnected markets – labor, consumption goods and credit – this implies that there are two differences with respect to the traditional theory (see Diamond, 1982 and Pissarides, 1990): it goes beyond the partial equilibrium approach and is cast in dynamic terms.

However, there are subtle differences even when they use the same concept. In fact, the matching process used in the canonical theories is different from that used by the ABM, where no matching function is operative. As is well known, the matching function is an analytical device that couples agents on the two sides of the market in the search-and-matching models of the labor market. In the ABM, on the contrary, search is not only costly but the firms that the searcher can visit are limited and can change at random, so that the network structure is continuously evolving over time, even though the number of firms is constant.

This search model is inserted into a general disequilibrium model, where agents interact on three interconnected markets: labor, consumption goods and credit. These markets are dominated by two kinds of uncertainty: between markets and within markets. This induces the fixing of prices and wages by rules of thumb, while at the same time producing a lack of coordination, generating an excess of supply and therefore unemployment.

Within this context, the canonical stylized facts characterizing the labor market are generated. In fact, both a Phillips curve and an Okun curve are generated as emergent properties of the system. Furthermore, a Beveridge curve, showing a negative relationship between the rate of vacancies (approximated by the ratio between the number of job openings and the labor force at the beginning of the period) and the rate of unemployment, is also generated.

The model also replicates regularities concerning job flows:

1. Layoffs (i.e. job destruction) and hiring (job creation) have a strong positive correlation both in levels and in differences.
2. Layoffs show higher volatility and are more correlated to unemployment than hiring, suggesting that production downscaling might be the major force behind unemployment fluctuations.

This a typical Keynesian result generated by a complex model where there are interactions between deterministic and stochastic elements that can only be studied by means of simulations. In this perspective, it is also important to mention the results of some experiments, illustrated in Table 13.1.

If the number of workers applications, which captures the market rigidities due to search costs and defines the size of the individual labor market, is decreased, path-dependency in the labor market increases.

If the labor market becomes more flexible by reducing the duration of contract, the economy is characterized on average by higher levels of unemployment and lower output, revealing the presence of coordination failure on a grand scale due to aggregate demand spillover.

Finally, a greater nominal wage flexibility leads to higher rate of unemployment, lower gross domestic product (GDP) and lower inflation. As stressed by Delli Gatti et al. (2015):

Table 13.1   The results of Monte Carlo experiments

Increase	Path-dependency	Unemployment	GDP	Inflation
Rigidity	+			
Job duration		+	−	
Wage flexibility		+	−	−

higher wage flexibility produces two contrasting effects: on one hand, as signalled by the lower inflation rate and firm default rate, it allows firms to reduce the wage bill, and thus costs, when facing periods of weak demand, but, on the other hand it reduces workers' income and depresses aggregate demand, offsetting the positive effect exerted on the supply side. (p. 128)

It follows that within this model unemployment is essentially an aggregate demand problem and not due to labor market frictions. Furthermore, the conventional wisdom of insisting on flexibility is also rejected because it can generate a negative impact.

4. A SIMPLER MODEL FOR THE FLOWS

Some of the results described in the ABM can be replicated by referring to a simpler model, which can be named macro top-down (see Chapter 8). Let us define vacancies as the difference between some desired level of employment and the level of last year's actual employment:[1]

$$V_t = N_t^* - N_{t-1}$$

If one divides through by N_{t-1}, one gets:

$$v_t = \frac{N_t^*}{N_{t-1}} - 1 \tag{13.1}$$

Let us define the rate of growth of desired employment as a function of the rate of growth of demand (g) and the rate of growth of steady state productivity (marked by 0).

$$gN_t^* = \frac{(1 + g_t)}{(1 + \tau_0)} - 1 \tag{13.2}$$

The hiring rate is defined in the following way:

$$h_t = h_0 + \lambda_1(v_t - v_0) \tag{13.3}$$

The firing rate is given by:

$$fir_t = \frac{\tau_t}{1 + \tau_t} \tag{13.4}$$

The rate of growth of actual employment is given by:

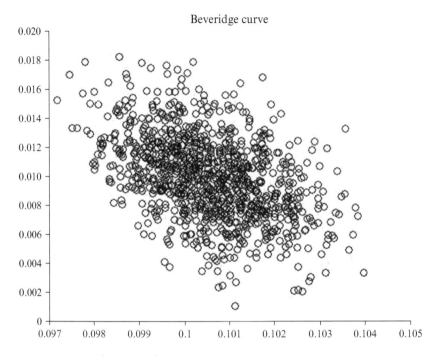

Figure 13.1   The Beveridge curve

$$gN_t = h_t - fir_t \tag{13.5}$$

The rate of growth of labor supply and the rate of unemployment are defined as in the previous chapters:

$$\sigma_t = \sigma_0 - \rho_1(u_{t-1} - u_0) \tag{13.6}$$

$$u_t = 1 - (1 - u_{t-1})\frac{(1 + gN_t)}{(1 + \sigma_t)} \tag{13.7}$$

Finally, g_t and τ_t are driven by a stochastic variable normally distributed.

The system can generate a Beveridge curve (see Figure 13.1) – where v_t and u_t are, respectively, on the y and x axis – even though no matching function has been assumed.

In this case, the value of the correlation is negative and equal to 0.40.[2]

This value increases with the values of λ_1 and ρ_1 and is stronger the higher the volatility of the rate of growth is with respect to that of productivity.

5.   FLOWS IN A GROWTH MODEL

The previous model can be inserted into an endogenous growth model, like the ones discussed in Chapter 11. In this case, only equation (13.2) is modified, in the following way:

$$N_t^* = \frac{(1 + Eg_t)}{(1 + \tau_0)}$$ (13.2) bis

The model has been simplified by ignoring the dynamics of prices. In this case, the same parameters have been used (while λ_1 has been set equal to 0.01), while dropping those relating to the variables that have been ignored. The dynamics of the system are illustrated in Figure 13.2.

The implicit assumption of the model is that firing takes place in those firms where there has been an increase in productivity, while hiring takes place in those expanding demand. This is the top-down part of the model. Macro considerations affect behavior and this feedbacks on the system.

In fact, assume that the equation describing firing is modified in the following way:

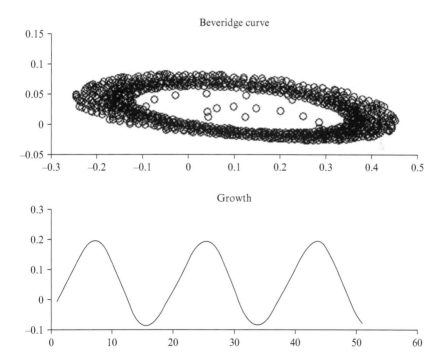

Figure 13.2   The Beveridge curve in a growth model

$$fir_t = \xi_1 \frac{\tau_t}{1 + \tau_t} \qquad \qquad (13.4) \text{ bis}$$

In other words, there is less flexibility in the model. The impact on the system is not reflected so much in the Beveridge curve that replicates the result of Figure 13.2. The difference is in the shape of the growth pattern. In the case of a smaller value of ξ_1, fluctuations are less volatile. This result is also in keeping with that obtained by Delli Gatti et al. (2015) with the ABM, which can be considered complementary to the approach followed in this chapter.

6. TWO CAVEATS

The results of the previous analysis give rise to two caveats. The first concerns the role of flexibility. Within the hypotheses of the model, flexibility may imply instability.

However, it is well known that many a concept in economics plays a double role. Flexibility may be destabilizing, but at the same time it can create an environment more favorable to technical change. In the previous analysis this effect has been ignored, and this is also true for Delli Gatti et al. (2015).

When both aspects are considered the results become more complex. This conclusion is strengthened if one also considers human capital, another aspect totally neglected so far.

This is the second caveat. In fact, technical change destroys old human capital, while it may stimulate the formation of a new one, within a broader Schumpeterian perspective. In this case, both the level of unemployment and the mismatches between aggregate demand and aggregate supply become important. These changes affect the role of the so-called thwarting forces, as has been seen with information technology and globalization.

7. THREE DISTINCT PROBLEMS

In the analysis of Part IV, there emerged three kinds of unemployment that are worth distinguishing:

1. unemployment in a strict sense;
2. structural unemployment or unemployment due to mismatches;
3. hidden unemployment, in the sense that it appears as a fall in the participation rate.

In chapters 11 and 12, unemployment was the result of two opposing forces: the rate of growth on the one hand, and the productivity growth on the other. These forces typically refer to aggregate demand. Labor supply partly depends (negatively) on unemployment. It follows that it mainly covers type 1 and partially type 3.

A more detailed analysis of technical change in Chapter 12 stressed the importance of type 2.

The three kinds of unemployment are distinct even though they are not independent. This raises many problems when policy and institutions are devised in order to tackle the problem.

A low level of employment, not necessarily accompanied by a higher rate of unemployment, is probably closer to a state of poverty of the population. The chances of getting employed are so low that people are discouraged from looking for a job and from declaring themselves as unemployed. Since these people do not disappear, they live in a state of poverty.

Unemployment is a source of inequality and poverty. This is exactly the dimension considered by Minsky in his *Ending Poverty: Jobs, Not Welfare* (2013). It is worth considering.

8. JOBS, NOT WELFARE

The articles collected by the Levy Economics Institute and edited by Papadimitriou, Kregel and Wray in *Ending Poverty: Jobs, Not Welfare* were written mostly in the 1960s, when the debate on the fight against poverty was high on the agenda of the Kennedy and Johnson administrations.

Four main statements come out of the book. The first is that when there is a serious problem of poverty, this is fundamentally due to the lack of employment. The second is that in this case welfare measures that sustain income, which might be useful in recessionary periods, are not valid because they cannot cope with a long-run problem. Third, in this context, is that those measures directed towards increasing employability might also not work. In fact, this is only the second step of a strategy that must have as the first step the creation of jobs. Last, the State must act as an employer of last resort.

As one can see, the framework is the same as that considered in Part IV of this book, that is, unemployment within a growth perspective. However, the problems are much more simplified for the simple reason that technical change and globalization were far from being present at those times. Given this different context, it is worth deepening the analysis in order to understand whether the measures suggested are both viable and effective.

For the purposes of the present book, it is worth considering whether they help defeat unemployment while at the same time strengthen those thwarting devices that counter instability.

9.   THE EMPLOYER OF LAST RESORT

One of the most urgent priorities is the necessity of defining a full employment target, also named "tight" full employment. Once this target is set, it must be reached by the State acting as an employer of last resort. This would parallel the role of the lender of last resort played by the Federal Reserve. This is the main proposition in Minsky (2013). In other words, there is a conviction that the traditional policies are not effective because their impact is too indirect and therefore either too slow or totally insufficient. Some of these ideas were developed further by Minsky in his 1975 book on Keynes when he discussed the socialization of investment (p. 156), a theme well discussed by Keynes himself and strongly related to the problem we are discussing.

There is no doubt that this policy was pursued during the Great Depression. However, it did not take place during the 1960s, when welfare measures were privileged and when tax reductions started to become the chosen option. It surely did not happen during the Great Recession, when the neo-liberal vision still had a strong tail wind in its favor. On that occasion, after a short period in which fiscal policy intervened heavily, the main pivot was monetary policy with its quantitative easing.

The role of the State as employer of last resort does not seem to have vast support. One might have the impression that this is the result of a radical position held by Minsky in his Berkeley period, when this was the prevailing sentiment. However, even though this objection may have some foundation, it does not cancel the necessity of examining the proposal to a fuller extent.

10.   CHALLENGES

There are four economic challenges that an employer-of-last-resort strategy, similar to that used in the New Deal years, has to face if implemented nowadays.

First, the international environment is different. The economy is open within a context of globalization. This implies that problems of competitiveness must be taken into consideration along with the necessity of increasing the number of jobs. In other words, the trade-off between productivity and number of jobs may have deteriorated.

Second, technical change is much more pervasive nowadays. Even though it is hard to measure its impact on productivity, it is undoubtedly true that the information technology revolution has affected most of the sectors of the economy, shaking the nature of permanent jobs. This implies that there is not only a problem of quantity of jobs but also of quality of job opportunities.

Third, technical change does not have only macro implications on jobs but also deep micro impacts since it affects each employee. And this makes employability a much more serious problem than Minsky thought when he wrote those articles.

The final challenge, considered by Minsky himself, may be the presence of a steeper Phillips curve aggravating the trade-off between inflation and unemployment and so generating the possibility of more frequent business cycle episodes. So far this has not happened, and we do not know what are the respective roles of the Great Recession and the impact of globalization. In spite of that, this challenge cannot be dismissed as irrelevant even though it does not create problems in a short-run perspective.

The alternative strategy of operating only through monetary channels also has many drawbacks. It takes longer to return to pre-crisis levels. Furthermore, it implies increasing inequalities because it tends to inflate capital values. Finally, it does not seem able to counter the erosion of employment brought about by globalization and technical change.

It is also for this reason that policies of job guarantees are being re-proposed (see Tcherneva, 2018). Their implementation within an employer-of-last-resort kind of strategy must find those institutional forms that are in keeping with the new economic environment.

NOTES

1. It is worth stressing the similarity of this definition with that of desired investment given in Chapter 11.
2. The shock has a σ equal to 0.03, while for the τ shock this value is smaller. Furthermore $\lambda_1 = 0.2$, while $\rho_1 = 0.5$.

PART V

The economics of Minsky in a dynamic setting

14. The financial instability hypothesis, inequality and the Great Recession

1. THE FINANCIAL INSTABILITY HYPOTHESIS REVISITED

Even when restricting the analysis to the Great Recession, the amount of literature exploring the causes of this event remains vast.[1] We want to highlight the contribution of Cynamon and Fazzari (2016), who not only put aggregate demand and inequality at the center of the analysis, but have the ambition to create a convincing narrative of the Great Recession. Their analysis is based upon the Minskyan financial instability hypothesis, enriched with inequality considerations (see Bellofiore and Ferri, 2001a, 2001b and Taylor, 2004). As stressed by Fazzari and Greenberg (2015, p. 56):

> The exposition of the "Minsky cycle" usually begins after a financial crisis with high levels of risk aversion among lenders and relatively strong balance sheets among potential borrowers. In this environment decisions to extend credit are more likely to be successful. Validation of new lending encourages more aggressive practices, greater lending and more demand stimulus. Lending and spending evolve into a self-reinforcing boom that pulls output and employment up with it, but the boom is accompanied by rising fragility that ultimately leads to a financial crisis and recession.

The challenge consists in extending this analysis to the housing market and to consumer spending (on these points, see also Lavoie, 2014). However, this attempt by Cynamon and Fazzari is worth considering, the key relationship being that between inequality and finance. In this context, the analysis put forward by Cynamon and Fazzari (2016) is based on the following points:[2]

1. Rising inequality in the personal distribution of income occurred largely due to slower income growth for the bottom 95 percent.
2. Instead of cutting consumption, these people increased their debt/income ratio.
3. This was possible because of changes in the credit market.

4. The overall process generated unsustainable dynamics that caused the Great Recession.
5. The ensuing de-leveraging helps explain the presence of headwinds to growth.

These points are worth considering and deserve deepening, both methodologically and analytically. In particular, they must be cast into dynamic terms that allow the existence of complex patterns (see Setterfield et al., 2016 and Ryoo, 2016).

2.   THE CONSUMER AGE

The increase in consumer expenditures and the historic increase in household debt that took place in the US led Cynamon and Fazzari (2008) to label the period from the 1980s to the eve of the Great Recession the "Consumer Age". In fact, during this period, real personal consumption expenditures rose at an annual rate of 3.4 percent while all other components of demand expanded at 2.5 percent (see Fazzari and Greenberg, 2015).

In this period, two relevant stylized facts became relevant. The first is that the US experienced strong growth relative to other advanced countries, while recessions were milder with respect to the past. This period is also known as the "Great Moderation". The second is that a substantial upward movement in households' debt/income ratios replaced the steady ratio of the previous period (see Cynamon et al., 2013).

Three themes deserve further exploration. The first concerns stylized facts. In fact, the centrality of household debt that characterized the Great Recession is a stylized fact that was not present in the Great Depression, when the importance of firms' indebtedness was prevalent. The second refers to the role that inequality has had on this process. And finally, the third concerns the impact on the financial instability hypothesis.

All these seem to challenge Minsky's financial instability hypothesis in its primitive form. The first one is a challenge stemming from empirical data. The second implies the need to consider explicitly elements that are included in Minsky's black box of tools. To further open this black box was the main objective of Part IV of the book.

3.   THE ROLE OF INEQUALITY

As has been shown by Ferri (2016), the analytical framework within which inequality has been studied is very much supply oriented. This is true not only of Piketty's (2014) benchmark work, but also of those contributions, such as that put forward by Stiglitz (2015), that tried to overcome some of the limitations of the French author's analysis. Once aggregate demand is brought back to the forefront to achieve an integrated framework, instability and more complex endogenous dynamics cannot be ignored.

In what follows, the focus is on consumption expressed in terms of heterogeneous sources of personal income. In more detail, there is a basic heterogeneity where households are classified according to their source of income: labor or capital. This classical dichotomy is reinforced by the presence of wealth.

There are four forces at work in this particular subsystem underlying the macro result. The first is that households with labor income try to keep up with the consumption of wealthy people. Second, in so doing, they can get indebted. Third, this depends on the debt service and the state of the economy. Finally, there are common factors behind the two groups of people that may evolve in time.

As shown in Ferri (2016), the role of inequality depends not only on its impact on aggregate demand, but also on the phenomena which accompany it (the presence of household indebtedness) and the reaction of the whole system. In other words, the partial effects measured by the differences in the propensity to consume must be combined with the system effects deriving from the remaining part of the model.

The interaction of these forces can generate endogenous complex dynamics. Some lessons from the recent events characterizing the economy can be learned, while an evolutionary perspective can produce different scenarios within which the aftermath of the crisis can be considered. However, before facing these problems, it is legitimate to ask what the impact is on the financial instability hypothesis.

4. FINANCE AND CREDIT SUPPLY

A variety of technological, institutional and policy changes increased the credit flow to US households, especially mortgage lending. This is very important because it allowed the increase in consumer spending. According to Fazzari and Greenberg (2015, p. 56):

> Innovations in both information technology and the ability to share electronic information made possible the individual score. The standardized measure improved household access to credit. It also facilitated securitization of household loans because they could now be viewed as a generic commodity rather than the outcome of the personal relationship between borrower and lender.

The increasing values of housing also made the value of the collateral grow, and this meant that the credit lines had a lower cost, partly because of the tax benefit. Furthermore, it stimulated the so-called second mortgages that favored non-housing expenditures. It was easy for homeowners to refinance their mortgage, and this became a regular habit, so contributing to increasing the debt ratio.

This change of paradigm could not have happened were it not for the process of innovation that has invested in the financial sector. The process of liberalization of this market can only be understood within the globalization of the economy that took place and that strengthened capital mobility across the world. Furthermore, this process has also ignited a financialization of the economy, where the presence of derivative, sub-prime contracts and new rules for approving mortgages have contributed to providing finance at a cheap price. Finally, one has to stress that many of these processes took place in the shadow banking system, as Minsky had taught.

5.   THE AFTERMATH

The Great Recession has been characterized by at least four stylized facts, including greater duration, higher volatility, a jobless recovery and difficulty generating high rates of growth in the aftermath. Many factors have been identified by the literature as far as this last fact is concerned. Given the particular role that financial aspects have played in the Great Recession, de-leveraging ranks high among the explanations. This has been underlined not only by Cynamom and Fazzari (2016), but has also been stressed by many other authors (see, for instance, Lo and Rogoff, 2015).

There is also the role of the so-called investment hangover (Rognlie et al., 2014). This feature is not typical of the Great Recession only, but can accompany any kind of bubble.

Uncertainty has been mentioned too. This is a typical Keynesian aspect that was translated into risk during the canonical business cycles but has assumed a stronger resemblance to Knight's (1921) definition in recent times. Uncertainty particularly hinges upon investment and is influenced by the presence of structural transformation at the world level, erratic economic policies and geo-political risks.

Finally, the presence of a floor to the nominal rate of interest (see Eggertsson and Mehrotra, 2014, Krugman, 2013 and Schmitt-Grohé and Uribe, 2012) has also been mentioned. This introduces the role of economic policy explicitly into the analysis and at the same time re-opens the thesis of secular stagnation. In fact, the presence of a zero bound on the nominal rate of interest can cause a natural rate of interest, that is, the short-term real rate of interest consistent with full employment according to Summers (2013), to be negative. If this state of affairs persists, then the long-lasting slump hypothesis can be brought back.

If the extrapolation of these effects to a secular tendency seems to be unwarranted, this does not imply that they cannot affect the economy for a period longer than the short run, by interacting with the structural forces underlying the process of increasing inequality pre-existing the Great Recession, as will be underlined in the next chapter.

6. BORROWING AND EMULATION EFFECTS IN THE CONSUMPTION FUNCTION

In order to deepen the analysis, one can start immediately with a specification expressed in intensive form. In other words, c_t is defined as current consumption (in real terms) deflated by last year's output:

$$c_t = \frac{C_t}{Y_{t-1}}$$

Given the above definition (see also Minsky, 1982), the following specification is suggested (see Ferri, 2016):[3]

$$c_t = c* + \frac{(1 + \lambda_t)}{(1 + g_{t-1})}(1 + \theta_0)(c_\pi \alpha_{t-1} + c_\beta \beta_{t-1}) \tag{14.1}$$

It is a consumption function based upon heterogeneity. In fact, the richest part of the society has a consumption propensity that heavily depends on profit share (α) and the wealth ratio (β), while the remaining part tries to consume a proportion of it, labeled θ_0. According to Landis and Gladstone (2017), these consumers are called "extroverts", and they are more so the lower the percentile they occupy on the scale of income percentile. It follows that θ_0 heavily depends on income inequality. Finally, there are the "introverts" that consume a fixed proportion $c*$.

The variable λ_t is a function of the following type:

$$\lambda_t = \lambda_1 - \lambda_2 \left(\frac{R_r d_{t-1}}{1 - \alpha_{t-1}} - \frac{R_0 d_0}{1 - \alpha_0} \right) \tag{14.2}$$

The parameter λ_1 reflects the rate of growth of credit expansion,[4] while λ_2 represents a self-correcting mechanism at work. If the ratio of interest paid on debt ($R_t d_t$) as a share of wage income rises with respect to its steady state value (indicated by 0), the value of λ_t diminishes.

7. DEBT AND WEALTH

Debt arises within wage earners (Auclert and Rognlie, 2018 and Mian and Sufi, 2018). It does not impact on profit earners. It follows that their wealth ratio is simply equal to the capital/output ratio since capital gains are excluded in the present model (see Ferri, 2016 for a different hypothesis).

It follows that:

$$\beta_t = v_t \tag{14.3}$$

The dynamics of debt depend on both a macro inequality (i.e. the ratio of capital share vis-à-vis the labor share) and a personal distribution inequality governing consumption. Rich wage earners are "introverts" and have a constant propensity to consume (c^*). They pay interest that increases debt and therefore impacts on c_t via λ_t.

Debts are financed by the banking system, which uses profit as a safety cushion. (This operation remains in the background in the present chapter.) The debt ratio (d_t) evolves according the following equation:

$$d_t = \frac{d_{t-1}(1+R_t)}{(1+\pi_{t-1})(1+g_{t-1})} + c^* + \frac{(1+\lambda_t)\theta_0}{(1+g_{t-1})}(c_\pi\alpha_{t-1} + c_\beta v_{t-1}) - (1-\alpha_{t-1}) \tag{14.4}$$

From this equation, it turns out that the greater the labor share, the smaller is the debt ratio. Furthermore, the presence of the inflation rate in the denominator (π_t) and the simultaneous presence of the nominal rate of interest in the numerator remind us that nominal values have been deflated by the current period nominal value of the output.

From the accumulation equation, the capital/output ratio dynamics evolve according to the formula

$$v_t = v_{t-1}\frac{(1+\delta)}{(1+g_{t-1})} + i_t \tag{14.5}$$

In other words, the capital/output ratio is variable, and this implies that the Kaleckian mechanism of adjustment based upon capacity utilization is at work.

8.   A RECURSIVE DYNAMIC MODEL

To obtain a dynamic model, the above equations must be inserted into a larger framework. The first step consists in introducing the equilibrium conditions between aggregate demand and aggregate supply:[5]

$$g_t = c_t + i_t - 1 \qquad (14.6)$$

Since consumption has already been specified, the investment ratio has to be considered. It has been specified in the following way:

$$i_t = i_{t-1} + \gamma_1 \left\{ E_t r_t - \left[\left(\frac{(1+R_t)}{(1+\pi_t)} \right) - 1 \right] + \eta_0 \right\} + \gamma_2 (g_{t-1} - g_0) \quad (14.7)$$

This specification is a generalization of the accelerator formula because it introduces the gap between profit and the real rate of interest, given a given risk premium (η_0) (see Taylor, 2004). Profit expectations are given by the usual adaptive formula:

$$E_t r_t = (1 - \rho_1) r_{t-1} + \rho_1 r_0 \qquad (14.8)$$

The profit share has been assumed to be a pro-cyclical function of the rate of growth:

$$\alpha_t = \alpha_0 + \mu_1 (g_{t-1} - g_0) \qquad (14.9)$$

while the rate of profit is measured by:

$$r_r = \frac{\alpha_t}{p_{k,0} v_t} - \delta \qquad (14.10)$$

where $p_{k,0}$ is the steady state value of the relative price of capital with respect to the general price of goods.

The inflation rate is represented by an equation à la Phillips of the type

$$\pi_t = \pi^* + \varphi_1 (\pi_{t-1} - \pi_0) - \varphi_2 (u_{t-1} - u_0) \qquad (14.11)$$

where π^* is the target rate of inflation, and the subscript 0 refers to the steady state value. The nominal rate of interest is determined according to a (simplified) Taylor equation of the type:

$$R_t = R^* + \psi_1 (\pi_t - \pi_0) \qquad (14.12)$$

For given productivity, unemployment evolves according to the following equation:

$$u_t = u_{t-1} - (1 - u_{t-1}) \frac{1 + g_t}{1 + \sigma_t}$$ (14.13)

The rate of growth of labor supply is given by:

$$g_{\sigma_t} = \zeta_1 - \zeta_2 u_{t-1}$$ (14.14)

A dynamic and recursive system of 14 equations in 14 unknowns (π_t, R_t, Er_t, i_t, λ_t, c_t, g_t, d_t, v_t, β_t, α_t, r_t, σ_t, and u_t) is obtained.

9.   SIMULATIONS

The model is recursive, and its dynamics can be simulated starting from a steady state situation, disturbed by a one-period stochastic shock to the investment equation. The dynamics are illustrated in Figure 14.1.
The parameters that have been used are shown in Table 14.1.

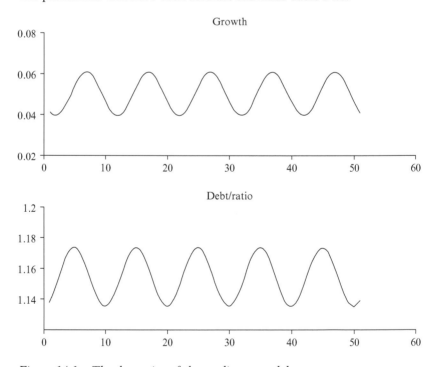

Figure 14.1   The dynamics of the nonlinear model

Table 14.1   The values of the parameters, exogenous variables and steady states

$\varphi_1 = 0.80$; $\varphi_2 = 0.20$	$g^* = 0.04$
$\psi_1 = 1.6$	$v^* = 1.5$; $\delta = 0.1565$
$\gamma_1 = 1.318$; $\gamma_2 = 1.3$; $\rho_1 = 0.1$	$d_0 = 0.9767$; $c^* = 0.15$
$c_\pi = 0.15$; $c_\beta = 0.05$; $\xi_1 = 0.106$ $\xi_2 = 1.1$; $\lambda_2 = 1.095$; $\lambda_1 = g^*$	$R_0 = 0.03$ $\alpha_0 = 4.30$; $\pi_0 = 0.005$

Figure 14.1 shows the last 50 runs of a simulation of 10 000 periods. Three points are worth underlining. The first is that there is both acceleration and deceleration that do not lead to runaway situations. On the contrary, and this is the second point, the dynamics fluctuate endogenously within bounds. The third point is that this is the result of nonlinearities and thwarting forces and not of the presence of physical bounds.

The model refers essentially to a deflationary environment where inflation fluctuates around a very low rate. In this context, the dynamics are driven by consumption, fueled by emulative effects and borrowing. Investment generates further dynamics that depend on two loops: the rate of profit and inflation. The overall dynamics can remain bounded, according to the values of the parameters.

In this framework, there is a positive correlation between the debt ratio and growth. This seems to be more in keeping with Minsky (1986a) than with Steindl (1952), as illustrated by Lavoie (2014). It is worth stressing that this result depends on both the specification of the model and the values of the parameters used.

10. LINEARIZING THE MODEL

The system can be linearized around its steady state values. Both the steady state and the multipliers are shown in the Appendix at the end of this chapter. The system can be written in the following way, where all the variables represent deviations from steady state values:

$$\pi_t = \varphi_1 \pi_{t-1} - \varphi_2 u_{t-1} \tag{14.15}$$

$$R_t = \psi_1 \pi_t - \psi_2 u_{t-1} \tag{14.16}$$

$$Er_t = (1 - \rho_1)r_{t-1} \tag{14.17}$$

$$i_t = \gamma_1 Er_t - \gamma_1 R_t + \gamma_1 \pi_t + \gamma_2 g_{t-1} \tag{14.18}$$

$$\lambda_t = -L1R_t - L2d_{t-1} + L3\alpha_{t-1} \tag{14.19}$$

$$c_t = C1\alpha_{t-1} + C2v_{t-1} + C3\lambda_t - C4g_{t-1} \tag{14.20}$$

$$g_t = c_t + i_t \tag{14.21}$$

$$d_t = D1d_{t-1} + D2R_t - D3\pi_{t-1} - D4g_{t-1} + D5\alpha_{t-1} + D6v_{t-1} + D7\lambda_t \tag{14.22}$$

$$v_t = V1v_{t-1} + i_t - V2g_{t-1} \tag{14.23}$$

$$\beta_t = v_t \tag{14.24}$$

$$\alpha_t = \alpha_1 g_t \tag{14.25}$$

$$r_t = R1\alpha_t - R2v_t \tag{14.26}$$

$$\sigma_t = -\zeta_2 u_{t-1} \tag{14.27}$$

$$u_t = U1u_{t-1} - U2g_t + U3g_{Ns,t} \tag{14.28}$$

This recursive model is a linearization of the previous model. It is composed of first order linear difference equations. It can be put in the following compact matrix form:

$$Ax_t = Bx_{t-1}$$

or

$$x_t = A^{-1}Bx_{t-1}$$

Some eigenvalues of this system are complex conjugate and have unitary modulus, while the remaining are less than 1. Thus the fixed point has a bifurcation analogous to the Neimark bifurcation, with limit cycles being generated (see Kuznetsov, 2004).

The parameters capable of generating a unitary modulus are those given in Table 14.1, with only small changes (in fact, $\gamma_2 = 1.399$).

The signs of their impact on the unitary modulus are shown in Table 14.2

Table 14.2   The impact on the unitary modulus $|\lambda|$ of an increase in the parameter

Parameters	Impact
γ_1	+
γ_2	+
c_π	+
c_β	+
λ_2	−
Φ_1	+
Φ_2	−
ψ_1	−
ξ_2	−
μ_1	+

The changes to the parameters do not alter the nature of the fluctuations, and this is the reason why the model is robust. Furthermore, their impact on the unitary modulus $|\lambda|$ is variegated and in keeping with the results that have been already commented on.

In particular, it is worth stressing that an increase in c_π and c_β makes $|\lambda| > 1$, and this creates bubbles. The reason behind this result is that the emulative effect gets reinforced. On the other hand, an increase in λ_2, which moderates the use of finance, has a stabilizing effect.

11.   THE ROLE OF INCOME DISTRIBUTION

So far a pro-cyclical profit share has been assumed (see also Ferri, 2011 and 2013) along with the presence of an exogenous steady state value of income distribution (α_0) Given the nature of the debt function, a positive correlation between growth and debt has been obtained.

One might wonder whether this result is robust to changes in the nature of the steady state. For instance, α_0 can be assumed to be endogenous. In this case, it is equal to:

$$\alpha_0 = \frac{c_0 - c^* - c_\beta v_0 (1 + \theta_0)}{(1 + \theta_0) c_\pi} \tag{14.29}$$

While the debt equation remains the same (see Appendix):

$$d_0 = \frac{c^* + \theta_0\Gamma - (1 - \alpha_0)}{\Delta}$$ (14.30)

where

$$\Gamma = c_\pi\alpha_0 + c_\beta v_0$$

$$\Delta = 1 - \frac{(1 + R_0)}{(1 + \pi_0)(1 + g_0)}$$

Three observations are worth making at this stage of the analysis. First, the dynamics of the model are the same as that obtained with an exogenous steady state value of the profit share and the correlation between g and d remains positive. It must be stressed that this is a system result. It depends on both the behavior of consumers and the reaction of the system. In turn, this depends on the overall nature of the model, the specification of the equations and the values of the parameters. For instance, an increase in λ_2 causes the correlation to increase. It follows that the behavior of consumers matters, but the sign of the correlation depends on the nature of the overall model. It also follows that the comparison with Steindl's results cannot be reduced to a different micro–macro foundation.

Second, the endogeneity of α_0 allows the presence of an exogenous θ_0 that measures the degree of "emulation" in the consumption function. When it increases, the instability of the model grows, given the parameters shown in Table 14.1. Finally, equations (14.29) and (14.30) show the limitations that changes in the values of the parameters cannot violate in order to obtain meaningful results.

12. POSSIBLE EVOLUTION OF THE SYSTEM

It is very important to understand whether the dynamics of the system can be changed. In other words, it is essential to investigate which changes can be considered in order to modify the evolution of the system. To pursue this aim, two changes are needed. The first one consists in referring to a multi-purpose strategy. The second one implies the need for modifications in the structure of the model.

As far as the first is concerned, two changes are put forward. On the one hand, the degree of inequality in the system, measured at both the macro

Table 14.3 Different evolutions of the system

Parameters	New values	$|\lambda|$	Problems
$g^* = 0.04$	$g^* = 0.03$	$|0.9204|$	Debt explosion
$\alpha_0 = 0.40$	$\alpha_0 = 0.35$	$|1.028|$	Explosion
$c^* = 0.15$	$c^* = 0.18$	$|1.0079|$	Explosion
$\theta_0 = 3.49$	$\theta_0 = 3.4$	$|\lambda| < 1$	α_0 increases

and the micro level, is reduced. In other words, the values of α_0 and θ_0 are decreased. On the other hand, the rate of growth of financial support is also reduced.

To verify the impact of these changes, the model must undergo some changes. First, c^* is endogenized so that its steady state value is given by the following expression:

$$c^* = c_0 - (1 + \theta_0)\Gamma \qquad (14.31)$$

With this modification, both α_0 and θ_0 can change since they have become exogenous variables. In particular, the values of $g^* = 0.03$(ex 0.04), $\alpha_0 = 0.35$ (0.40) and $\theta_0 = 3$ (3.49) bring about a system where the eigenvalues are still complex conjugate, but they have values which are less than the unitary modulus. In other words, the system asymptotically reaches, by means of smaller fluctuations, a new steady state characterized by a lower but stable rate of growth.[6]

This multi-purpose strategy can be compared with the mono strategies shown in Table 14.3.

None of these strategies seem to be effective. They are based upon the *ceteris paribus* assumption. This implies that the values of all the other variables are supposed to be given. In this perspective, reducing the rate of growth of finance stabilizes the rate of growth but makes the debt explode.

The second strategy, which only reduces the macro inequality, makes the system unstable. The third strategy, which is based upon an increased weight of the "introverts", destabilizes the system. Finally, the last strategy stabilizes the system by reducing the degree of emulation, which is linked to personal income inequality, at the cost of increasing macro differences.

13.   RUNAWAY SITUATIONS

A dynamic model driven by a consumption function based upon two fundamental forces – (1) emulation and (2) financial aspects – has been presented. These two forces presuppose a monetary economy of production marked by inequality in income and wealth. Inserted into a dynamic model, this consumption function can generate complex dynamic patterns, where the possibility of bubbles and runaway situations is indeed very likely. In a sense, it is a generalization of Minsky's financial instability hypothesis.

In this context, the role of the different parameters has been examined. Furthermore, two important issues have been considered. On the one hand, the importance of the behavior of income distribution has been stressed. On the other, the correlation between growth and the debt ratio has also been taken into consideration. The sign of this correlation depends not only on the reactions of the consumer, but also on the properties of the system and the nature of the other components, income distribution being one of the most important.

Finally, the possible evolution of the system has been considered where the reduction of macro and micro inequalities, accompanied by financial moderation, can stabilize the system.

At least two lines of further inquiry can be envisaged. One concerns the supply of credit and the role of the banking system in general, which should be explicitly considered (this is also the recommendation put forward by Fazzari and Greenberg, 2015, p. 56). This attempt would represent some steps towards what Minsky called a process of integration that characterizes a monetary economy of production. The presence of the banking sector will be very important to understand the dynamics of runaway situations, where financial contagion takes place (see Cominetta, 2016) and fire selling becomes a necessity. Without an explicit consideration of this sector, one has to limit its impact on the endogenous changes in the parameters, as Minsky taught in his doctoral dissertation.

A second consists in deepening the interactions between aggregate demand and aggregate supply in order to better understand the evolution of the system (see Dosi et al., 2017). Like the model of Fazzari et al. (2018), the system includes endogenous aggregate demand and endogenous aggregate supply. However, in the present case, productivity is given, and this hypothesis should be dropped if one wants to extend the time horizon of the analysis.

Both of these will be dealt with in the next chapter.

MATHEMATICAL APPENDIX

A1. Calibration and Steady State

The model is calibrated in such a way so as to produce a steady state growth $g_0 = 0.04$ and an inflation rate $\pi_0 = 0.005$. The first result is obtained by putting $g^* = 0.04$ into equation (14.1). From equation (14.5), one obtains:

$$i_0 = \frac{v^*(g^* + \delta)}{(1 + g^*)}$$

From (14.6), one gets:

$$c_0 = g_0 - i_0 + 1$$

From (14.10), one obtains:

$$r_0 = \frac{\alpha_0}{v^*} - \delta$$

Inflation is obtained from equation (14.7), after having defined r_{f0} as the long-run real financial rate of interest (assigned a value of 0.0250; the gap between r_0 and r_{f0} is equal to the risk premium). In this case the steady state inflation rate is equal to:

$$\pi_0 = \frac{(1 + R_0)}{(1 + r_{f0})} - 1$$

Where R_0 is given. From (14.4), one gets:

$$d_0 = \frac{c^* + \theta_0 \Gamma - (1 - \alpha_0)}{\Delta}$$

where

$$\Delta = 1 - \frac{(1 + R_0)}{(1 + \pi_0)(1 + g_0)}$$

From (14.1), one obtains:

$$\theta_0 = \frac{c_1 - c^*}{\Gamma} - 1$$

where

$$\Gamma = c_\pi \alpha_0 + c_\beta v_0$$

In this context

$$u_0 = \frac{\xi_1 - g_0}{\xi_2}$$

A2.　The Multipliers

The multipliers have the following expression (in absolute values).
　For equation (14.19), one has:

$$L1 = \lambda_1 \frac{d_0}{(1 - \alpha_0)}$$

$$L2 = \lambda_2 \frac{R_0}{(1 - \alpha_0)^2}$$

$$L3 = \lambda_2 \frac{R_0 d_0}{(1 - \alpha)^2}$$

For equation (14.20), one has:

$$C1 = c_\pi \frac{(1 + \theta_0)(1 + \lambda_0)}{(1 + g_0)}$$

$$C2 = c_\beta \frac{(1 + \theta_0)(1 + \lambda_0)}{(1 + g_0)}$$

$$C3 = \frac{\Gamma(1 + \theta_0)(1 + \lambda_0)}{(1 + g_0)}$$

$$C4 = \frac{\Gamma(1 + \theta_0)(1 + \lambda_0)}{(1 + g_0)^2}$$

For equation (14.22), one has:

$$D1 = \frac{(1 + R_0)}{(1 + \pi_0)(1 + g_0)}$$

$$D2 = \frac{d_0}{(1 + \pi_0)(1 + g_0)}$$

$$D3 = \frac{d_0(1 + R_0)}{(1 + \pi_0)^2(1 + g_0)}$$

$$D4 = \frac{(1 + \lambda_0)\theta_0}{(1 + g_0)^2}\Gamma + \frac{d_0(1 + R_0)}{(1 + \pi_0)(1 + g_0)^2}$$

$$D5 = \frac{(1 + \lambda_0)\theta_0 c_\pi}{(1 + g_0)} - 1$$

$$D6 = \frac{(1 + \lambda_0)\theta_0 c_\beta}{(1 + g_0)}$$

$$D7 = \frac{\theta_0}{(1 + g_0)^2}\Gamma$$

For equation (14.28), one has:

$$U1 = \frac{1 + g_0}{1 + \sigma_0}$$

$$U2 = \frac{1 - u_0}{1 + \sigma_0}$$

$$U3 = \frac{(1 - u_0)(1 + g_0)}{(1 + \sigma_0)}$$

For equation 14.23, one has:

$$V1 = \frac{1 - \delta}{1 + g0}$$

$$V2 = \frac{v_0(1 - \delta)}{(1 + g_0)^2}$$

Finally, for equation (14.26), one has:

$$R1 = 1/v_0$$

$$R2 = \frac{\alpha_0}{v_0^2}$$

NOTES

1. See Cristini et al. (2015), Ferri (2011), Hall (2011) and Palley (2016). For a survey, see Lavoie (2014).
2. According to Mason (2018), this account is not valid in general, but it is tailored to the period 2002–08, a time span which is central to our research interest.
3. See Setterfield et al. (2016) for a Kaleckian approach.
4. This has been stressed by Keen (2011) and by Stiglitz (2015).
5. Consumption and investment are the only flow variables deflated by last period income Y_{t-1}.
6. The values of the parameters are the same as those in Table 14.1, except $\gamma_1 = 4.2$, $\gamma_2 = 0.7285$, $\lambda_2 = 0.9$.

15. A meta-model of the financial instability hypothesis

1. EXTENDING THE ANALYSIS

If one wants to insert the financial instability hypothesis into a dynamic context and obtain a general model capable of including the specific examples considered so far, one has to refer to the two basic principles on which the financial instability hypothesis is based.

In fact, Minsky (1992) refers to the two principles as "theorems", saying that there are two theorems at the root of the financial instability hypothesis:

> The first theorem. . . is that the economy has financing regimes under which it is stable, and financing regimes in which it is unstable. The second theorem . . . is that over period of prolonged prosperity, the economy transits from financial relations that make for a stable system to financial relations that make for an unstable system. (pp. 7–8)

These two theorems stimulate the consideration of inserting the financial instability hypothesis within a theoretical model based upon regime switching. This approach could be made so general so as to include the cases considered thus far as particular situations. In other words, it could be considered a meta-model with respect to these different specifications. Furthermore, within this framework, new analytical aspects should be considered. In particular, the analysis should be extended in three directions. First, the role of income distribution should be endogenized. An attempt in this direction has been made by Fazzari et al. (2008) and reconsidered in Chapter 14. However, further investigation is needed. Second, expectations should be made to overcome the dichotomy perfect foresight–backwardness. In Chapter 3 we referred to the perfect foresight hypothesis. That is, we made the hypothesis that there is a correlation between expectations and ex-post data. This hypothesis is extreme and is useful only for special environments. However, in an uncertain world it is untenable, and therefore some form of learning must be introduced into the analysis. Finally, the specifications of the various equations should be enriched, starting from the investment equation.

2.   INCOME DISTRIBUTION

We have seen how in the era of the "Great Moderation" the rapid increase in capital share was outstanding. I use the term "capital share" and not simply "profit share" because in this period it was "capital gains" that were a key component, not just because of gains in the Stock Exchange, but also because of the increasing value of land and housing. In a parallel way, the wage share declined. In Chapter 14, we saw how the only way to maintain the level of consumption in spite of the falling wage share was through increasing household debt. In this perspective, investment was driven by profit (in other words, there has been a profit-driven growth, to use the terminology suggested in the literature – see Lavoie, 2014) and supplemented by consumption, sustained by debt. The combination of these forces has contributed to creating potential instability in the real side of the economy.

Two points deserve to be considered. The first is that the forces underlying the pattern of capital share are complex. They include both globalization and the information technology revolution (see Dew-Becker and Gordon, 2005, Guscina, 2006 and McAdam and William, 2008). The second is that this pattern is not an "iron law" and might well change.

In what follows, the profit share has been specified in the following way:

$$\alpha_t = \alpha_0 + \gamma_1 (Eg_t - g_0) \tag{15.1}$$

It stresses a pro-cyclical behavior of the profit share (α).

In this environment, where only firms get indebted, the debt equation also assumes a different specification to that considered in the last chapter:

$$d_t = \frac{d_{t-1} R_{t-1}}{(1 + g_{t-1})(1 + \pi_{t-1})} + \frac{i_{t-1} - \kappa_1 \alpha_{t-1}}{(1 + g_{t-1})} \tag{15.2}$$

In fact, the debt ratio increases with investment and decreases with the profit share, corrected by the parameter κ_1 that represents the retention rate.

3.   LEARNING

A large number of learning devices exist, so one cannot pretend to be exhaustive. However, in what follows, one particular learning technique will be presented. Let us assume that agents do not have a complete knowledge of the model and therefore use simple rules to forecast the future output growth and inflation. We suppose, as is done in De Grauwe (2008), that the agents can be either optimistic or pessimistic (see also Chapter 9). The optimists' forecast is given by the following relationship:

$$\overline{E}_t^{opt} g_{t+1} = g_{2,t}^*$$

In other words, they expect that a bigger rate of growth is always prevailing. On the other hand, the pessimists forecast a smaller rate, which can even be negative:

$$\overline{E}_t^{pess} g_{t+1} = g_{1,t}^*$$

The market forecast is obtained as a weighted average of these two forecasts, that is:

$$\overline{E}_t g_{t+1} = \alpha_{opt,t}\, \overline{E}_t^{opt} g_{t+1} + \alpha_{pess,t}\, \overline{E}_t^{pess} g_{t+1}$$

$$\alpha_{opt,t} + \alpha_{pess,t} = 1 \tag{15.3}$$

Following Brock and Hommes (1997), a selection mechanism is introduced. In fact, agents compute the forecast performance by referring to the mean squared forecasting error:

$$U_{opt,t} = -\sum_{k=1}^{\infty} \chi_k \left[g_{t-k} - \overline{E}_{opt,t-k-1}\, g_{t-k} \right]^2 \tag{15.4}$$

$$U_{pess,t} = -\sum_{k=1}^{\infty} \chi_k \left[g_{t-k} - \overline{E}_{pess,t-k-1}\, g_{t-k} \right]^2 \tag{15.5}$$

where χ represents geometrically declining weights.

The proportion of optimistic agents is determined à la Brock and Hommes (1997):

$$\alpha_{opt,t} = \frac{\exp(\gamma U_{opt,t})}{\exp(\gamma U_{opt,t}) + \exp(\gamma U_{pess,t})} \tag{15.6}$$

As we have shown in Chapter 9, there is an analogue equation for pessimistic agents (see 9.16).

4.   REGIME SWITCHING

In order to generate a broader model of the financial instability hypothesis, a regime switching technique is introduced (see Ferri, 2011). This technique is based upon three strategic elements:

1.   there are multiple equilibria (two, at least);
2.   there is a threshold dividing them;
3.   some equations switch in the various states.

In the present case, different thresholds will be considered. Furthermore, they can either be deterministic or stochastic. We start from the following deterministic one, which is given by the inequality:

$$\kappa_1\alpha_{t-1} - \kappa_1\kappa_2\left(\frac{\alpha_{01} + \alpha_{02}}{2}\right) > R_{t-1}d_{t-1}$$

The left-hand side of the equation represents the excess of the available profit share over a long-run average, weighted by some risk factor κ_2. If this number exceeds the debt service, the financial system is robust and Regime 2 is prevailing. It is the regime where hedge finance is dominant, and it is characterized by a higher profit share, high rate of growth and lower debt ratios.
The opposite happens in Regime 1.

5.   THE SWITCHING EQUATIONS AND THE META-MODEL

There are two fundamental switches in the system. The first is the value of the exogenous rate of growth of autonomous demand, g^*, which therefore becomes:

$$g_j^*$$

where $j = 1,2$ indicates the prevailing regime.
The second takes place in the parameters of the investment equation, which introduces financial aspects along with real factors:

$$i_t^j = \{1 + \beta_{1j}((\alpha_t - \alpha_{0j}) - (R_td_t - R_{0j}d_{0j}))\}\beta_{2j}\{v^*(1 + Eg_t)^2 - (1 - \delta)v_t\} \tag{15.7}$$

where $j = 1,2$.

In other words, the speed of the adjustment of investment is made dependent on the net cash flow of the firms. This equation remains in the same vein as the investment function rooted in the Harrod model discussed in Part IV, corrected by the presence of financial aspects discussed in Chapter 14. This effect is null in steady state.

It must be stressed that in Regime 1 firms are liquidity constrained (as suggested by Aghion and Banerjee, 2005).

All the various equations forming the meta-model are represented in a compact way below:

$$R_t = R_j^* + \gamma_1 (E\pi_t - \pi_j^*) - \gamma_2 (u_{t-1} - u_{0,j}) \tag{15.8}$$

$$\alpha_t = \alpha_{t-1} + \gamma_1 (Eg_t - g_{0j}) \tag{15.9}$$

$$r_t = \frac{(1 + R_t)}{(1 + E\pi_t)} - 1 \tag{15.10}$$

$$d_t = \frac{d_{t-1} R_{t-1}}{(1 + g_{t-1})(1 + \pi_{t-1})} + \frac{i_{t-1} - \kappa_1 \alpha_{t-1}}{(1 + g_{t-1})} \tag{15.11}$$

$$v_t = \frac{v_{t-1}(1 - \delta)}{(1 + g_{t-1})} + \frac{i_{t-1}}{(1 + g_{t-1})} \tag{15.12}$$

$$i_t^j = \{1 + \beta_{1j}(\alpha_t - \alpha_{0j}) - (R_t d_t - R_{0j} d_{0j})\} \beta_{2j} \{v^*(1 + Eg_t)^2 - (1 - \delta)v_t\} \tag{15.13}$$

$$c_t = c_1 (1 + Eg_t) + c_2 (R_t d_t - R_0 d_0) \tag{15.14}$$

$$f_t = \frac{f_{t-1}}{(1 + g_{t-1})}(1 + g_j^*) \tag{15.15}$$

$$g_t = f_t + i_t + c_t - 1 \tag{15.16}$$

$$\tau_t = \theta_0 + \theta_1 \frac{i_{t-1}}{v_{t-1}} \tag{15.17}$$

$$\sigma_t = \rho_0 - \rho_1 u_{t-1} \qquad (15.18)$$

$$gN_t = \frac{(1 + g_t)}{(1 + \tau_t)} - 1 \qquad (15.19)$$

$$u_t = 1 - (1 - u_{t-1}) \frac{(1 + gN_t)}{(1 + \sigma_t)} \qquad (15.20)$$

$$\pi_t = \varphi_1 E\pi_t - \psi_1 (u_t - u_{0j}) + (1 - \varphi_1)\pi_{t-1} \qquad (15.21)$$

The system contains 14 unknowns in 14 equations.

6.   THE DYNAMICS OF THE META-MODEL

The model is recursive and can be simulated. A preliminary step consists in introducing the parameters of the meta-model. This is in keeping with what has been done in the previous chapters.

These parameters determine the different values of the steady states given in Table 15.2, and, of course, influence the dynamics of the model.

Regime 1 is the "bad" regime where growth is low, inflation is higher and the debt ratio is substantial. Regime 2 has the opposite characteristics. However, they also have different dynamic properties, as will be shown.

Table 15.1   The values of the parameters

Benchmark values	
$c_1 = 0.608$	$\theta_0 = 0.001$
$c_2 = 0.05$	$\theta_1 = 0.20$
$\delta = 0.10$	$\rho_0 = 0.04$
$v^* = 1.5$	$\rho_1 = 0.30$
$g_{01}^* = 0.02 \quad g_{02}^* = 0.04$	$\psi_1 = 2.8$
$\beta_{11} = 0 \quad \beta_{12} = 0.8$	$\psi_2 = 0.85$
$\beta_{21} = 0.8 \quad \beta_{22} = 1$	$\gamma_1 = 0.05$
$\varphi_1 = 0.70$	$\sigma_1 = 0.1$
$\kappa_1 = 0.6$	$\kappa_2 = 0.76$
Expectations: $\gamma = 600$	$\rho = 0.5$

Table 15.2   The steady state values in the two regimes

	Regime 1	Regime 2
α_0	0.19	0.3217
i_0	0.1440	0.216
g_0	0.02	0.04
π_0	0.07	0.02
d_0	3	1.5
R_0	0.08	0.03
u_0	0.1496	0.0719

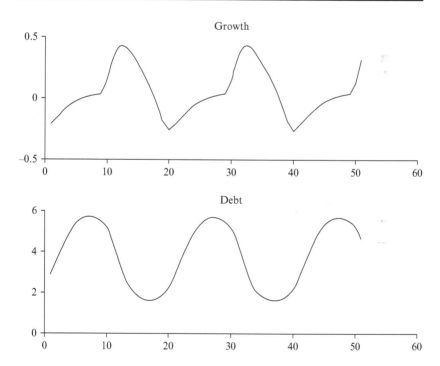

Figure 15.1   The dynamics of the meta-model

To this purpose, it is important to start from the dynamics of the whole model, which are shown in Figure 15.1.

The following points are worth stressing. The first is that the model is capable of generating bounded fluctuations. However, and this is the second point, these fluctuations are more volatile than those considered so far. This means that the model can deal with significant financial crises having a big impact on real variables. Finally, the system is robust in the sense that changes in the parameters maintain the properties of the model.

7. PROPERTIES OF SINGLE REGIMES

At this stage of the analysis it is important to "de-structure" the model in order to understand the forces behind it. In particular, let us consider the properties of each regime considered in isolation. In what follows, attention is focused on Regime 1, also called the "bad regime", which is characterized by negative properties: a low rate of growth and a high debt ratio. Its dynamics are illustrated by Figure 15.2.

The parameters are the same as those given in Table 15.1, except that the value of both v^* and d_{01} have been lowered ($v^* = 1.235$ and $d_{01} = 2$).

This reduction tends to stabilize the system. However, in spite of this

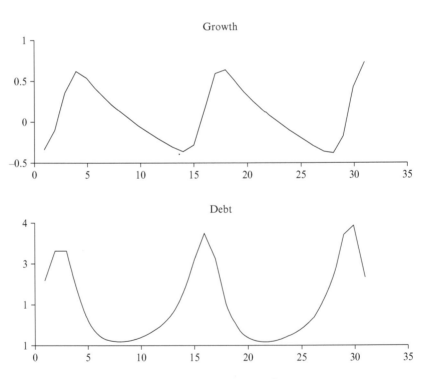

Figure 15.2   The dynamics within the "bad state"

reduction, the dynamics of the model are explosive. In other words, this is in keeping with Minsky's theorem according to which the dynamics of a fragile financial regime are unstable. The low level of growth accompanied by a high level of debt is at the root of the instability. On the contrary, Regime 2 considered in isolation is bounded, that is, either stable or oscillating.

It is important to stress that the destabilizing forces are endogenous in these kinds of models. The sentence "stability is destabilizing" coined by Minsky for financial crises, which seems to have raised much perplexity, is actually very common in all nonlinear models. For instance, the stability of income is the source of instability in the accelerator–multiplier model, to mention a well-known example that Minsky studied deeply.

8.   ALTERNATIVE SPECIFICATIONS

A strategic element behind the results of the meta-model are not only the dynamical properties of each regime, but also the kind of threshold chosen.

The one suggested before seems to be in keeping with Minsky's definition of financial fragility, where cash flows are compared to the debt service. However, in the literature one usually also finds other kinds of specifications. Two of them will be considered – one is based upon analytical aspects, while the other implies a different methodological perspective. The first alternative consists in introducing the following threshold:

$$d_{t-1} < d_{02}$$

This inequality defines Regime 2 as that state where the (last period) debt ratio is lower than a certain level, in this case represented by the steady state value of Regime 2. If one uses the same parameters as in Table 15.1, one obtains very similar dynamics.

The second alternative consists in introducing a different kind of threshold including a stochastic component. In this case, the above expression becomes:

$$d_{t-1} < d_{02} + \varepsilon_t$$

where ε_t is a normally distributed variable.

Figure 15.3 shows the last 30 runs of a simulation based on a Monte Carlo approach consisting of 1000 runs. The system is bounded. This means that the values of the parameters included in Table 15.2 along with

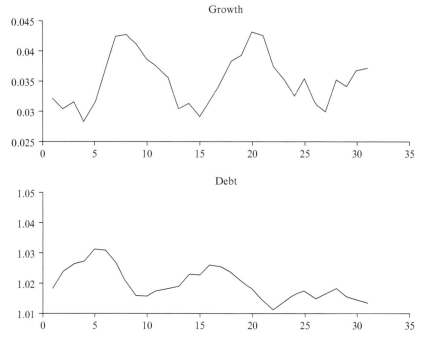

Figure 15.3   The dynamics with a stochastic debt threshold

the presence of a stochastic threshold can generate financial business cycles.

Or one might use a stochastic threshold of the type that is more in keeping with the deterministic one:

$$\alpha_{t-1} > R_{t-1} d_{t-1} + \varepsilon_t$$

In this case, with the same kinds of parameters underlying Figure 15.3 (which in turn are the same as those in Table 15.1, except that $v^* = 1.1$), the picture in Figure 15.4 is obtained.

Here, the variability is greater, even though the dynamics remain bounded.

9.   A CRISIS DETECTOR?

It is well known that the concept of threshold is probably the most controversial aspect of the analysis carried out so far. In a sense, it may raise the

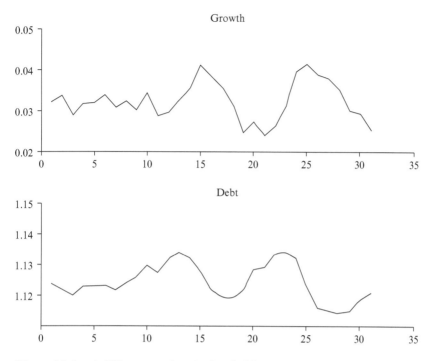

Figure 15.4   A different stochastic threshold

same perplexities as those induced by the presence of ceilings and floors. In the case of threshold, however, the concept is more flexible because it does not refer necessarily to the presence of physical objects. They are simple signals that may trigger different behavior.

In a recent paper, Aldasoro et al. (2018) have considered the threshold based upon debt described in the previous model. In fact, in their analysis the threshold is represented by a long-run value of the ratio between total debt and gross national product (GNP).

The thesis put forward is that when the actual ratio is above this level, in other words when there is a positive gap, the likelihood of an unsustainable credit boom increases in a decisive way. In this case, the gap is used as a crisis detector. According to the authors, it would have predicted 80 percent of the crises since 1980 in the countries and periods for which data are available.

Two points are worth stressing. The first is that the gap also predicted many crises that never arrived. In over 850 instances, the gap exceeded its long-run value but nothing happened. This is the reason why a stochastic threshold has been used in the previous analysis.

The second point is that there is heterogeneity among countries, a problem not present in the analysis in this chapter. Apart from institutional differences, the existence of different rates of growth should be mentioned. In this context, China seems to be an outlier. The credit gap has predicted at least three out of zero crises, reinforcing Samuelson's joke about the stock market's capabilities of forecasting crises, having predicted nine out of America's last five recessions.

According to *The Economist*: "If a financial crisis eventually strikes China, many people will be caught out – not because of a lack of warnings, but because of too many" (May 5, 2018).

It follows that the threshold must, fundamentally, be considered as an easy way of introducing nonlinearities, which are at the root of the endogenous explanations of the business cycles. The addition of a stochastic component is useful to diminish the mechanical aspect of the mechanism.

10. A USEFUL DEVICE?

Ferri and Tramontana (2018) have shown that regime switching makes the analysis of endogenous fluctuations more robust compared to similar analysis that only considers one regime.

For a model that aims to study great events, such as the Great Depression or the Great Recession, this may sound paradoxical. We are looking for runaway situations more than robust fluctuations. In a deeper analysis, the two concepts are not in contradiction.

In fact, it is worth having a model that is robust to parameter changes, otherwise the results become too shaky. It is not worthwhile considering models generating financial fluctuations that depend on a particular configuration of parameters. The larger the interval the single parameters are allowed, the more robust the model becomes. So the value added of the regime switching device remains.

In order to generate runaway situations typical of the great events, the parameters must be allowed larger intervals. The problem is to understand what these larger intervals mean.

11. MISSING VARIABLES

In his dissertation, Minsky explained how his accelerator–multiplier model was rooted in a monetary economy of production even though the monetary and financial sectors were not explicitly considered. This hypothesis did not imply that these sectors were powerless, but rather that their impact was indirect and manifested itself through changes in the parameters of the real equations.

In other words, long before the so-called Lucas critique, Minsky (1954/2004) recognized that parameters may change and that this may not only be due to policy changes, as underlined by Lucas, but may also be due to changes in the structure of the economy.

In the specific case that we are looking at, the financial sector is not considered. We already know that its role is very important in such extreme events.

In particular, in the meta-model the role of the banking system has not been explicitly considered, except for the steady state value of the investment in Regime 1. In this case, the credit crunch can constrain the value of investment.

In the buoyant regime, on the contrary, the various economic units can have all the credit they want, at a rate of interest fixed by the authorities.

In this sense, the banking system endogenously creates the amount of finance required by the economy. This approach is in keeping with Minsky's idea of the functioning of the banking system (see Wray, 2016).

The substance of that working is not changed with the appearance of so-called shadow banking. Contrary to Krugman's opinion, it is not empirical aspects that characterize Minsky's contribution, but his endogenous vision of the banking system's working.

12. RUNAWAY SITUATIONS

The complexity of Minsky's analysis does not depend only on his effort to consider the dual role of the different phenomena, and in this specific case the role of flexibility and instability of financing, but it depends also on the role of their variables in the various circumstances.

According to Minsky, for instance, money may matter in many circumstances but not in others. This is why the presence of a monetary economy of production need not include an explicit financial sector. Each unit can be considered as a bank. Furthermore, when money does matter, it may act through changes in the parameters of the real functions, as suggested by Minsky in his dissertation.

It goes without saying that the explicit presence of a banking system would make the analysis more complete (see Ryoo, 2016). However, it would become indispensable should one want to analyze the details of runaway situations. In this case, the particular nature of the debt involved, the channels of the banking system and the presence of fire-selling activities are all elements that can contribute to explaining the details and the development of the runaway situations.[1] The liquidity crises can only be found in such a context, while in the meta-model only solvency problems were encountered.

Also in this case, the possibility of a crisis depends on the details of the institutional arrangements. For instance, the difference underlined in a BIS (Bank of International Settlements) study between developed and developing economies may depend on such arrangements, including the role of the thwarting system in place.

The presence of a money manager capitalism, as Minsky has named this stage of the evolution of this complex financial and economic system, does not necessarily mean the explosion of new crises. The system can be reformed under the awareness of the continuous tension between endogenous innovations and attempts at reforms.

13.   A SYNTHESIS

The introduction of a regime-switching strategy has important implications for the structure of the model, which also depends on the theoretical choices that have been made. The overall result is that the following have been considered:

1.   A lesson from the regime switching model is that changes in the environment have an impact on the behavior of agents, a warning that the Lucas critique has always made. However, the changes of regime are rather complex and cannot be anticipated. They contribute to feeding uncertainty into the model and to imposing a learning strategy on the behavior of agents.
2.   These learning mechanisms contribute to consolidating the endogenous dynamics of the model. This is in keeping with the endogenous explanations of fluctuations in general and, as said before, with the endogenous explanation of the financial instability analysis stressed by Minsky.
3.   The financial instability analysis, based upon the link between income distribution, cash flows and debts, must be integrated within a macro model where both aggregate demand and aggregate supply aspects matter.
4.   The supply side is characterized by the presence of imperfect competition, where there are idle resources and where both price and quantity adjustments are important. In this context, the dynamics of productivity are not only a technological phenomenon, but they are also related to the pattern of aggregate demand.

5. The analysis is mainly carried out within a medium-run perspective, where the role of institutions is supposed to be a given. However, the study of their evolution would help in bridging the gap between medium- and long-run types of analyses.

NOTE

1. As has already been mentioned, Fisher (1933), Galbraith (1961) and Kindleberger (1978) described those processes in a debt-deflation context. For the recent experience, see the works cited in Chapter 3.

16. Final considerations and challenges

1. A HEDGEHOG

In a paper presented for the Festschrift *Financial Conditions and Macroeconomic Performance: Essays in Honor of Hyman P. Minsky*, Dymsky and Pollin (1992) labeled Hyman Minsky a hedgehog, a metaphor put forward by Isaiah Berlin, who referred back to the Greek poet Archilochus. According to the poet, the fox knows many things, but the hedgehog knows one big thing. The "big thing" known by Minsky, as has been illustrated in this book, is that the financial instability is capable of generating the so-called Minsky moments, as set out in his financial instability hypothesis. Although originating during the Great Depression, these moments were predicted to happen again. And they did.

One can trace a parallel with the work of the physicist Stephen Hawking, who concentrated his research on black holes and on the singularities in the space–time underlying them. For most of the physicists this was just a mathematical curiosum that did not lead anywhere. The same happened to Hyman Minsky. His relative isolation within the field was mainly due to his insistence on asking the question "Can 'it' happen again?", a historical curiosum that did not seem to impassion fellow members of the profession. However, differently from Hawking, the singularity has happened again, and this is at the root of the rediscovery of Minsky, both in the media and in the profession.

2. SCHADENFREUDE?

One might wonder whether the focus on the Great Depression was a form of schadenfreude. On the contrary, it was his personal experience of the misery and the suffering of that period that induced him to become an economist in order to avoid them. However, his interest was not historical, but analytical and methodological. Underlying the question "Can 'it' happen again?" was the big question concerning the endogenous instability of the economic system. In this perspective, the likelihood of depression is just the tip of the iceberg of the endogenous system instability. This represents the dividing line with the rest of the profession, which is focused on a macroeconomics dominated by the stability assumption. In this paradigm, the dynamics are driven by shocks, and for a "Great Recession" to take place one needs bigger shocks than usual. The theory of the rare events or the so-called black swans essentially tried to sidestep Minsky's analysis in spite of paying him lip service.

This is one the reasons why the Minsky moment in the economy has not had a deeper analytical impact in the profession.

3.   QUEEN ELIZABETH'S QUESTION

When Queen Elizabeth asked at the London School of Economics why the economists did not forecast the crisis, the audience was at a loss for a moment. Many answers were put forward, but few satisfactory. The answer could not be that this time a bigger shock than usual was to blame and therefore the crisis was unforecastable.

The explanation must go deeper than this. And in this perspective, Hyman Minsky's financial instability hypothesis was the best alternative available.

Minsky, of course, did not forecast the Great Recession. Nobody could have done so. However, different from most of the theories of economists, this result was in the range of the theoretical possibilities of Minsky's financial instability hypothesis.

Even among those who rediscovered Minsky, there is no consensus on the significance of his contribution. Its nature is not only empirical. In fact, he was among the few insisting on the endogenous evolution of the financial system, where shadow banking was becoming out of control. Even though this represents an important aspect of his work, and deserves merit, it is not the most essential aspect. The core of his work is his analytical contribution rooted in the endogenous instability of the system.

4.   THE FINANCIAL INSTABILITY HYPOTHESIS

The financial instability hypothesis, when taken into account, has raised many objections, as has been illustrated in this book. Two of them deserve further attention.

The first is that it is a micro theory that does not hold in a macro environment. In a Kaleckian framework, to which Minsky referred, investment creates profits, and if debt lets investment take place, there is no increase in the debt ratio because profit also rises. This is the so-called paradox of debt that seems to prevent the financial instability hypothesis from being operative, since the increasing leverage ratio, one of the pillars of the theory, cannot materialize.

The results of our simulations go against this objection. This does not imply that the debt paradox cannot be generated. It all depends on the complexity of the interaction between real and monetary factors that takes place in a dynamic environment. If one assumes that financial conditions change in an expansion phase, then the financial instability hypothesis becomes a macro possibility where the relative speeds of investment, cash flows and debt service are not necessarily the same.

The other objection refers to the endogeneity of the hypothesis. Or in other words, the statement that stability is destabilizing seems paradoxical. As Minsky wrote in his *John Maynard Keynes* (1975): "Stability – even of an expansion – is destabilizing in that more adventuresome financing of investment pays off to the leaders, and others follow. Thus an expansion will, at an accelerating rate, feed into the boom" (p. 127).

Two points are worth stressing. The first is that it is important to consider the presence of heterogeneous agents in the above sentence. There are laggards that try to catch up with the successful firms and this strengthens the expansion.

The second point is that the proposition just seems to be a catchy slogan. On the contrary, it is at the root of every nonlinear theory of business cycles. It is the habit of working with exogenous theory of the business cycle that makes the proposition sound unfamiliar.

5.   THEORY VERSUS STORYTELLING

It has become fashionable nowadays to talk about storytelling. I think that it is an essential task of economics not only to refer to models, or in general to mathematical formalization, but also to explain the sequence of events underlying the results. The important thing is not to create opposition between the two. In this perspective, Minsky has been considered a master in the art of storytelling, even though his language was sometimes complex – an economist that tried to bypass formalization as much as possible, in spite of his mathematical degree (see, for instance, Foley, 2001).

This book has presented many of the analytical attempts made by Minsky on different occasions. The reason why he did not push the process of formalization to a deeper level has to do more with the nature of his theory than with his lack of capability.

6. REDISCOVERING POLITICAL ECONOMY

Minsky's vision of a sophisticated economy, in which monetary and real aspects interact, creating complex dynamics where endogenous destabilizing forces are countered by the presence of thwarting policies and institutions, cannot be reduced to simple models. The number of interacting markets along with the presence of thwarting forces are sufficient to create complex dynamics. However, there are two further factors that feed these complex dynamics. The first is that the various variables are not considered in a unilateral perspective but within a broader context. For instance, finance is both a means of flexibility and a source of instability. Technical change is a source of flexibility but may reduce employment. Investment stimulates aggregate demand but also increases capacity. It is well known that these opposing forces are at the root of any business cycle.

The second is that, in his view, economic models were not simply mechanical devices, for the simple reason that parameters can change and variables can be made to be present or to disappear. Minsky claimed that the parameters can change well before the Lucas critique was put forward. Differently from this critique, which was at the root of the rational expectation theory, Minsky insisted that expectations were only one source of this instability. Furthermore, the solution was not to look for an Archimedes lever made of given tastes and production, but rather to accept a changeable world. This is after all political economy.

In this environment, there can be other sources of instability, and some of them can be represented by the interference of variables that were omitted in the analysis. For instance, take monetary aspects or the banking sector. A true systemic analysis should take these into consideration. However, for special environments, they can be omitted, as Minsky recognized. This choice does not imply that the nature of the monetary economy of production, stressed by Keynes, is violated. It simply implies that their influences are channeled through changes in the parameters of the remaining equations.

These changes play an important part in Minsky's dynamics.

7. THE "LEITMOTIV"

The "leitmotiv" of the book has been to underline, deepen and extend Minsky's dynamic analysis in order to find the most appropriate environment for his financial instability hypothesis. The starting point was three papers that Minsky and I co-authored, which have then been updated and then deepened. The objective was to bridge the gap existing between

Minsky's *Stabilizing an Unstable Economy* (1986) and his *Can "It" Happen Again* (1982). In the former the financial instability hypothesis is put forward, while in the latter the basis of his economics of nonlinear dynamics is set out.

These dynamic aspects have not only been deepened, but also extended. In fact, this book includes an attempt to enter the toolbox of instruments that Minsky did not fully exploit in his dynamic analysis, which was based upon three pillars:

1. a medium-run perspective, long enough to capture the evolution of all the aspects of a financial crisis;
2. the necessity of overcoming the one-sidedness of theory either based upon aggregate demand or aggregate supply;
3. the completeness of the market considered.

It follows that the analysis refers to disequilibrium processes stretching over a medium-run period, where aggregate demand and aggregate supply interact and where real and financial forces coexist. Within this context, not only the financial instability hypothesis finds the appropriate soil in which to flourish, but the relationship with the labor market becomes more important.

8.   DEBT, CASH FLOWS AND INCOME DISTRIBUTION

The financial instability hypothesis has been mainly dealt with by experts in finance. However, it is rather important to stress its link with the classical theme of income distribution, a topic that has been at the center of economic analysis since Ricardo (see Stockhammer et al., 2008). The financial instability analysis is based upon the dynamic comparison between cash flows, debt service and the payments of debts. This relationship calls into question variables such as the expected rate of profit, the rate of growth and the rate of interest. In other words, these variables depend on income distribution either directly or indirectly.

In the course of the analysis, different hypotheses have been made about income distribution. Exogeneity has been the starting point. In this case its relevance has appeared from the stability analysis. Later on, the endogenous hypothesis has been put forward. From the meta-model presented in Chapter 15, two points are worth stressing. First, the results obtained depend on the hypothesis concerning the relative value of the steady state share in the two regimes, and on the endogenous mechanisms at the root of their dynamics. Second, the results can be different according to whether they relate to leveraged producers or leveraged consumers.

Beyond these technical considerations, there are broader implications that should be considered. They refer to the economic forces underlying the model. For instance, the attempt to sustain consumption by means of debt has created an unsustainable economic situation, above all in the US economy.

In trying to explain the instability of the model, the behavior of the monetary authorities has been called into question. Their policy, based upon a very low rate of interest, was at the root of the speculative bubble that eventually burst into a recession. Even though this interpretation is important, it should be integrated with the consideration of a falling labor share. This pattern is not compatible with growing consumption, even though the debt process can mitigate the divergence between consumption and growth for a period of time.

The debt process should be seen from two points of view. The financial sector has increased the possibilities of getting indebted, while the dynamics of the labor share has compelled the consumer to incur debts. To this macro aspect, one should also add the micro income distribution where the increase in disparities has certainly contributed to exacerbating the situation (see also Dew-Becker and Gordon, 2005).

9. OPENING THE BLACK BOX

The results obtained depend also on the nature of the growth model chosen to incorporate the financial instability analysis. The pursuit of this line of research has been called "entering the black box of Minsky's tools of analysis". We have not only tried to explicitly consider income distribution but have also tried to take into account simultaneously both the natural rate of growth (i.e. that referring to the labor market) and what Harrod called the warranted rate of growth (i.e. the growth rate of the product market). The analysis has been completed by making the assumption that the latter is endogenous. In this case, very interesting results emerge.

First, unemployment and growth can coexist. They can remain bounded, while unemployment plays the role of "reserve army", which helps keep wages under control and assures the availability of resources. In this perspective, the labor supply must also be considered since it is an endogenous variable, which, together with the rate of unemployment, gives an idea of the amount of spare resources available for the system. Second, one can show that this link between spare resources and growth is complex because it also depends on the pace of technical change. Technical change can have an impact on both the macro measure of unemployment and the number of mismatches existing in the system. Third, unemployment has a complex nature: at the same time it represents availability of resources, it is a source of inequality and it can imply poverty.

The first aspect of unemployment's complex nature has been analyzed in Part IV, where its dual role in the reconciliation between aggregate demand and aggregate supply aspects and the stability of the system have been considered. The second aspect has been stressed in Part V, where the relationship between unemployment, inequality and the financial instability hypothesis has been examined. The third aspect, that is, the relationship between unemployment and poverty, a theme treated in Minsky's (2013) posthumous book, opens the way to the role of the so-called thwarting forces.

10.   THE THWARTING FORCES

Minsky's deep ideas on dynamics were based on two assumptions. On the one hand, the system is endogenously unstable. On the other, instability can be checked by the presence of thwarting forces and appropriate institutions.

According to Minsky, the long-run legacy of the Great Depression has been represented by those institutional changes that favored post-war growth and that were implemented by the triad big government, big firms and big unions. This set up had a double impact on the economy. First, it prevented extreme events, such as the Great Depression, from happening. Second, it allowed the existence of an endogenous business cycle that had profound differences compared with pre-World War II experiences.

The lender-of-last-resort role of the Federal Reserve, along with the built in fiscal stabilizers, supported the idea that devastating events were initially considered unlikely and then impossible. These results did not represent "the state of nature", as erroneously thought by Lucas (1987) and most of the supporters of the so-called DSGE (discrete stochastic general equilibrium) models, but they were conditioned on the presence and the effectiveness of those thwarting forces. This is the reason why Minsky always used a question mark when dealing with the question "Can 'it' happen again?"

The institutional set up of the "New Deal" lasted until the early 1970s. The change of paradigm that succeeded the Keynesian world reached the conclusion that the system was self-regulating. This conviction was an important component in the deflagration of the Great Recession.

The Great Recession is not obviously a mere repetition of the Great Depression. This has two implications. On the one hand, it obliges the financial instability hypothesis to be reformulated in order for it to fit different stylized facts. On the other, it calls for the presence of new thwarting forces which have to face three problems that were not present in the Great Depression:

1. globalization;
2. the information technology revolution;
3. financialization.

These changes affect all the markets, from the product market to labor and financial markets, and therefore call for important institutional changes that have not been devised yet. Furthermore, the presence of the financialization of the economy makes it likely that the conditions for the financial instability hypothesis to remain operative will persist.

11. THE FINANCIALIZATION OF THE ECONOMY

It is correct to claim that recessions are deeper and longer when the financial system in general and the banking sector in particular are involved. This statement does not necessarily imply that the crisis is financial. As we have tried to explain, in a monetary economy of production the monetary and the real aspects are too linked to allow misleading separations. Integration is the "leitmotiv" of the book, even though "finance" has been kept backstage.

As Minsky (1954/2004) often underlined, this situation does not imply that the financial sector does not matter, but simply that its impacts are felt through changes in the values of the parameters, especially those referring to the investment function. It is obvious that in this case one can see only the tip of an iceberg.

There are several advantages in considering explicitly the financial and the banking sectors. One is that the economic system is more and more run by what Minsky called the "money managers", who are the dominant feature in the process of financialization of the economy. This process is also bound to dominate the near future, and therefore it becomes strategic to take it into consideration in an explicit way.

Another advantage is that the presence of this sector allows a better understanding of the passage from expansion to instability that characterizes the financial instability hypothesis. Minsky said that stability turns endogenously into instability. This principle, which characterizes nonlinear models, finds important mechanisms when the financial sector is explicitly considered and when important hypotheses on "crowd" expectations are put forward.

The same holds for the descending phase, when the impact of the crisis on the financial system contributes to creating a powerful feedback in the real economy that is absent in the canonical experiences.

The contribution by Caballero and Simsek (2009) is very important in this regard. These authors identify three kinds of externality: liquidity, fire externality and complexity externality.

The first stems from the interlinkages of the financial system: when a bank chooses to raise external liquidity rather than trying to generate liquidity from its internal resources it spreads distress into the system. The second kind of externality is derived from the impact that fire sales by a bank have on the balance sheets of the remaining ones. More interesting is the final kind of externality. According to the Caballero and Simsek (2009, p. 1):

> . . .complexity, a feature strongly disliked by investors during downturns for the uncertainty it generates, rises endogenously during the crises: as asset prices implode, more financial institutions (banks, for short) within the financial network may go under, which increases each bank's likelihood of being hit by an indirect shock from a counterparty risk.

There is no doubt that these contributions must be framed within a macro perspective in order to complete our analysis, which has been carried out based on the assumption that the financial system is considered as given.

12.   DEALING WITH COMPLEXITY

If one wants to overcome the dichotomy between hydraulic Keynesianism and the so-called DSGE models, into which macroeconomics is divided, one must insert the financial instability hypothesis into a complex dynamic context. In fact, the financial instability hypothesis is rooted within endogenous destabilizing processes that are countered by the presence of thwarting forces. Their interaction creates complex dynamics that need to be explored.

In the present book, the so-called meta-model, which should act as a theoretical framework for the various forms in which the financial instability hypothesis can manifest itself, analyzes the complex dynamics by means of a regime-switching technique.

This technique seems to be in keeping with Minsky's (1992) thoughts for several reasons, three of which are mentioned here. First, the economy is characterized by different financing regimes that possess different types of stability or instability. Second, the model is capable of explaining why over periods of prolonged prosperity the economy transits from financial relations that make for a stable system to financial relations that make for an unstable system. Third, the system can remain bounded, something Minsky always tried to consider since his first studies on accelerator–multiplier models.

The idea of referring to a regime-switching device in order to generate particularly complex dynamics is not new (see Ferri, 1997 and 2011). It is a piecewise linear technique that allows complex dynamics to be obtained without those difficulties that sometimes characterize nonlinear specifications. In other words, it is easier to find economic justifications for these kinds of assumptions. If one looks at the micro dimension, one realizes that many choices by consumers, firms or workers can be described within this framework (see, for instance, Van Ours et al., 1993 and Aoki and Yoshikawa, 2007). There is a threshold beyond which agents change behavior in a more or less radical way. However, smoothness by aggregation normally prevents this pattern emerging at a macro level.

This is why it is difficult to discover these patterns in macro econometrics. However, there are periods when extreme events happen, and these make the hypothesis of regime switching more palatable even at a macro level. There remain two difficulties. The first is that at this macro dimension, regime switching must compete with the hypothesis of structural breaks that sometimes characterize the time series (see Hamilton, 1994). Structural breaks refer to irreversible changes, while regime switching implies that change is reversible. This property is not easily detectable in quantitative analysis. The second difficulty is that extreme events do not necessarily generate enough data to detect the hypothesis. For these reasons, simulations become an essential tool of analysis.

The idea that the system can have reversible changes can be enlightening. First, regime switching acts as a sort a meta-mechanism of dynamic adjustment for the economic systems. In fact, changes in the various equations when certain thresholds have been passed prevent the system from exploding, even though it can evolve in a complex way.

Second, the dynamics within and between regimes are endogenous, and this is in keeping with Minsky' s intuition that the tendency of financial agents to a Ponzification of the economy can be a generalized phenomenon.

Finally, regime switching is more than a technical device capable of generating complex dynamics, since it also implies a particular philosophy of history, where rules, institutions and not just economic incentives can have a role.

13.   ALTERNATIVE APPROACHES

Regime switching is certainly not the only technique which is adequate for dealing with complex dynamics. The so-called agent-based models (ABMs) constitute a valid companion, as has been shown, for instance, in Chapter 13.

According to the ABM approach:[1]

1.   "The system is composed of interacting units";
2.   "The system exhibits emergent properties, that is, properties arising from the interactions of the units that are not properties of the individual units themselves" (Judd and Tesfatsion, 2006, p.836).

If heterogeneity is introduced, the analysis becomes more complex and the methodological issues more demanding. In fact, the study of the interactions between agents in an environment where the information required by the Walrasian or the Arrowian general equilibrium is not available is at the core of new approaches, where since it is not possible to obtain closed-form solutions, the only alternative is carrying out simulations.

Undoubtedly, the ABM approach is interesting. It combines heterogeneity with dynamic interaction. And as Delli Gatti et al. (2011) have shown, it is possible to insert Minsky's financial instability hypothesis based upon heterogeneous agents into a dynamic analysis, where the macro results are not isomorphic to micro behavior (see also Chiarella and Di Guilmi, 2011).

Furthermore, the ACE approach allows not only the consideration of Schumpeterian technical change (see Dosi et al., 2012) in a monetary economy of production, but also lets the banking system play a strategic role (see also Gurgone et al., 2018).

14.   CONCLUDING REMARKS

The core of Minsky's analysis is the dynamics of an accumulating capitalist economy, with complex and evolving financial, product and labor markets, where complex patterns can be generated. The financial instability hypothesis, his well-known theory, is best understood within this perspective.

In fact, Minsky always tried to blend his early research on the dynamics of business cycles with various macroeconomic theories, ranging from Keynes's analysis of investment under conditions of uncertainty to the Kaleckian theory of profits, which represent the macro support to his theory.

In this book, the successive steps of this complex theory have been examined from a particular methodological point of view, centered on a dynamic perspective.

Minsky has offered different solutions to these methodological problems arising from the presence of heterogeneous agents interacting within a dynamic system. These solutions range from top-down to bottom-up methods, some of them characterized by a two-way process and others much simpler. All these attempts seem to be in keeping with Victoria Chick's thesis, according to which these solutions can only represent compromises that are not valid under any circumstance.

In this perspective, this variety of approaches is a sign of richness, characterized, however, by two unifying principles. On the one hand, microeconomics tend to be macrofounded. In other words, micro behavior reflects the state of the economy, which is characterized by complex real and financial interrelationships coupled by the presence of particular institutions. On the other hand, macro dynamics are dominated by a complex set of forces that can thwart instability, which is not an iron law of economics but a likely event.

To reconcile these principles, new compromises need to be reached, while new justifications must be looked for.

Agents can change behavior according to the prevailing environment, and this contributes to changing the environment itself. The environment has sometimes been depicted in a restrictive way as the world of expectations. In fact, it refers to expectations, social norms and rules of the game. In this complex world, agents make decisions: macro has an impact on micro. However, the interactions between micro units eventually constitute the macro environment. Only in equilibrium is there a fixed point mapping the two worlds. But this is probably where most economic events are not interesting.

NOTE

1. For surveys of the ABM approach, see Dawid and Delli Gatti (2018) and Di Guilmi (2017).

Bibliography

Aghion, P. and A. Banerjee (2005), *Volatility and Growth*, Oxford: Oxford University Press.

Aghion, P. and P. Howitt (1998), *Endogenous Growth Theory*, Cambridge, MA: MIT Press.

Aldasoro, I., C. Borio and M. Drehmann (2018), 'Early warning indicators of banking crises: expanding the family', *BIS Quarterly Review*, March, Basel: BIS.

Alichi, A., K. Kantenga and J. Solé (2016), 'Income polarization in the United States', IMF Working Paper, WP/16/121, Washington, DC: IMF.

Allain, O. (2015), 'Tackling instability of growth: a Kaleckian model with autonomous demand expenditures', *Cambridge Journal of Economics*, 39, 1351–71.

Andreassen, M.G. (2017), *Modelling Minsky's Financial Instability Hypothesis: A Criticism of Previous Efforts and Complexity Economics as an Appropriate Alternative*, Dissertation, Durham: University of Durham.

Aoki, M. (1996), *New Approaches to Macroeconomic Modeling*, Cambridge: Cambridge University Press.

Aoki, M. and H. Yoshikawa (2007), *Reconstructing Macroeconomics*, Cambridge: Cambridge University Press.

Arrow, K. and G. Debreu (1954), 'Existence of an equilibrium for a competitive economy', *Econometrica*, 23, 265–90.

Arrow, K. and F. Hahn (1971), *General Competitive Equilibrium*, San Francisco, CA: Holden-Day.

Arthur, W.B. (1994), 'Inductive reasoning and bounded rationality', *American Economic Review*, 4, 406–11.

Asada, T.P., C. Chen, C. Chiarella and P. Flaschel (2006), 'Keynesian dynamics and the wage–price spiral: a baseline disequilibrium model', *Journal of Macroeconomics*, 28, 90–130.

Auclert, A. and M. Rognlie (2018), 'Inequality and aggregate demand', Working Paper 24280, Boston, MA: National Bureau of Economic Research.

Barro, R.J. and H.I. Grossman (1971), 'A general disequilibrium model of income and distribution', *American Economic Review*, 61, 82–93.

Basili, M. and C. Zappia (2010), 'Ambiguity and uncertainty in Ellsberg and Shackle', *Cambridge Journal of Economics*, 34, 449–74.

Baumol, W.J. and J. Benhabib (1989), 'Chaos: significance, mechanism and economic applications', *Journal of Economic Perspectives*, 3, 77–105.

Beavis, B. and I. Dobbs (1990), *Optimization and Stability Theory for Economic Analysis*, Cambridge: Cambridge University Press.

Bellofiore, R. and P. Ferri (eds) (2001a), *Financial Keynesianism and Market Instability: The Economic Legacy of Hyman Minsky, Volume I*, Cheltenham, UK and Northampton, MA, USA: Edward Elgar Publishing.

Bellofiore, R. and P. Ferri (eds) (2001b), *Financial Fragility and Investment in the Capitalist Economy: The Economic Legacy of Hyman Minsky, Volume II*, Cheltenham, UK and Northampton, MA, USA: Edward Elgar Publishing.

Bernanke, B. (2005),'The global saving glut and the US current account deficit', Sandridge Lecture, Richmond, VA: Virginia Association of Economists.

Bils, M., P.J. Kelnow and B.A. Malin (2018), 'Resurrecting the role of the product market wedge in recessions', *American Economic Review*, 108, 1006–30.

Blanchard, O.J. (1997), 'The medium-run', *Brookings Papers on Economic Activity*, 1997 (2), 89–158.

Boyer, R. and J. Mistral (1984), *The Present Crisis: From an Historical Interpretation to a Prospective Outlook*, Paris: Cepremap.

Brainard, W. and J. Tobin (1986), 'Pitfalls in financial model building', *American Economic Review*, 58, 99–122.

Brock, W. and C. Hommes (1997), 'A rational route to randomness', *Econometrica*, 65, 1059–95.

Bronfenbrenner, M. (ed.)(1969), *Is the Business Cycle Obsolete*, New York: John Wiley and Sons.

Brunner, K. (1968), 'The role of money and monetary policy', *Federal Reserve Bank of St. Louis Review*, July.

Brunner, K. and A.H. Meltzer (1972), 'Friedman's monetary policy', *Journal of Political Economy*, 80, 837–51.

Brusco, S. (1982), 'The Emilian model: productive decentralization and social integration', *Cambridge Journal of Economics*, 6, 167–84.

Caballero, R.J. and A. Krishnamurthy (2008), 'Collective risk management in a flight to quality episode', *Journal of Finance*, 63(5), 2195–230.

Caballero, R.J. and A. Simsek (2009), 'Fire sales in a model of complexity', Working Paper 15479, Cambridge, MA: National Bureau of Economic Research.

Carlin, W. and D. Soskice (2018), 'Stagnant productivity and low unemployment: stuck in a Keynesian equilibrium', *Oxford Review of Economic Policy*, 34, 169–94.

Carrol, C.D. (1992), 'The buffer stock theory of saving: some macroeconomic evidence', *Brookings Papers on Economic Activity*, 1992 (2), 61–156.

Caskey, J. and S. Fazzari (1987), 'Aggregate demand contractions with nominal debt commitments: is wage flexibility stabilizing?', *Economic Inquiry*, XXV, 583–97.

Cerra, V. and S.C. Saxena (2017), 'Booms, crises and recoveries: a new paradigm of the business cycle and its policy implications', IMF Working Paper, WP/17/250, Washington, DC: IMF.

Charles, S. (2016), 'Is Minsky's financial instability hypothesis valid?', *Cambridge Journal of Economics*, 40, 427–36.

Chiarella, C. and C. Di Guilmi (2011), 'The financial instability hypothesis: a stochastic microfoundation framework', *Journal of Economic Dynamics and Control*, 35, 1151–71.

Chick, V. (1973), *The Theory of Monetary Policy*, London: Gray-Mills Publishing.

Chick, V. (2016), 'On microfoundations and Keynes' economics', *Review of Political Economy*, 28, 99–112.

Clower, R.W. (1965), 'The Keynesian counterrevolution: a theoretical appraisal', in F. Hahn and F. Brechling (eds), *The Theory of Interest Rates*, London: Macmillan.

Cominetta, M. (2016), 'Financial contagion: a new perspective (and a new test)', Working Paper 12, Frankfurt: European Stability Mechanism.

Cooley, T.F. (ed.) (1995), *Frontiers of Business Cycle Research*, Princeton, NJ: Princeton University Press.

Cripps, F. and W.A.H. Godley (1976), 'A formal analysis of the Cambridge economic policy group model', *Economica*, 35, 335–48.

Cristini, A., S.M. Fazzari, E. Greenberg and R. Leoni (eds) (2015), *Cycles, Growth and the Great Recession: Economic Reflections in Time of Uncertainty*, London: Routledge.

Cynamon, B.Z. and S.M. Fazzari (2008), 'Household debt in the consumer age: source of growth and risk of collapse', *Capitalism and Society*, 3, 1–30.

Cynamon, B.Z. and S.M. Fazzari (2016), 'Inequality, the Great Recession and slow recovery', *Cambridge Journal of Economics*, 40, 373–99.

Cynamon, B.Z., S.M. Fazzari and M. Setterfield (eds) (2013), *After the Great Recession: The Struggle for Economic Recovery and Growth*, New York: Cambridge University Press.

Davidson, P. (1972), *Money and the Real World*, New York: John Wiley and Sons.

Dawid, H. and D. Delli Gatti (2018), 'Agent-based macroeconomics', Bielefeld Working Papers in Economics and Management, No. 02-2018.

Day, R.H. (1982), 'Irregular growth cycles', *American Economic Review*, 72, 406–14.

Day, R.H. (1983), 'The emergence of chaos from classical economic growth', *Quarterly Journal of Economics*, 98, 201–13.

Day, R.H. and W. Shafer (1986), 'Keynesian chaos', *Journal of Macroeconomics*, 7, 277–95.

De Grauwe, P. (2008), 'Animal spirits and monetary policy', Working Paper 2418, Brussels: CESIFO.

De Grauwe, P. (2011), 'Animal spirits and monetary economy', *Economic Theory*, 47 (2–3), 423–57.

Delli Gatti, D., S. Desiderio, E. Gaffeo, P. Cirillo and M. Gallegati (2011), *Macroeconomics from the Bottom Up*, Milan: Springer.

Delli Gatti, D. and M. Gallegati (1997), 'At the root of the financial instability hypothesis: induced investment and business cycles', *Journal of Economic Issues*, 31, 527–34.

Delli Gatti, D., M. Gallegati and S. Desiderio (2015), 'The dynamics of the labour market in an agent-based model with financial constraints', in A. Cristini, S.M. Fazzari, E. Greenberg and R. Leoni (eds), *Cycles, Growth and the Great Recession: Economic Reflections in Time of Uncertainty*, London: Routledge, 117–129.

Delong, J. and L. Summers (1986), 'Is increased price flexibility stabilizing', *American Economic Review*, 76, 1031–44.

Delong, J. and L. Summers (2012), 'Fiscal policy in a depressed economy', *Brookings Papers on Economic Activity*, 43, 233–97.

Dew-Becker, I. and R.J. Gordon (2005), 'Where did the productivity go? Inflation dynamics and the distribution of income', *Brookings Papers on Economic Activity*, 2005 (2), 67–150.

Di Guilmi, C. (2017), 'The agent-based approach to post-Keynesian macro modeling', *Journal of Economic Surveys*, 31, 1183–200.

Di Guilmi, C.M. and L. Carvalho (2015), 'The dynamics of leverage in a Minskyan model with heterogeneous firms', University of Sydney Working Papers, 2015-15.

Diamond, P.A. (1982), 'Aggregate demand management in search equilibrium', *Journal of Political Economy*, 90, 798–812.

Dieci, R. and X. He (2018), 'Heterogeneous agent models in finance', in C. Hommes and B. Le Baron (eds), *Handbook of Computational Economics*, Vol. 4, Amsterdam: Elsevier, 257–328.

Dosi, G., G. Fagiolo and A. Raventini (2012), 'Schumpeter meeting Keynes: a policy-friendly model of endogenous growth and business cycles', *Journal of Economic Dynamics and Control*, 34, 1748–67.

Dosi, G., M. Napolitano, A. Roventini and T. Treibich (2017), 'Micro and macro policies in the Keynes + Schumpeter evolutionary models', *Journal of Evolutionary Economics*, 27, 63–90.

Duesenberry, J.S., G. Fromm, L.R. Klein and E. Kuh (eds) (1965), *The Brookings Quarterly Econometric Model of the United States*, Chicago: Rand McNally Company.

Duffie, D. and H. Sonnenshein (1989), 'Arrow and general equilibrium theory', *Journal of Economic Literature*, XXVII, 565–98.

Dutt, A.K. (2006), 'Aggregate demand, aggregate supply and economic growth', *International Review of Applied Economics*, 26, 319–36.

Dutt, A.K. (2010), 'Reconciling the growth of aggregate demand and aggregate supply', in M. Setterfield (ed.), *Handbook of Alternative Theories of Economic Growth*, Northampton, MA, USA: Edward Elgar Publishing, 220–40.

Dymsky, G. and R. Pollin (1992), 'Hyman Minsky as hedgehog: the power of the Wall Street paradigm', in S. Fazzari and D.B. Papadimitriou (eds), *Financial Conditions and Macroeconomic Performance: Essays in Honor of Hyman P. Minsky*, New York: M.E. Sharpe, 27–62.

Economist, The (1988), 'New economists: the Cambridge tendency', December 24, London.

Economist, The (2016a), 'Secrets and agents', July 23, London.

Economist, The (2016b), 'Minsky's moment', July 30, London.

Economist, The (2018), 'Where will the next crisis occur?', May 5, London.

Eggertsson, G.B. and P. Krugman (2013), 'Debt, deleveraging, and the liquidity trap: a Fisher-Minsky-Koo approach', *Quarterly Journal of Economics*, 127, 1469–513.

Eggertsson, G.B. and N.R. Mehrotra (2014), 'A model of secular stagnation', Working Paper 20574, Cambridge, MA: National Bureau of Economic Research.

Eichengreen, B. (2015), 'Secular stagnation: the longview', Working Paper 20836, Cambridge, MA: National Bureau of Economic Research.

Eusepi, S. and B. Preston (2009), 'Labor supply heterogeneity and macroeconomic co-movement', Working Paper 15561, Cambridge, MA: National Bureau of Economic Research.

Eusepi, S. and B. Preston (2015), 'Consumption heterogeneity, employment dynamics and macroeconomic co-movement', *Journal of Monetary Economy*, 71, 13–32.

Fama, E. (1970), 'Efficient capital markets: a review of theory and empirical works', *Journal of Finance*, 25, 383–417.

Farebrother, R.W. (1973), 'Simplified Samuelson conditions for cubic and quartic equations', *The Manchester School of Economics and Social Studies*, 41, 396–400.

Farmer, R.E.A. (1999), *Macroeconomics and Self-Fulfilling Prophecies*, Cambridge, MA: MIT Press.

Fazzari, S. and M.J. Athey (1987), 'Asymmetric information, financing, constraints, and investment', *Review of Economics and Statistics*, LXIX, 481–7.

Fazzari, S., P. Ferri and E. Greenberg (1998), 'Aggregate demand and firm behavior: a new perspective on Keynesian microfoundations', *Journal of Post Keynesian Economics*, Summer, 20, 527–58.

Fazzari, S., P. Ferri and E. Greenberg (2008), 'Cash flow, investment and the Keynes–Minsky cycles', *Journal of Economic Behavior and Organization*, 63, 555–72.

Fazzari, S., P. Ferri and E. Greenberg (2010), 'Investment and the Taylor rule in a dynamic Keynesian model', *Journal of Economic Dynamics and Control,* 34, 2010–22.

Fazzari, S.M., P. Ferri, E. Greenberg and A.M. Variato (2013), 'Aggregate demand, instability and growth', *Review of Keynesian Economics*, 1 (1), 1–21.

Fazzari, S.M., P. Ferri and A.M. Variato (2018), 'Demand-led growth and accommodating supply', FMM Working Paper 15-2018.

Fazzari, S.M. and E. Greenberg (2015), 'Are macroeconomic models with ceilings and floors useful in understanding the Great Recession', in A. Cristini, S.M. Fazzari, E. Greenberg and R. Leoni (eds), *Cycles, Growth and the Great Recession: Economic Reflections in Time of Uncertainty*, London: Routledge, 45–65.

Fazzari, S., G.R. Hubbard and B.C. Petersen (1988), 'Financing constraints and corporate investment', *Brookings Papers on Economic Activity*, 1988 (1), 141–95.

Fazzari, S. and D.B. Papadimitriou (eds) (1992), *Financial Conditions and Macroeconomic Performance: Essays in Honor of Hyman P. Minsky*, New York: M.E. Sharpe.

Ferrero, G., M. Gross and S. Neri (2017), 'On secular stagnation and low interest rates: demography matters', Working Paper No. 2088, Washington: IMF.

Ferri, P. (1983), 'The consumption–wage gap', *Journal of Post Keynesian Economics*, 5, 579–89.

Ferri, P. (1992), 'From business cycles to the economics of instability', in S. Fazzari and D.B. Papadimitriou (eds), *Financial Conditions and Macroeconomic Performance*, New York: M.E. Sharpe, 105–20.

Ferri, P. (1997), 'Ceilings and floors', in D. Glasner (ed.), *Business Cycles and Depressions: An Encyclopedia*, New York: Garland, 86–8.

Ferri, P. (2000), 'Wage dynamics and the Phillips curve', in R.E. Backhouse and A. Salanti (eds), *Macroeconomics and the Real World*, Oxford: Oxford University Press, 97–112.

Ferri, P. (2001), 'Ceilings and floors, growth and the Nairu', in R. Bellofiore and P. Ferri (eds), *Financial Fragility and Investment in the Capitalist Economy: The Economic Legacy of Hyman Minsky, Volume II*, Cheltenham, UK and Northampton, MA, USA: Edward Elgar Publishing, 53–68.

Ferri, P. (2008), 'The economics of nonlinearity', in R. Scazzieri, A.K. Sen and S. Zamagni (eds), *Markets, Money and Capital: Hicksian Economics for the 21st Century*, Cambridge: Cambridge University Press, 309–27.

Ferri, P. (2010), 'Growth cycles and the Financial Instability Hypothesis (FIH)', in D.B. Papadimitriou and L.R. Wray (eds), *The Elgar Companion to Hyman Minsky*, Cheltenham, UK and Northampton, MA, USA: Edward Elgar Publishing, 206–21.

Ferri, P. (2011), *Macroeconomics of Growth Cycles and Financial Instability*, Cheltenham, UK and Northampton, MA, USA: Edward Elgar Publishing.

Ferri, P. (2013), 'Income distribution and debt in a fragile economy: market processes and macro constraints', *Journal of Economic Interaction and Coordination*, 8, 219–30.

Ferri, P. (2016), *Aggregate Demand, Inequality and Instability*, Cheltenham, UK and Northampton, MA, USA: Edward Elgar Publishing.

Ferri, P., A. Cristini and A. Variato (2015), 'Endogenous fluctuations, markups, capacity and credit constraints', *Journal of Economic Interaction and Coordination*, 11, 273–92.

Ferri, P., A. Cristini and A. Variato (2018), 'Growth, unemployment and heterogeneity', mimeo, Bergamo, Italy: University of Bergamo.

Ferri, P., S.M. Fazzari, E. Greenberg and A.M. Variato (2011), 'Aggregate demand, Harrod's instability and fluctuations', *Computational Economics*, 38, 209–20.

Ferri, P. and E. Greenberg (1989), *The Labor Market and Business Cycle Theory*, New York: Springer.

Ferri, P. and E. Greenberg (1992), *Wages, Regime Switching and Cycles,* New York: Springer-Verlag.

Ferri, P., E. Greenberg and R.H. Day (2001), 'The Phillips curve, regime switching, and the Nairu', *Journal of Economic Behavior and Organization*, 46, 23–37.

Ferri, P. and H.P. Minsky (1988), 'Business Cycles and Economic Instability', Bergamo: University of Bergamo, unpublished book.

Ferri, P. and H.P. Minsky (1989), 'The breakdown of the IS–LM synthesis: implications for post-Keynesian economic theory', *Review of Political Economy*, 1, 123–43.

Ferri, P. and H.P. Minsky (1992), 'Market processes and thwarting systems', *Structural Change and Economic Dynamics*, 3, 79–91.

Ferri, P. and F. Tramontana (2018), 'Debt persistence in a deflationary environment: a regime-switching model', *Computational Economics*, 52 (2), 421–42.

Ferri, P. and A. Variato (2010a), 'Uncertainty and learning in stochastic macro models', *International Advances in Economic Research*, 16 (3), 297–310.

Ferri, P. and A. Variato (2010b), 'Financial fragility, the Minskian triad and economic dynamics', *International Journal of Political Economy*, 39 (2), 70–82.

Fisher, I. (1933), 'The debt-deflation theory of Great Depressions', *Econometrica*, 1 (4), 337–57.

Foley, D. (2001), 'Hyman Minsky and the dilemmas of contemporary economic method', in R. Bellofiore and P. Ferri (eds), *Financial Keynesianism and Market Instability: The Economic Legacy of Hyman Minsky, Volume I*, Cheltenham, UK and Northampton, MA, USA: Edward Elgar Publishing, 47–59.

Foley, D. (2008), 'Review of "Reconstructing Macroeconomics" by M. Aoki and Y. Yoshikawa', *Journal of Economic Behavior and Organization*, 68, 319–28.

Friedman, M. (1956), 'The quantity of money: a restatement', in M. Friedman (ed.), *Studies in the Quantity Theory of Money*, Chicago: University of Chicago Press.

Friedman, M. (1959), *A Program for Monetary Stability*, New York: Fordham University Press.

Friedman, M. (1968), 'The role of monetary policy', *American Economic Review*, 58, 1–17.

Frisch, R. (1933), 'Propagation problems and impulse problems in dynamic economics', in *Economics Essays in Honor of G. Cassel*, London: Allen and Unwin.

Gabaix, X. (2008), 'Variable rare disasters: an exactly solved framework for ten puzzles in macro-finance', Working Paper 13724, Cambridge, MA: National Bureau of Economic Research.

Galbraith, J.K. (1961), *The Great Crash 1929*, Boston, MA: Houghton Mifflin.

Gallegati, M. and A. Kirman (eds) (1999), *Beyond the Representative Agent*, Cheltenham, UK and Northampton, MA, USA: Edward Elgar Publishing.

Gandolfo, G. (1996), *Economics Dynamics*, New York: Springer.

Geneakoplos, J. (2003), 'Liquidity default and crashes: endogenous contracts in general equilibrium', Cowles Foundation Discussion Paper, No. 1316, New Haven, CT: Yale University, Cowles Foundation.

Geneakoplos, J. (2010), 'The leverage cycle', Cowles Foundation

Discussion Paper No. 1715, New Haven, CT: Yale University, Cowles Foundation.

Giordano, R.M. (1987), *The Federal Reserve's Response to the Stock Market Crash: Financial Market Perspectives*, December, New York: Goldman Sachs Economic Research Group.

Gleick, J. (1987), *Chaos: Making a New Science*, New York: Viking.

Goodfriend, M. and R.G. King (1997), 'The new neoclassical synthesis and the role of monetary policy', in B. Bernanke and J.J. Rotemberg (eds), *NBER Macroeconomic Annual*, Cambridge, MA: MIT Press, 231–83.

Goodwin, R.M. (1950), 'Non-linear theory of the cycle', *Review of Economics and Statistics*, 32, 316–20.

Goodwin, R.M. (1967), 'A growth cycle', reprinted in *Essays in Economic Dynamics* (1983), London: Macmillan, Ch. 14.

Gordon, R. (2015), *The Rise and Fall of American Growth: The US Standard of Living since the Civil War*, Princeton, NJ: Princeton University Press.

Greenwald, B. and J.E. Stiglitz (1987), 'Keynesian, new Keynesian and the new classical economics', *Oxford Economic Papers*, 39, 119–32.

Gurgone, A., G. Iori and S. Jafarey (2018), 'The effect of interbank networks on efficiency and stability in a macroeconomic agent-based model', *Journal of Economic Dynamics and Control*, 91, 257–88.

Gurley, J.G. (1961), 'Review of M. Friedman's "A Program for Monetary Stability"', *Review of Economic Statistics*, 43, 307–8.

Guscina, A. (2006), 'Effects of globalization on labour's share in national income', IMF Working Paper, WP/06/294, Washington, DC: IMF.

Hahn, F.H. and R.C.O. Matthews (1965), 'The theory of economic growth: a survey', in *Surveys of Economic Theory*, Vol. 2, London: Macmillan, 1–124.

Hall, R.E. (2011), 'The long slump', *American Economic Review*, 101, 431–69.

Hamilton, J.D. (1989), 'A new approach to the economic analysis of non-stationary time series and the business cycle', *Econometrica*, 57, 357–84.

Hamilton, J.D. (1994), *Time Series Analysis*, Princeton, NJ: Princeton University Press.

Hansen, A. (1938), *Full Recovery or Stagnation*, New York: W.W. Norton & Co.

Harrod, R.F. (1939), 'An essay in dynamic theory', *Economic Journal*, 49, 14–33.

Hicks, J.R. (1937), 'Mr Keynes and the classics: a suggested interpretation', *Econometrica*, 5, 147–59.

Hicks, J.R. (1950), *A Contribution to the Theory of the Trade Cycle*, Oxford: Oxford University Press.

Hicks, J.R. (1965), *Capital and Growth*, Oxford: Clarendon Press.

Hicks, J.R. (1974), *The Crisis in Keynesian Economics*, Oxford: Basil Blackwell.

Hicks, J. (1983), 'Micro and macro', in *Classics and Moderns*, Oxford: Basil Blackwell.

Hicks, J. (1989), *A Market Theory of Money*, Oxford: Clarendon Press.

Hobsbawn, E. (1994), *Age of Extremes: The Short Twentieth Century*, London: Penguin Books.

Hommes, C. and G. Sorger (1998), 'Consistent expectations equilibria', *Macroeconomic Dynamics*, 2, 287–321.

Howitt, P. and O. Ozak (2009), 'Adaptive consumption behavior', Working Paper 15427, Cambridge, MA: National Bureau of Economic Research.

Hsu, J.H., D.A. Matsa and B.T. Melzer (2018), 'Unemployment insurance as a stabilizer of the housing market', *American Economic Review*, 108, 49–89.

IMF (2018), *World Economic Outlook*, April, Washington, DC: IMF.

Ingrao, B. and G. Israel (1985), 'General economic equilibrium theory: a history of intellectual paradigmatic shifts, I, II', *Fundamenta Scientiae*, 6, 1–45 and 89–125.

Ingrao, B. and G. Israel (1987), *La Mano Invisibile*, Bari: Laterza.

Jones, C.L. and P.M. Romer (2009), 'The new Kaldor facts: ideas, institutions, population, and human capital', Working Paper 15094, Cambridge, MA: National Bureau of Economic Research.

Jorgenson, D. (1963), 'Capital theory and investment behavior', *American Economic Review*, 53, 247–9.

Jorgenson, D.W., K. Fukao and M.P. Timmer (eds) (2016), *The World Economy: Growth or Stagnation*, Cambridge: Cambridge University Press.

Judd, K. and L. Tesfatsion (2006), *Handbook of Computational Economics, Vol. 2, Agent-Based Computational Economics*, Amsterdam: North Holland.

Kaldor, N. (1957), 'A model of economic growth', *Economic Journal*, 67, 591–624.

Kaldor, N. (1961), 'Capital accumulation and economic growth', in F.A. Lutz and D.C. Hague (eds), *The Theory of Capital*, London: St Martin's Press, 177–222.

Kaldor, N. (1978), 'Causes of the slow rate of growth in the UK', in *Further Essays on Applied Economics*, London: Duckworth, vii–xxix.

Kalecki, M. (1971), *Selected Essays in the Dynamics of the Capitalist Economy*, Cambridge: Cambridge University Press.

Keen, S. (2011), 'Debunking macroeconomics', *Economic Analysis and Policy*, 41, 147–67.

Keynes, J.M. (1921), *A Treatise on Probability*, London: Macmillan.

Keynes, J.M. (1936), *The General Theory of Employment, Interest and Money*, London: Macmillan.

Keynes, J.M. (1937), 'The general theory of employment', *Quarterly Journal of Economics*, 51, 209–23.

Kindleberger, C.P. (1978), *Manias, Panics and Crashes*, New York: Basic Books.

Kirman, A.P. (1992), 'Whom or what does the representative individual represent?', *Journal of Economic Perspectives*, 6, 117–36.

Knight, F.H. (1921), *Uncertainty and Profit*, Boston, MA: Houghton Mifflin.

Kregel, J. (1973), *The Reconstruction of the Political Economy: An Introduction to Post-Keynesian Theory*, London: Macmillan.

Kregel, J.A. (1980), 'Economic dynamics and the theory of steady growth: an historical essay on Harrod's "knife-edge"', *History of Political Economy*, 12, 97–123.

Kregel, J. (1982), 'Money, expectations and relative prices in Keynes's monetary equilibrium', *Economie Appliquée*, 35(3), 449–65.

Kregel, J. (1983), 'Effective demand: origins and development of the notion', in J. Kregel (ed.), *Distribution, Effective Demand and International Economic Relations*, London: Macmillan.

Kregel, J. (1984), 'Expectations and rationality within a capitalist frame-work', in E.J. Nell (ed.), *Free Market Conservatism: A Critique of Theory and Practice*, London: Allen and Unwin.

Kregel, J. (1987), 'The changing place of money in Keynes's theory from the Treatise to the General Theory', in G. Gandolfo and F. Marzano (eds), *Keynesian Theory of Planning Models and Quantitative Economics*, Padova: Giuffrè.

Krugman, P.R. (2013), 'Secular stagnation, coalmines, bubbles, and Larry Summer', Blog Post.

Kuznetsov, Y.A. (2004), *Elements of Applied Bifurcation Theory*, New York: Springer-Verlag.

Landis, B. and J.J. Gladstone (2017), 'Personality, income and compensating consumption', *American Economic Review*, 86, 349–73.

Lavoie, M. (2014), *Post Keynesian Economics: New Foundations*, Cheltenham, UK and Northampton, MA, USA: Edward Edgar Publishing.

Lavoie, M. and M. Seccareccia (2001), 'Minsky's financial fragility hypothesis: a missing macroeconomic link?', in R. Bellofiore and P. Ferri (eds), *Financial Fragility and Investment in the Capitalist Economy: The Economic Legacy of Hyman Minsky, Volume II*, Cheltenham, UK and Northampton, MA, USA: Edward Elgar Publishing, 76–98.

Layard, R., S. Nickell and R. Jackman (1991), *Unemployment*, Oxford: Oxford University Press.

Leijonhufvud, A. (1968), *On Keynesian Economics and the Economics of Keynes*, Oxford: Oxford University Press.

Leijonhufvud, A. (1987), 'Whatever happened to Keynesian economics – and does it have a future?', mimeo, Siena: International School of Economic Research.

Liu, Z. and P. Wang (2011), 'Credit constraints and self-fulfilling business cycles', Working Paper 2010-22, San Francisco, CA: Federal Reserve Bank.

Lo, S. and K. Rogoff (2015), 'Secular stagnation, debt overhang and other rationales for sluggish growth, six years on', BIS Working Paper 482, Basel: BIS.

Lucas, R.E. (1972), 'Expectations and the neutrality of money', *Journal of Economic Theory*, 4, 103–24.

Lucas, R.E. (1976), 'Econometric policy evaluation: a critique', Carnegie-Rochester Conference Series on Public Policy, 2, 19–46.

Lucas, R.E. (1981), *Studies in Business-Cycle Theory*, Cambridge, MA: MIT Press.

Lucas, R.E. (1987), *Models of Business Cycles*, Oxford: Blackwell.

Lucas, R.E. and T.J. Sargent (1981), *Rational Expectations and Econometric Practice*, Minneapolis, MN: University of Minnesota Press.

Malinvaud, E. (1977), *The Theory of Unemployment Reconsidered*, Oxford: Basil Blackwell.

Mankiw, N.G. (1987), 'Recent developments in macroeconomics: a very quick refresher course', Working Paper 2474, Cambridge, MA: National Bureau of Economic Research.

Mankiw, N.G. and D. Romer (1991), *New Keynesian Economics*, Cambridge, MA: MIT Press.

Mason, J.W. (2018), 'Consumption debt, household debt, income inequality, national income accounting', Working Paper 900, Annandale-on-Hudson, NY: Levy Economics Institute.

Matthews, R.C.O. (1959), *The Trade Cycle*, Cambridge: Cambridge University Press.

May, R.M. (1976), 'Simple mathematical models with very complicated dynamics', *Nature*, 261, 459–67.

McAdam, P. and A. William (2008), 'Medium run redux: technical change, factor shares and frictions in the Euro area', European Central Bank, Working Paper Series, 915, Frankfurt: European Central Bank.

McCombie, J.S.L. (2002), 'Increasing returns and the Verdoorn law from a Kaldorian perspective', in J. McCombie, M. Pugno and B. Soro (eds), *Essays on Verdoorn's Law*, Basingstoke: Palgrave Macmillan, 64–114.

McKenzie, L. (1959), 'On the existence of general equilibrium for a competitive market', *Econometrica*, 27, 54–71.

Mendoza, E.G. (2006), 'Endogenous sudden stops in a business cycle model with collateral constraint: a Fisherian deflation of Tobin's Q', Working Paper 12564, Cambridge, MA: National Bureau of Economic Research.

Merton, R.C. (1973), 'An intertemporal capital asset pricing model', *Econometrica*, 41, 867–87.

Mian, A.R. and A. Sufi (2018), 'Finance and business cycles: the role of driven household demand', Working Paper 24322, Boston, MA: National Bureau of Economic Research.

Minsky, H.P. (1954/2004), *Induced Investment and Business Cycles*, Cheltenham, UK and Northampton, MA, USA: Edward Elgar Publishing.

Minsky, H.P. (1957), 'Monetary systems and accelerator models', *American Economic Review*, 47, 859–83.

Minsky, H.P. (1959), 'A linear model of cyclical growth', *Review of Economics and Statistics*, 41, 137–45.

Minsky, H.P. (1969), 'Private sector asset management and the effectiveness of monetary policy: theory and practice', *Journal of Finance*, 24, 223–38.

Minsky, H.P. (1975), *John Maynard Keynes*, New York: Columbia University Press.

Minsky, H.P. (1982), *Can 'It' Happen Again?*, New York: M.E. Sharpe.

Minsky, H.P. (1986a), *Stabilizing an Unstable Economy*, New Haven, CT: Yale University Press.

Minsky, H.P. (1986b), 'The relevance of Kalecki: the usable contribution', a paper prepared for a Conference at the University of Perugia, April.

Minsky, H.P. (1988), 'Schumpeter: finance and evolution', paper prepared for the conference: 'Evolution of technology and market structure in an international context', University of Siena, May 24–7.

Minsky, H.P. (1992), 'The financial instability hypothesis', Working Paper No. 74, Anandale-on-Hudson, NY: Levy Economics Institute.

Minsky, H.P. (2013), *Ending Poverty: Jobs, Not Welfare*, Annandale-on-Hudson, NY: Levy Economics Institute.

Minsky, H.P. and P. Ferri (1984), 'Prices, employment, and profits', *Journal of PostKeynesian Economics*, 6, 489–99.

Mitchell, W.C. (1913), *Business Cycles*, Berkeley, CA: University of California Press.

Modigliani, F. (1944), 'Liquidity preference and the theory of interest and money', *Econometrica*, XII, 45–88.

Modigliani, F. and M. Miller (1958), 'The cost of capital, corporation finance and the theory of investment', *American Economic Review*, 48, 261–97.

Muth, J.F. (1961), 'Rational expectations and the theory of price movements', *Econometrica*, 29, 315–35.

Nikolaidi, M. (2017), 'Three decades of modeling Minsky: what we have learned and the way forward', *European Journal of Economics and Economic Policies: Intervention*, 14, 222–37.

Palley, T.I. (2012), 'Growth, unemployment and endogenous technical progress: a Hicksian resolution of the Harrod's knife-edge', *Metroeconomica*, 63, 512–41.

Palley, T.I. (2016), 'Inequality, the financial crisis and stagnation: competing stories and why they matter', *Real-World Review*, 74, 1–19.

Papadimitriou, D.B. (1992), 'Minsky on himself', in S. Fazzari and D.B. Papadimitriou (eds), *Financial Conditions and Macroeconomic Performance*, New York: M.E. Sharpe, 13–26.

Papadimitriou, D.B. (2004), 'Introduction', in H.P. Minsky, *Induced Investment and Business Cycles*, Cheltenham, UK and Northampton, MA, USA: Edward Elgar Publishing.

Papadimitriou, D.B. and L.R. Wray (eds) (2010), *The Elgar Companion to Hyman Minsky*, Cheltenham, UK and Northampton, MA, USA: Edward Elgar Publishing.

Pasinetti, L.L. (1962), 'Rate of profit and income distribution in relation to the rate of economic growth', *Review of Economic Studies*, 29, 267–79.

Pasinetti, L.L. (1981), *Structural Change and Economic Growth: A Theoretical Essay on the Dynamics of the Wealth of Nations*, Cambridge: Cambridge University Press.

Pasinetti, L.L. (1993), *Structural Economic Dynamics*, Cambridge: Cambridge University Press.

Passarella, M. (2010), 'The paradox of tranquility revisited: a Lotka-Volterra model of the financial instability', *Rivista degli Economisti*, XV, 69–104.

Patinkin, D. (1956), *Money, Interest, and Prices*, Evanston, IL: Row, Peterson and Company.

Pesaran, M. and S. Potter (1997), 'A floor and ceiling model of US output', *Journal of Economic Dynamics and Control*, 2, 661–95.

Phelps, E.S. (1970), 'Money wage dynamics and labor market equilibrium', in Phelps et al. (eds), *Microfoundations of Employment and Inflation Theory*, New York: Norton.

Piketty, T. (2014), *Capital in the Twenty-First Century*, Cambridge: Cambridge University Press.

Piore, M. and J. Sable (1985), *The Industrial Divide*, Cambridge, MA: MIT Press.

Pissarides, C.A. (1990), *Equilibrium Unemployment Theory*, Oxford: Basil Blackwell.

Preston, B. (2005), 'Adaptive learning, forecast-based instrument rules and monetary policy', *Journal of Monetary Economics*, 53, 507–35.

Ramsey, F.P. (1928), 'A mathematical theory of saving', *Economic Journal*, 38, 543–59.

Reder, M.V. (1982), 'Chicago economics: permanence and change', *Journal of Economic Literature (JEL)*, 20, 1–38.

Reinhart, C.M. and K. Rogoff (2011), 'From financial crash to debt crisis', *American Economic Review*, 101, 1676–706.

Robinson, J. (1956), *The Accumulation of Capital*, London: Macmillan.

Rognlie, M., A. Shleifer and A. Simsek (2014), 'Investment hangover and the Great Recession', Working Paper 20569, Cambridge, MA: National Bureau of Economic Research.

Romer, C.D. and D.H. Romer (2017), 'New evidence on the aftermath of the financial crises in advanced countries', *American Economic Review*, 107, 3072–118.

Romer, D. (1996), *Advanced Macroeconomics*, New York: McGraw-Hill.

Romer, P.M. (1986), 'Increasing returns and long run growth', *Journal of Political Economy*, 94, 1002–37.

Rose, H. (1967), 'On the non-linear theory of the employment cycle', *Review of Economic Studies*, 34, 153–73.

Ryoo, S. (2016), 'Demand-driven inequality, endogenous saving rate and macroeconomic instability', *Cambridge Journal of Economics*, 40, 201–25.

Samuelson, P.A. (1939), 'Interaction between the multiplier analysis and principle of acceleration', *Review of Economic Statistics*, 21, 75–8.

Samuelson, P.A. and R.M. Solow (1960), 'Analytical aspects of anti-inflation policy', *American Economic Review*, 50, 127–94.

Schmitt-Grohé, S. and M. Uribe (2012), 'The making of a great contraction with a liquidity trap and a jobless recovery', Working Paper 18544, Cambridge, MA: National Bureau of Economic Research.

Schularick, M. and A.M. Taylor (2009), 'Credit booms gone bust: monetary policy, leverage cycles and financial crises, 1870–2008', Working Paper 15512, Cambridge, MA: National Bureau of Economic Research.

Schumpeter, J.A. (1934), *The Theory of Economic Development*, Cambridge, MA: Harvard University Press.

Schumpeter, J.A. (1951), *Ten Great Economists: From Marx to Keynes*, New York: Oxford Economic Press.

Serrano, F. (1995), 'Long period effective demand and the Sraffian super-multipliers', *Contributions to Political Economy*, 14, 67–90.

Setterfield, M. (ed.) (2010), *Handbook of Alternative Theories of Economic Growth*, Cheltenham, UK and Northampton, MA, USA: Edward Elgar Publishing.

Setterfield, M., Y.K. Kim and J. Rees (2016), 'Inequality, debt servicing and the sustainability of steady state growth', *Review of Political Economy*, 28, 1, 45–63.

Skott, P. (2010), 'Growth, instability, and cycles: Harrodian and Kaleckian models of accumulation and income distribution', in M. Setterfield (ed.), *Handbook of Alternative Theories of Economic Growth*, Cheltenham, UK and Northampton, MA, USA: Edward Elgar Publishing, 108–31.

Slutsky, E. (1937), 'The summation of random causes as a source of cyclical processes', *Econometrica*, 5, 105–46.

Smith, A. (1776), *An Inquiry into the Nature and Causes of the Wealth of Nations*, reprinted in E. Cannan (ed.) (1961). London: Methuen.

Solow, R.M. (1956), 'A contribution to growth theory', *Quarterly Journal of Economics*, 70, 65–94.

Solow, R.M. (2000), 'Towards a macroeconomics of the medium run', *Journal of Economic Perspectives*, 14, 151–8.

Sraffa, P. (1932a), 'Dr Hayek on money and capital', *Economic Journal*, 42, 42–53.

Sraffa, P. (1932b), 'A rejoinder', *Economic Journal*, 42, 249–51.

Steindl, J. (1952), *Maturity and Stagnation in American Capitalism*, New York: Monthly Review Press.

Stiglitz, J.E. (2015), *The Great Divide*, London: Allen Lane.

Stiglitz, J.E. and B. Greenwald (2003), *Towards a New Paradigm in Monetary Economy*, New York: Columbia University Press.

Stockhammer, E., O. Onaram and S. Ederer (2008), 'Functional income distribution and aggregate demand in the Euro Area', *Cambridge Journal of Economics*, 33, 139–59.

Summers, L. (2013), 'Why stagnation might prove to be the new normal', *The Financial Times*, December 15.

Tavani, D. and L. Zamparelli (2017), 'Endogenous technical change in alternative theories of growth and distribution', *Journal of Economic Survey*, 31, 1–42.

Taylor, L. (2004), *Reconstructing Macroeconomics: Structuralist Proposals and Critiques of the Mainstream*, Cambridge, MA: Harvard University Press.

Taylor, L. and S.A. O'Connell (1985), 'A Minsky crisis', *Quarterly Journal of Economics*, 100, Supplement, 871–85.

Tcherneva, P.R. (2018), 'The job guarantee: design, jobs, and implementation', Working Paper 902, Annandale-on-Hudson, NY: Levy Economics Institute.

Tobin, J. (1968), 'Discussion', in S. Rousseaus (ed.), *Proceedings of a Symposium on Inflation: Its Causes, Consequences, and Control*, New York: New York University.

Tobin, J. (1975), 'Keynesian models of recession and depression', *American Economic Review*, 65 (2), 195–202.

Tobin, J. (1980), *Asset Accumulation and Economic Activity*, Chicago: University of Chicago Press.

Toporowski, J. (2008), 'Minsky's induced investment and business cycles', *Cambridge Journal of Economics*, 32, 725–37.

Toporowski, J. and A. Denis (2016), 'Microfoundations: introduction', *Review of Political Economy*, 28, 90–91.

Tramontana, F., L. Gardini and P. Ferri (2010), 'The dynamics of the Nairu model with two switching regimes', *Journal of Economic Dynamics and Control*, 34, 681–95.

Turnovsky, S.J. (2000), *Methods of Macroeconomic Dynamics*, Cambridge, MA: MIT Press.

Van Eeghen, P.H. (2014), 'Why DSGE analysis cannot accurately model financial-real sector interaction', *Real-World Economics Review*, 67, 17–40.

Van Ours, J.C., G.A. Pfann and G. Ridder (eds) (1993), *Labor Demand and Equilibrium Wage Formation*, Amsterdam: North Holland.

Variato, A. (2001), 'Hyman Minsky: what kind of (post) Keynesian?', in R. Bellofiore and P. Ferri (eds), *Financial Keynesianism and Market Instability: The Economic Legacy of Hyman Minsky, Volume I*, Cheltenham, UK and Northampton, MA, USA: Edward Elgar Publishing, 75–105.

Variato, A.M. (2004), *Investimenti, Informazione, Razionalità*, Milan: Giuffrè.

Vercelli, A. (2001), 'Minsky, Keynes and the structural instability of a sophisticated monetary economy', in R. Bellofiore and P. Ferri (eds), *Financial Fragility and Investment in the Capitalist Economy: The Economic Legacy of Hyman Minsky, Volume II*, Cheltenham, UK and Northampton, MA, USA: Edward Elgar Publishing, 33–52.

Weintraub, R. (1979), *Microfoundations*, Cambridge: Cambridge University Press.

Weintraub, S. (1966), *A Keynesian Theory of Employment Growth and Income Distribution*, Philadelphia: Chilton.

Weintraub, S. (1978), *Capitalism's Inflation and Unemployment Crisis*, Boston, MA: Addison-Wesley Publishing Co.

Weintraub, S. (1981a), 'An eclectic theory of income shares', *Journal of Post Keynesian Economics*, 4, 10–24.

Weintraub, S. (1981b), 'Bedrock in the money wage-money supply inflation controversy', *Banca Nazionale del Lavoro Quarterly Review*, 139, 439–46.

Woodford, M. (2009), 'Convergence in macroeconomics: elements of the new synthesis', *American Economic Journal of Macroeconomics*, 1, 242–66.

Wray, L.R. (2016), *Why Minsky Matters*, Princeton, NJ: Princeton University Press.

Index

ABM (agent-based models) 105, 121,
    167–9, 220
accelerator–multiplier model
    article reproducing formula of 43
    ceiling and floor version 82
    explosive relation 60
    income as source of instability in 203
    rooted in monetary economy of
        production 206–7
    slightly altered version of Samuelson
        123
    trade cycle 55, 103
    tranquillity paradox at root of 34
    use as metaphor 49
adapters *see* drivers, adapters and
    constraints
agent-based models (ABM) 105, 121,
    167–9, 220
aggregate demand
    and aggregate supply
        equilibrium conditions between
            183
        in growth theory 135–8, 142–3
        interdependence between 113, 115,
            119, 134, 190, 208, 214
        unemployment generated by
            138–9, 144–5, 149, 160, 166,
            168–9, 172–3, 216
    and inequality 159, 177, 179
    investment stimulating 213
    and market power 87–8, 92
Aghion, P. 114, 119, 135, 147, 166, 199
Akerlof's market for lemons 1
anti-laissez faire theorem 89–91
Aoki, M. 105–7, 119, 219
Arrow, K. 48, 84, 93
asset prices 70–72
asymmetric information 20, 34, 69,
    77, 79
autonomous demand 136–8, 142–4,
    146, 157–8, 160, 198–200

"balance sheet" perspective 20
banking system
    debts financed by 182
    as players in Great Recession 27
    quantitative easing measures 28
    role of 18, 34–5, 190, 207–8, 220
    shadow 27, 180, 207, 211
    trade union settlement dominating
        86–7
    see also central banks
bargaining and market power 52–5
Beveridge curve 168, 170–72
black box
    enriching 134
    entering 4, 10, 133
    opening 215–16
black swans 28–9, 211
"Boltzmann–Gibbs" distribution
    107
bottom-up approaches 103–4, 106–7,
    166, 221
bounded unemployment 144–5
Brock, W. 117–18, 197
business cycles
    canonical 19–20, 27, 33–4, 180
    ceiling and floor theory of 124–5
    debt deflation theory of 75
    endogenous–exogenous dichotomy
        17
    financial instability hypothesis
        contributions to 17
        as endogenous explanation of 15
        insertion of 20, 24–5
    government modifying nature of 53
    and hypotheses about expectations
        22
    impact of sudden, extreme events
        28–9, 33
    and induced investment 100–103
    Minsky's contribution to 14, 44–5,
        96, 101–4, 107, 112–13, 220

two theorems
  anti-laissez faire and "limitation
    upon the attainable" theorems
    89–91
  at root of financial instability
    hypothesis 195

uncertainty
  bankers and businessmen 81
  in capitalist economy 69
  complexity generating 218
  concept of 34
  DSCE models ignoring 112
  exclusion of 15, 34
  financialization of economy
    increasing 35
  implying presence of imperfect
    competition 118
  influences upon 180
  in investment function 20
  Keynes' emphasis on 68, 72, 79, 81,
    92, 96, 98, 107, 220
  learning process 117–18
  macro environment characterized
    by 99
  markets dominated by two kinds of
    168
  in medium run perspective 116–17
  in Minsky's papers 46, 98
  and regime switching 208
  role of unemployment 138
unemployment 149–61
  ABM approach 167–9
  bounded 144–5, 215
  caveats 172
  complex relationship with growth
    135, 215

in financial Keynesianism model
    21–4
flows
  in growth model 171–2
  simpler model for 169–70
generated by aggregate demand and
    supply 138–9, 144–5, 149, 160,
    166, 168–9, 172–3, 216
and heterogeneity 138–40, 165
and inequality 135, 138–9, 145, 160,
    173, 216
and job creation 173–4
Keynesian 67–70, 77
literature review 165–6
natural rate of 66, 78–9
in recursive dynamic model 184
relation with poverty 173, 216
state as employer of last resort 174–5
and technical change 149, 215–16
three kinds of 172–3
updating 11, 43, 49–50, 213–14
  see also prices, profit and
    employment

Variato, A.M. 20, 31, 34, 50, 148
Vercelli, A. 8
vision *see* Minsky, H.P.: vision

wage rates and prices 56–8, 72, 74–5
wage share dynamics 41–2
Walrasian general equilibrium 49, 66,
    68, 74, 78, 93, 220
wealth 179, 182, 190
Weintraub, S. 60–62
Wray, L.R. 2, 5, 10, 12, 32, 173, 207

Yoshikawa, H. 105, 107, 119, 219